London Longings

a memoir

-Forgetting the Former Things 1-

Published by Leanne J Minton, July 2025

Cover by Rhodes Design

ISBN 978-0-473-74609-4 (pbk)

The names of several key people have been changed to protect their identity and privacy.

Dedication

For all those grieving a severed relationship

He heals the broken hearted
and binds up their wounds.
Psalm 147:3

PROLOGUE

'I'll go anywhere, God—anywhere in the world
if You'll find a man to truly treasure me.'

My husband had left me for the 'other woman.' It was such a clichéd and commonplace scenario but no less hurtful. Raw and visceral, the pain was made more intense by the fact it was the second time he'd done so. I was finally convinced to relinquish my hold on what—if I was honest—had been a miserable marriage.

In the oppressive loneliness that followed and in my hunger for companionship and touch, my vow was profoundly heartfelt. But it represented more the enormity of my desire rather than an actual belief God would honour it.

I never expected I'd be required to uphold my part of the bargain.

PART ONE

March 1983 –
April 1996

1983

Chapter One

The autumn evening was unseasonably warm so I was able to wear my favourite summer dress to the young adults' group barbeque. I wouldn't know many people there as I attended a different church, so the boldly coloured dress would give me confidence.

'Welcome, Leanne. I'm glad you could make it.' The group leader met me at the door of her home and ushered me through to the large sunny lounge where about 15 to 20 young people were gathered. The hostess handed me a glass of orange juice and I took one of the last seats, glad to be able to sit and have something to hold in my hands.

Looking around I saw a few guys and girls I knew across the room. I made eye contact with them and smiled. Next to me were two guys I hadn't met before. One seemed to be doing most of the talking and keeping the other amused. Of only average height and build he nevertheless seemed to take up a lot of space, sitting with his legs spread and an arm outstretched. His denim shorts revealed his tanned and muscled legs. Like my schoolgirl crushes, he was dark haired with deep brown eyes and a cheeky smile.

His friend noticed me looking in their direction and said hello. He asked my name, then introduced himself as Wayne and his friend as Karl.

'What do you both do?' I asked.

Wayne looked at Karl. 'He's a political science student and I'm—'

'A bean counter,' Karl interrupted.

'At least my skills are useful!' countered Wayne with a grin.

They joked good-naturedly for a few minutes, making me laugh.

'And you?' Wayne asked.

'I'm a secretary for a Christian organisation.'

'They don't bring any Christian musicians to New Zealand, do they?'

'No, unfortunately.' Despite the negative answer the topic gave me an opening. 'Talking about music, did either of you see Larry Norman last year at the town hall?'

Both guys looked blank. Blast! What else could I find to talk about? I had no notion of what political science was and didn't fancy showing my ignorance by asking questions about it.

To my surprise Karl continued with the music theme. 'I don't know who that Larry guy is but I'd love to see Dire Straits.'

'Oh yes, me too!' I said, risking a direct gaze at Karl. 'They're one of my favourite bands.'

'Mine, too,' Wayne said. 'I'd pay good money to see them.'

'Sure you can afford it?' Karl teased, leaning back and clasping his hands behind his head. 'Isn't your money all tied up in bonds and shares?'

'Very funny! At least I'm earning.'

They were still bantering when our hostess stepped into the doorway from the kitchen and cleared her throat. 'Excuse me everyone, the food is now ready so would you please come through and help yourselves?'

We all stood, Wayne stretching out his arm in front of me. 'Beauty before age.'

'Thank you.' I felt my cheeks warm. The compliment was lovely but I wished it had been from Karl.

'*Now* it's age before beauty,' Karl said, indicating that Wayne should go before him.

Wayne rolled his eyes at me but he did as he was bid. In the kitchen we each took a plate and made our selections before heading back to take our seats.

Wayne looked sideways at the mass of food piled on Karl's plate and lifted an eyebrow. 'Sure you have enough?'

'Yes, I'm on a seafood diet.'

I paused in cutting into my beef sausage. 'What's that?'

Karl looked at me without expression. What was he thinking? Was it painfully obvious how eager I was to talk to him? 'Whatever you see you eat.'

I laughed to cover my embarrassment. Did he think me foolish to have fallen for such an obvious joke?

Going home that night I realised it wasn't the only thing for which I'd fallen. Throughout the next few days my thoughts kept reverting to Karl. Had he been interested in me? Did the few smiles he'd given me mean anything? Had I looked pretty enough? I couldn't do much about my skin which was acne-prone but maybe I should have spent more time on my hair which was short and thick and hard to manage.

A few evenings later the phone rang in my flat. One of my flatmates answered. 'Leanne, it's for you.' She put her hand over the receiver. 'It's a man,' she whispered.

Exhilaration shot through me. Was it Karl? Please God, let it be Karl!

'Hello.' Had my voice just wobbled? I was 21 but had only dated once before.

'Hi Leanne, it's Wayne from the barbeque.'

Oh no!

'I was hoping you'd like to go out with me this weekend.'

My excitement vanished. Unable to find a reason to refuse, I accepted Wayne's invitation. I made an effort to be pleasant company as Wayne was a nice guy but I worried he'd mistake good manners for me being interested in him, and would ask me out again.

When the phone rang for me a couple of days afterwards I still hadn't come up with a plausible excuse. Shoulders tense and my stomach churning, I answered.

'Leanne, it's Karl.'

What? Really? I had to stop from giving a squeal of excitement.

'I was talking with Wayne and he said I should ask you out.' There was amusement in his voice. Was this some sort of joke?

'I'm ... I'm not sure I understand.'

Karl laughed. 'He said you spent the entire evening asking about me so he figured I might have more luck.'

I cringed. Had I really been so obvious, not to mention

thoughtless about Wayne's feelings?

'So, will you go out with me on Friday night to the movies?'

My answer was never in doubt. But in the days leading up to our date my mind was full of misgivings. With Wayne I'd been careful not to be flirtatious but that restriction wouldn't apply to Karl—I wanted him to get close. However, in doing so would he be turned off by my flawed skin? Would my glasses get in the way of him kissing me?

Karl had chosen the movie, *Tootsie*. I remember little of the film and mostly the overwhelming physical connection as Karl held my hand. It was as if nothing existed for me other than the warmth of his hand, the feel of his skin on mine and the sense it gave me of being desirable.

As we began dating on a regular basis, Karl sent me letters and cards in the mail and left notes for me to find in which he paid me compliments. He called me beautiful which bewildered me. Could he not see what I did when I looked in the mirror? A childhood friend had once called me 'Gateposts.' In explaining, she said my legs were so skinny there was room for a gate between them—I'd been filled with self-loathing. But Karl didn't seem to see me as critically as I saw myself and his compliments had become as necessary to me as food.

To these he added gifts.

The first came one afternoon while I was at work. Just after lunch I heard the sound of a motorbike in the office car park. Several of the young people that visited our organisation rode motorbikes so I didn't think anything of it and continued typing up the latest newsletter.

The door opened and closed. 'Hi gorgeous.'

My head shot up. 'Karl!'

His dark hair a little tousled from being shaken free of his helmet, he came around my desk to give me a kiss.

My delight was blighted by prickles of anxiety. Should I be kissing at work? If the director and youth workers saw us would I face their condemnation or amusement? I willed them to remain upstairs in their offices.

From behind his back he handed me a long, rectangular-shaped, gift-wrapped box. 'Here's a present for you.'

My heart singing, I unwrapped it to find a crystal vase. It was slender and very delicate. 'Thank you so much, Karl. It's lovely.'

'Just like you.'

He had to leave but he remained in my mind all afternoon. I could think of little else and kept making mistakes as I typed. My thoughts were further centred on him when, to complement the vase, he came back the next day with a stunningly scented red rose.

One evening Karl dropped me home on his motorbike. He bent to kiss me goodbye and as he leaned back he said, 'I love you, Leanne.'

How I'd longed for those words. 'I love you too, Karl.'

With my heart secured, a different side of Karl emerged. I shouldn't have been altogether surprised as there were aspects of his persona that should have given me pause. On our first date he boasted about fights he'd gotten into in supposedly friendly soccer matches; anger seemed a significant part of his makeup. He'd spoken of traumatic childhood events as a missionary kid but seemed to recount them as incidents to solicit my admiration of him rather than as incidents that had damaged him. He'd also mentioned various issues with his parents and siblings from which I pieced together some troubling family dynamics.

But by the time I'd come to realise Karl was a broken young man I was enthralled by him, and rather than being scared off, I'd made it my mission to save him. I had no knowledge then of the concept of being a rescuer, nor the irony that in the end it would be me who would need rescuing. For Karl had indeed seen my lack of confidence and began to capitalise on it.

One evening we were in my flat and watching television; in the ad breaks I was making a grocery list.

'What are you doing?' Karl suddenly demanded.

I turned to him in puzzlement. Wasn't it obvious? Why did he sound so accusatory?

'Sorry, what do you mean?'

He looked across at my notepad and stabbed his finger at the doodles I'd made. 'Those squiggles.'

'They're doodles,' I answered, still confused.

'They indicate a lack of sophistication. Children doodle,' Karl stated. 'I've read that they're a sign of an immature mind.'

How that stung! I simply enjoyed giving my brain something creative to do while I was thinking. How was that childish?

Karl continued, appearing not to notice my silence as I struggled to process my conflicting thoughts and emotions. 'You don't want other people thinking you're scatterbrained. I'm just trying to save you embarrassment.' He pressed further. 'How long have you been doing it?'

'Years,' I said, beginning to feel embarrassed.

'It's time to stop then,' he pronounced, his face as cold as his logic. Doodling had suddenly become some inferior habit, the product of a shallow mind. His opinion mattered hugely to me and I couldn't see how to change it as he had research to back him up. While I didn't understand how such a conclusion could have been reached, I also didn't see how I could refute it. I never thought to question that maybe the research didn't exist. So my resistance collapsed, as did part of my spontaneous, joyful nature.

And so the shaping of my behaviour had begun. Over months, it grew to full-blown verbal and emotional abuse. His arguments seemed logical and indisputable, and challenging them only led to hurtful comments about my poor thinking and over-exaggerated emotions.

But as distressing as it became, I never told anyone.

And that is now what I puzzle over most. Was it because it started so slowly and increased so gradually that it became normal? Or perhaps I simply interpreted it as typical of the storms that every relationship goes through. However, I suspect it was that I had no framework for dealing with abusive behavior, no understanding that some behavior was toxic. I lacked the knowledge that pursuing a relationship with the perpetrator, unless they were genuinely contrite and committed to change, would be destructive.

Initially I tried to discuss these hurtful interactions but my challenges were never successful. One afternoon at my flat I went into my bedroom to get something and was startled to find a large spider on my bedroom wall. Ever since encountering a poisonous spider when young, I'd had a strong fear of them. I fled from the room into the lounge and pleaded for Karl to go and kill it. He went as I'd asked but came back with it alive. When I shrank back in horror he followed, thrusting the spider at me in his outstretched hands.

'Don't!' I whimpered, almost in tears. I sought refuge behind the kitchen table. 'Take it away!'

He laughed, then went to the back door to release the spider.

I was heartbroken. How could Karl find pleasure in terrifying me? I pushed down my distress until my flatmates had gone to bed and we were alone in the lounge.

'How could you do that?' I asked.

'Do what?' Karl replied, eyes still on the television.

I felt upset at having to elaborate; I'd wanted to minimise my re-engagement with the trauma. 'You know! Chase me with the spider.'

'Oh, that. I was just having a bit of fun.'

'What? I was terrified!'

Karl turned around on the couch to face me. 'It was just a spider.'

I felt close to tears and swallowed hard. 'But I told you about what happened to me when I was young. You know how frightened I was.'

'I wasn't going to throw it on you.'

'How did I know?'

Karl sighed. 'Trust me.'

'Why should I? You were chasing me.' My eyes welled up and a tear escaped down my cheek.

'There's no reason to cry.' He sounded impatient. 'I got rid of the spider and you should be grateful. If you're really so scared you should go see a psychiatrist.'

'But—'

'You're spoiling our evening.' Karl turned back to face the television. 'There's nothing more to say. We're missing "Cheers."'

I stared at the television, my emotions a maelstrom. Tears slipped down my face, one after the other, as I sat there in silence. I'd tried so hard to help Karl see what a destructive episode it was but he'd thwarted me at every turn.

This feeling of frustrated helplessness was to become commonplace. Karl ignored or minimised my pain, twisted my words, deviated from the topic and went off on tangents, all the while peppering those ploys with dismissive, hurtful comments. Bewildered by this battering of my reason and emotion, I was unable to continue our discussions; tears were my only recourse.

Then afterwards began the desperately hard work of forgiving him.

I'd come to know and love God as a six-year-old and I wanted to please Him by forgiving Karl. I realized too that it was wise, as bitterness is both ugly and unhealthy. So I forgave Karl once, twice, seventy times seven it seemed, all the while praying he would change. But he didn't. And, equally sadly, neither did I. I had no grasp of the second part of Jesus' commandment, "to love others *as you love yourself.*" If I'd truly loved myself, I would have stopped subjecting myself to Karl's treatment.

Even worse, I'd made the process of freeing myself significantly more difficult by having slipped into a sexual relationship with Karl. The knowledge it was wrong troubled me immensely, but the need to fill the aching void in my soul was greater.

In 1985 I married Karl.

Chapter Two

Nothing changed afterwards and in fact things only got worse. It wasn't helped by the fact that a few years later we relocated from friends and family and went to live in a large city where Karl had been offered a job. I didn't know then that removing one's partner from their support system is a common tactic used by abusers and I suspect now this was one of the reasons for our move. Even though I didn't share what was going on in our marriage, if we'd stayed nearby perhaps close friends and family might have detected what was happening.

After a year of office work, which had been my employment since leaving school, I began primary teacher training, and the difficulties Karl and I had were exacerbated by the stress of my studying. Admittedly there were some good times, as Karl had a great sense of humour and could be fun to be with; he was the life and soul of a party. But I never knew when he would turn on me with harsh criticism, false accusations, and painfully wounding comments. He was the very definition of mercurial and I was constantly on edge.

One night we were invited out for a meal at a couple's home. As we sat around the dining table, I'd just started a new topic of conversation when my right foot was sharply trod on.

It could only have been Karl. Why would he deliberately do that? My heart hurt even more than my foot.

My friend noticed my grimace. 'Are you okay?' she asked.

'Yes, I'm fine thanks,' I said, forcing a smile. Shifting on my chair I tucked my feet protectively under it and made myself continue to talk when what I really wanted to do was escape to their bathroom and weep.

Karl's behaviour caused deeper and deeper wounds. I began to get angry and our rows became very heated, with me sometimes losing control and lashing out physically when he verbally attacked me.

On one occasion I threw a phonebook at Karl. He ducked and it crashed into the wall of our flat, making a hole in the plaster. I felt sick at the damage I'd caused and the cost to repair it, as well as fear of the repercussions had I hurt Karl.

We were stuck in a very destructive cycle and still I told no one.

One autumn we went to stay with my parents. On the first morning I woke up to sunlight slanting onto the carpet from the edge of the curtains. It had been forecasted to be a warm, windless day. Perfect!

Karl stirred beside me.

'Good morning!'

He grunted.

'Hey, it's a beautiful day. We can help mum and dad collect pinecones. That's always fun.'

He turned over and stared at me coldly. 'What's fun about it?'

Why was he so grumpy? With him being in that mood, how could I answer without him picking holes in my reply?

'Well, it's nice to be outside on a lovely autumnal day. And it's fun to do chores together. We can chat—'

'Why don't they just buy cones instead? The weather's been wet so they'll be covered in dirt. And we can just as easily talk here.' He made a sound of impatience and turned to lay heavily on his back. 'Besides, I don't have any gloves. I'll just stay here.'

Why was he making such a big deal out of small things? Where was the happy-go-lucky man he showed to everyone else but me?

'Why do you have to spoil things?'

'I'm not. You're making too big a deal out of it.'

How was wanting my husband's company making a big deal? But the real spectre was trying to explain his behaviour to mum and dad. If I began, it could unravel until my greatest fears manifested. Facing the shame over hiding our chaos for so long. Being crushed by a version of, 'You've made your bed, now lie in it.' And—concealed so deeply I barely registered its presence—acknowledging the terror that once exposed, Karl would leave.

Tears threatened at the back of my eyes. I sniffed.

'There you go crying again! You really have a problem, Leanne. You don't get your own way and you turn on the tears. Well, you're not manipulating me.'

At that I did begin to cry, albeit quietly. I wanted to sob out loud, give voice to the frustration and hurt that flooded me, but I kept silent so mum and dad wouldn't hear.

'Oh, for goodness sake! I knew I shouldn't have come.' Karl

thumped his pillow and turned over to face away from me.

I heard footsteps come down the hallway.

'Hey you two, you're missing out on the best part of the day,' dad called out cheerily.

'Yes,' I replied, swallowing my tears and forcing a laugh. 'We must stop being so lazy and get up.'

It hurt to be missing the lovely day as well as special time with mum and dad. But mostly my heart ached because of Karl's behavior. It was like I was a caged mouse that he owned and tormented—sometimes I felt I even hated him.

During all this time I never considered divorce because I thought that the only permissible condition in the Bible was infidelity. Even if I hadn't taken such a simplistic view, I didn't have enough emotional strength to make a stand. With little or no experiential knowledge of God's passionate love for me, I neither loved nor respected myself very much. I had no heart revelation that God's love would have seen me through the painful process of removing myself from Karl's abuse.

In His amazing mercy I believe God hastened the inevitable course of our relationship.

It began with a bizarre series of events in 1994 when I'd been staying with my parents again. Karl couldn't join me because he was in Singapore, checking out the exciting possibility of an international job. He'd rung several times, telling me of the humid heat, the lush vegetation and landmarks he saw from his taxi.

When Karl returned, his flight got in a few hours before me and he was waiting at the airport when I arrived. I hurried towards him, eager to hear more about his Singaporean position.

His smile didn't reach his eyes and there was a distant look in them. Oh no, what was wrong? I put my bag down and went to hug him. His hug was perfunctory and lacked any warmth.

I stepped back, puzzled. 'Are you okay?'

'Just tired. Let's get out of here.' He took my bag but not my hand and walked quickly to the exit.

In the car I tried again. 'So, tell me more about your job.'

'There's not much to say.' Karl put the car in reverse then drove out of the car park. 'They want me for the sales position.'

'Congratulations.' I shifted in my seat to look at him more easily. 'When do you start? How much time do we have to pack up? I'll need to let my school know I'm resigning.'

'Leanne, just leave it alone! I'm jetlagged.'

He didn't speak again and by the time we arrived home I was fed up with his icy silence and desperate for answers.

'What's going on?' I said, after I shut the front door. 'You're acting weird.'

Karl put down my luggage and turned to me. 'You're not able to work in Singapore. You can't go.'

I'd already accepted that Karl had said I couldn't work there for visa reasons and I'd been dreaming about how to spend my days as a lady of leisure. As I love to sing I'd toyed with the idea of taking singing lessons to strengthen my voice. But the idea I *wouldn't* be able to go didn't make sense and I told him so.

'You'd hate it. It's hot and sticky.'

'But I love hot weather!' I frowned, going to sit on the couch. 'What on earth are you talking about?'

'Just what I said.' He continued to stand. 'I'm taking the job but you can't go. You'd be bored and unhappy if you couldn't teach.'

'What sort of marriage is that? You there and me stuck here.' By now my whole body was tense with anger. This was ridiculous. 'Right, tomorrow I'm ringing the New Zealand Embassy to find out what's stopping me from working. There must be some misunderstanding.'

At that, Karl's face changed. From adamant, he now looked furtive.

'What?' I demanded.

He glanced away and was quiet. Finally he spoke. 'There *is* no job,' he sighed. 'I just need time by myself away from our marriage ... to sort myself out, find out what I want.' He looked back at me. 'It's not about you.'

Karl may as well have struck me. Inwardly I reeled—this can't be happening. Time paused with the surreal experience of standing outside of my body and watching myself suffer the shock.

A moment later I came to myself, questions bombarding my mind. How could it be nothing to do with me? If Karl loved me he'd never consider leaving. How would leaving help? Why couldn't he share what was going on? How long had he been considering abandoning me?

His blank face gave no acknowledgement of the devastation his casual and clichéd declaration had inflicted. I was overcome by a myriad of emotions: shock, disbelief, feeling unwanted, discarded, and the acute pain that I was "not enough."

One hellish week later he was gone.

Given the destructive state of our married life, one might have thought that life was better without Karl but his desertion hurt even more than our bad times and I wanted him back. With equal desperation I also wanted answers to questions that had arisen from his shock admission that there was no job in Singapore. I was shaken by the knowledge he'd faked all his phone conversations to me.

Just who was this man who I'd been married to for nine years? What else had he manufactured or hidden?

Summoning my courage, I rang his colleagues at work and one let slip that Karl was very friendly with a woman called Amanda. I'd thought I could not hurt any deeper but I was wrong. Terrified at what I would discover but unable to live with not knowing what was going on, I rang the company again and this time asked to speak to her. The receptionist put me through, thankfully not asking me what the call was about.

My shoulder muscles hunched tight, and my voice was tense—what if I froze up and couldn't even speak? God, help! Amanda answered and her pleasant manner encouraged me.

'Hi Amanda. This is Leanne, Karl's wife.' I plunged on before I ran out of courage. 'Um ... you may know that he's left me. The thing is, I have lots of questions I'd really like answers to. I'm wondering if you'd be kind enough to talk to me.'

She didn't hang up but she was silent.

'I'm sorry,' I added. 'I know this is very awkward and I'm asking a lot.'

'No, no ...' Amanda found her voice. 'It's okay. I was kind of curious to talk to you actually.'

That came as a surprise but a strangely welcome one. I began asking questions and she replied frankly.

One particular incident she relayed was even more outlandish than the imaginary job scenario, and involved Karl trying to pass himself off as the son of a foreign political figure. It was so ridiculous I had to laugh which was the last thing I thought I'd end up doing with the "other woman."

I discovered that through his falsehoods, Karl had created a separate identity for himself at work. Sometimes we'd given our tithes to his company because Karl had said that they were raising money for a charity. Instead, I learnt he'd used the money to shout drinks on a Friday afternoon for everyone in his office. To bolster this portrait of largesse, once out with a colleague Karl had pointed to a substantial house in a wealthy suburb as being our home. The truth was we rented a humble three-bedroom dwelling in a modestly-priced suburb.

As Amanda talked, I was able to make sense of past incidents. All the pieces, each one so puzzling by itself, now came together to make a complete picture—Karl was a compulsive liar.

Then came the self-blame.

How could I not have known? What was wrong with me that I didn't? Was I stupid or just naïve? Confusion contended with condemnation; relief with outrage that apparently our real life was not sufficient for him. The only glimmer of hope from our conversation was that Amanda had suspected Karl wasn't telling the truth and had broken off their relationship. No wonder she was willing to talk to me—she wanted to substantiate her gut feelings about Karl.

Unfortunately, this bombshell discovery was not sufficient to warn me away. My loneliness was too acute and I kept praying that Karl would return. After about four to five months he made contact and we began meeting up. I'd been seeing a wise and empathetic Christian counsellor, and with a new mindset I decided to take Karl back.

This decision came with a warning from my counsellor. 'Karl probably isn't going to change overnight. And so it's going to require change from you, too. Rather than be propelled into anger like in your past, let Karl see the full extent of the hurt he causes you.'

'You mean, "cry"?'

His eyes fill with compassion. 'Yes.'

Emotional exhaustion and fear warred within me. 'It'll be very hard to be so vulnerable again. Karl hates it when I cry.'

The counsellor nodded and smiled sadly in acknowledgement. 'I know. But God will give you the courage. And it's going to have one of two effects—either he'll be brokenhearted about hurting you and seek help, or he'll so dislike the mirror you are holding up to him that he'll leave you again.'

Distress engulfed me, overflowing in tears. The counsellor pushed the box of tissues closer to me.

'I know that's painful to contemplate, Leanne, but won't it be better than carrying on the way things were?'

'Yes. It's hard to admit and terrifying but ... yes.'

The counsellor smiled again. 'Remember there's always the chance he'll want to change.'

So, with God's help I steeled myself to give expression to my pain through tears. It was so difficult to break the habit of feeling angry as it had taken away much of the anguish and given me a feeling of being in control. However, that was an illusion because I couldn't manage the anger and it often became destructive.

One condition of me taking him back was that he attend joint counselling sessions. He agreed but after a few sessions he stopped coming.

I felt sick at what that might portend but took encouragement from the fact he'd consented to the counsellor's suggestion that we visit the country in which he'd grown up as a missionary kid. It seemed to be the catalyst for much of his emotional baggage and might unstop emotions and experiences that could then be dealt with.

The country of Karl's past was hot, noisy, and frantically busy. We spent several days in the small town in which he'd grown up. Afterwards we drove to a remote mountain village and stayed overnight with an elderly couple who Karl had known from his childhood. They were a super couple and I hugged them fondly as we said goodbye.

As we drove along the windy, narrow, gravel road enclosed by rainforest, I pondered Karl's reactions. So far there had been none. No recall of painful memories and no visible emotions either negative or positive—just an unexpected and disturbing silence. It was as if all the traumatic events Karl had described had never happened. Were they inventions like so many other events? But they'd been so real when he'd recounted them.

I decided to risk raising the topic. 'How are you feeling?'

'What do you mean?' He sounded defensive.

'Well, what are you feeling being here? Is it bringing back memories?'

He shrugged. 'Maybe.'

The noncommittal answer infuriated but also puzzled me. How could he feel nothing? 'But—'

'I can't talk about it now!' he snapped, changing down gears. 'The road's dangerous. I need to concentrate.'

It was the perfect excuse.

My hope of the trip acting as a bottle opener to pop the cork of Karl's painful past was coming to naught. I clung to the fact we still had a few days to go in which to discuss the issue.

It turned out we didn't.

That night, back in a major city and the comforts of a hotel, I was woken by Karl shouting at me to wake up. His tone frightened me and my whole body tensed.

'Why, what's the matter?' I switched on the bedside lamp and turned over to face him.

'I'm sick,' he said, clutching his stomach, his face contorted in pain.

Panic shot through me. When someone I loved was ill, I imagined it happening to me. It was hard to separate myself from their pain in order to figure out what to do.

'Are you nauseous?'

'No, maybe ... I don't know! Just do something!' From sitting up in bed, he lay down and curled up. 'I must have food poisoning,' he groaned.

In the midst of my scrambled thoughts, it came to me that I needed to be dressed in order to help him. Forget about make-up and just put on some clothes. Quickly.

'Are you feeling any better?' I asked, having pulled on shorts and a t-shirt and laced up my shoes.

'Are you stupid? Of course not!'

I pushed down my hurt. 'Okay, I'm going down to reception to ask for an ambulance.'

Not waiting for a reply, I grabbed the room key and shut the door behind me.

In the hospital Karl waited for hours before he was examined. He was more distraught than anyone I'd ever seen. At one point he hit the wall beside his bed with a closed fist. 'Just get a gun and shoot me!'

I recoiled at the level of pain he was experiencing, as well as what he'd asked of me. God, help!

Eventually he was seen but the diagnosis was unclear. They gave Karl some powerful medication and stabilised him sufficiently for us to catch our planned flight that evening back to the country's capital. We checked into our hotel then took a taxi to the hospital. After hours of agonised waiting, Karl was diagnosed with kidney stones and told he needed urgent surgery.

Again throwing myself on God for help, I found the clear thinking and competence to arrange the surgery with our insurance company in New Zealand. Karl was in no mood to appreciate how I'd gained access to a phone for international calls, managed the time difference involved and arranged for his surgery.

A few days later Karl was cleared to fly. But the worst of the trauma wasn't over. When we arrived back in New Zealand he had further severe pain and needed to be operated on again. What on earth had the Asian hospital staff done? Had they only got *some* of the stones?

I was never to find out. Karl told me not to come into the hospital. He was adamant about that which puzzled me greatly but I did as he asked.

Finally, the day came when he was due to be released from hospital. I rushed home from school, eager to see him. With Karl's recovery finally underway, we could book a session with the counsellor and make a new start by unlocking and working through Karl's childhood issues.

Entering our flat, I dropped my bag of schoolwork onto the lounge floor and hurried over to Karl. He was sitting on the couch and didn't get up. I assumed he was in discomfort until I noticed the look on his face was not one of pain but of coldness. A jolt of déjà vu shot through me.

'Sit down, Leanne.'

My heart constricted and then pounded. I did as he said, petrified at what he was going to say.

'I'm leaving. Our marriage is over.'

If Karl said more, I wasn't aware of it. Nothing registered other than the fact he was leaving me again. Being found wanting, not once but twice, produced a pain that was bone-deep. There was nothing left to say and so I fled to our bedroom, grabbed Karl's things and threw them into the spare room. I curled up alone in what had been our bed—alternately sobbing then groaning like a hurting animal—not knowing how I'd survive this a second time.

After a night of little sleep and tortuous thoughts there was one thing I *did* know—I couldn't bear to have Karl in the same house as me. His frosty contempt made me ache but worse was the contemplation that I might, in a moment of weakness, humiliate myself by breaking down and begging him to take me back. I could no longer hide from the fact our ten-year-old marriage was truly over. Any love and good times we'd shared were now soiled beyond redemption and utterly worthless. Before I left for school I informed him that by the time I came home that afternoon he had to be gone.

A few weeks later I was told that Karl was having an affair. To my despair was added anger and jealousy. There was torment in the negative comparison of myself to the other woman and the magnification of all my inadequacies. I veered back and forth from heartbroken love to scalding hatred.

Chapter Three

In the midst of all this I told God I no longer trusted Him. If He could let this happen to me, what else might He allow? I told Him angrily He'd have to earn my trust back. But at the same time I reached out daily to Him because, like Peter, I knew the answer to his rhetorical question, "To whom shall we go?" God was the only One who would always be with me in the endless years of misery I envisaged.

Preparing for school each morning was one of the worst times. As I went to apply mascara I'd see the sorrow in my eyes and they'd flood with tears. I'd have to stop and retreat to my room.

The first time it happened I sought comfort in music and God brought to mind Steve Apirana's version of "Something Beautiful." His slow and achingly raw rendition resonated with emotion and enabled me to empty myself of my own. It also offered the faintest hope that God might take all my brokenness and make something beautiful from it. By the end of the song God had cloaked me with His peace and I was able to complete my make-up and get to school on time.

This became the pattern of my mornings and through it came the miracle that I missed only one day of school in nine months.

Another avenue He gave to help process my grief was a new church. I'd found it too difficult to continue at my old one, especially after someone in leadership insensitively suggested that I might be better off without Karl. In hindsight he was right but that was *not* the time to tell me.

Shortly after I began attending, the pastor's wife invited me for coffee and gave me the chance to share my story.

'Well, Leanne,' she smiled kindly as I finished, 'come up for prayer after the service as often as you need. You're going through a tough time.'

'You might regret saying that if you see me every week.'

The woman shrugged. 'If that's what it takes, fine! Grief doesn't run to a set time schedule.'

My eyes welled up. This woman was so understanding. Thank you, God!

Accepting her heartfelt invitation in the weeks that followed, the tears I cried must have filled a multitude of the bottles mentioned in Psalms. And at home in my bed as I mined King David's words for comfort, I must have shed just as many.

In the intense despair of thinking life would never again hold anything other than pain, I once contemplated driving head on into an oncoming car. I was grateful to God the thought only lasted a few seconds. But my desolation became even bitterer a few weeks later.

Driving out of my street onto the main road, my eyes caught on a couple walking along the pavement. The man was similar to Karl—dark and about his height—no! It *was* Karl! My heart clenched in pain and I fought to keep my car from swerving. After the initial grief, a tsunami of rage coursed through me. How dare he walk hand in hand with his mistress only two blocks from my home? How many more times might I have to endure his callous flouting of my replacement?

This encounter coincided with the new principal at my school having just asked each member of staff what our plans were for the future. That evening I seriously contemplated his question. My social life was dismal. All my friends were married and I had no-one to listen to music or attend a movie with on Friday or Saturday nights. I'd tried a church singles group—and was grateful for a woman I met there who became a friend I could go out with—but the men were lacking in almost every way imaginable: dress sense, conversation, wit, and even energy.

There really was only one conclusion—to gain a larger pool of singles with which to socialise and make friends, I would have to leave New Zealand.

But where would I go?

As my mind began to open to life beyond my immediate pain, the answer came quickly—London. Its historical figures and ancient buildings fascinated me and I'd always wanted the chance to visit in person. In terms of work, I'd heard that primary school teachers were sought after so a job was guaranteed. And with two cousins already living in London, I had a familial backstop. With this goal to work towards, I surrendered my privacy and took in a flatmate to share the rent so I could save as much as possible.

Eleven months after Karl left, I was ready to depart.

In addition to my flight luggage I sent a box of personal items via courier. On impulse before sealing the box I took out Split Enz's greatest hits and played, "I Hope I Never (have to see you again)." The lyrics and haunting melody eloquently summed up my desperate need to leave.

After wiping away tears, I snapped the CD into its case and placed it back into the container.

I planned to be in London one year where I would build a new life for myself away from the possibility of seeing Karl. I would leave behind all the places that reminded me of him and all the cruel things he'd said and done.

'Stick with me kid and you'll go places,' he'd said.

We hadn't.

But now, without his help, I was embarking on a venture halfway around the world. Despite my fears about the monumental move I was making, I was shaking off the shackles I'd let him place on me.

PART TWO

April 1996 – December 2001

1996

Chapter Four

The deputy head teacher wished me luck and hurried away. I glanced around the classroom. It was my first day's supply teaching at a school near Old Street tube station in London's inner city. Drab and unwelcoming, the small room had little natural light. There were several windows on one wall but they were too high to enable you to look outside. Without a view the space was oppressive, like being in a basement. By early afternoon I was using the word, dungeon—imprisoned as I was with twenty-eight students.

Actually, that wasn't quite correct. One had gone home sick in the morning—I thought at first she was misleading me in order to skip class. My guilt over that error was soon forgotten in trying to manage two boys whose fight over Power Ranger cards had escalated dangerously. I sent a note to the head teacher and the boys were removed to another class, bringing the total down to twenty-five.

After lunch I took the roll then set the class the task assigned by their teacher—to study the Amazon rainforest. There weren't enough non-fiction books to go around so while I distributed them, I explained that each one had to be shared between two or three students.

'Miss,' yelled a boy near the front of the room, 'Tyrone won't share with me!' I looked over to see a book being yanked away from one boy by another.

What had the teacher been thinking? Why hadn't she photocopied relevant pages to ensure each child had their own copy? Maybe she was some teaching goddess who had them eating out of her hand. As I walked over to deal with the situation, the backchat began again, just like it had that morning.

'Why are we studying the rainforest anyway?' said a

disgruntled boy with a crew cut. 'None of us is ever gonna go there!'

'Speak for yourself, Eddie,' came a cheeky voice from the other side of the room. 'I'm going to be the next David Attenborough!'

Sniggers echoed around the class.

While I attempted to reason with the two students about the need to share and do so cooperatively, one of them interrupted. 'You talk funny, Miss! Where yer from?'

Before I could answer his question and then refocus him, a girl at the back screamed, 'Tell 'em all to shut up! It's too noisy.'

She was right.

And on it went. My eyes increasingly sought the clock on the back wall.

Eventually 3.30 pm arrived and the last student left the room. I sat down, shattered. What had I been thinking in taking on supply teaching work? I was useless. Useless and starving. At the classroom sink I ran some water into my cup and retrieved the last chocolate bar from my bag. I would rather have had a cup of tea but I didn't want to go to the staffroom and be subjected to questions about how my day went.

I ate and drank hurriedly, picked up the papers and pencils strewn over the floor, ensured all chairs were put on their desks, wrote a short note to the teacher, and fled.

That night in my room I shared my experience with Rieta, a Kiwi friend-of-a-friend who had been living in London for several years. Like me, she was a primary school teacher but unlike me she was a veteran of teaching in London.

'So, none of your class did a runner?' she asked. I must have looked as shocked as I felt, for she laughed and said that it wasn't unheard of for students to abscond when a relieving teacher was present.

'No,' I answered.

'And there weren't any fights? Nobody got hurt?'

'No.' I wondered where she was going with her questions.

Rieta smiled and relaxed back in her chair. 'Well, then, you did a good job.'

'What? I did *no* quality teaching. I couldn't remember *half* the kids' names. Most of them weren't even listening to me. I may as well not have even *been* there.' I took my glasses off and rubbed my eyes. 'Gosh, I'm tired.'

'It's tougher than back home, isn't it? Honestly, Leanne, as a supply teacher, and a foreign one at that, all you can hope for in some of those schools is that you keep the kids in class and prevent any fights.'

I grimaced. 'Really? Sounds like babysitting, not teaching.'

'In a way,' Rieta conceded. 'But at least the school hasn't had to split the class between other teachers. You know how disruptive and stressful that is.'

I nodded.

'It's a no-win situation. But the kids who want to learn will take whatever you can offer in between refereeing the others. Just do what you can and then walk away at the end of the day and don't worry.'

'I guess you should know,' I sighed, then gave a reluctant smile. 'Thanks, Rieta. It's just so different from class teaching.'

'Yes, there's certainly no relationship building.' She reached across for the packet of chocolate Hob Nobs she'd brought. 'Right, let's go to the kitchen and make a cup of tea to have with these and you can tell me how you're finding London.'

I'd been in London about four weeks. During the first of these I'd stayed with my cousin, Jill, and her husband, Dan. From their penthouse in Bermondsey they had an outlook in a million—a close and unobstructed view of the south tower of the impressive Tower Bridge. It was very near to the Tower of London which had been the backdrop to scores of historical novels I'd read. To be staying in such proximity to it was a rare gift and a foretaste of the history I had dreamt of experiencing. It cemented my sense that despite uncertainty about the immediate future, I was right to have come.

A few nights later Jill and Dan invited me to have a meal with friends of theirs. During conversation a man asked what had brought me to London. I gave my standard answer that I'd been deserted by my husband and was trying to rebuild my life, and was affronted when he asked whether I was happier now than when I'd been married. But when I contemplated my release from Karl's mercurial moods and my constant fear of his displeasure, I was astounded to hear myself answering that I *was* happier now.

The man's insightful question moved me from offence to gratitude, prompting me to regard the move to the UK as *my* adventure, not a choice forced on me.

With this healthier thinking, thoughts of Karl decreased significantly. After his desertion the leaden misery of it had descended on me within seconds of waking, snuffing out any light and beauty from my world. It was a very long six months before I awoke to experience another thought first.

Now hours passed before Karl intruded into my thinking for there was so much to take in: the cosmopolitan nature of the people around me; the accelerated pace of life; the juxtaposition of the brick, steel, and glass of modern buildings with those of medieval timber and stone; the new currency; the adjustment from private vehicle to public transport. Most confronting of all was the sheer number of people.

The pressure of living and moving amongst a multitude of others was accompanied by unarticulated but defined behaviour. No one looked you in the eye on the street, and in the enclosed spaces of public transport this unspoken code was strictly adhered to and often aided by the closing of one's eyes. I was slow to apprehend this etiquette until I found myself being blanked when I met people's gaze. A corollary to retreating to one's inner world was refraining from making pass-ing comments to strangers or engaging them in conversation.

As I pondered this novel behaviour and began to participate in it myself, I came to understand it functioned as a coping strategy because attempting to interact with the hundreds of passers-by and fellow passengers one encountered would be exhausting.

After a week of sight-seeing and familiarizing myself with the inner city, I settled down to the daunting business of finding a flat. I had no idea where to start. London was huge! Where would it be best to live? How would I go about it? I prayed that God would have something for me that would meet my requirements for

Christian flatmates and would be close to good transport links.

The obvious place to start was to ask Rieta. Amazingly, she knew of a place in a flat in north-west London with two of her friends, Gwen and Bridget. I'd have to share a room with one of them and the suggestion was made that a curtain could be rigged up to provide some separation. However, there were still times when sorrow overwhelmed me and I needed the relief of tears. Privacy was paramount and so I declined.

Then Rieta heard of accommodation close by in Kilburn. A local church rented out five bedrooms on its fourth storey, one of which had just become vacant, and after taking a look, I accepted gratefully. The bedrooms were small and modest but provided all the basics: a bed, a desk and chair, shelves and a free-standing wardrobe. Along with the bedrooms were two bathrooms, a laundry and tiny kitchen/living area. In addition to being secure, the accommodation was reasonably priced with power and heating included. Kilburn was also relatively close to central London, boasting multiple means of transport: two bus routes into the city, the Kilburn tube station on the Jubilee line, Brondesbury station on British Rail and Thameslink trains at West Hampstead, only a short walk away.

Negotiating this transport was initially intimidating but was an essential skill to master. At Jill's, the closest train station had been the sprawling terminus of London Bridge. It gave me access to the Underground's Northern lines, and British Rail to the east and south coasts and a myriad of places in between. Choosing from the large number of levels and platforms was bewildering. Jill did me a great service when she informed me of the difference between a Tube and train, because until then I'd thought they were interchangeable! It dawned on me that some of my confusion came from my faulty assumption that the Underground was entirely underground. Instead, the essential difference was that the Underground serviced London, and British Rail gave access to Greater London and further afield.

A further lesson was learnt—about the importance of direction—when I travelled to the inner-city office of a supply teacher agency called TimePlan. I'd joined up with them before leaving New Zealand and now needed to have an in-person interview.

At Baker Street I changed for a different Tube line. Once seated I consulted a fold-out Tube map and saw that the next station was Great Portland Street. As the train slowed down with a whine, the blurred station name came into focus. To my shock it was Edgeware Road.

A quick glance at my map showed I'd taken a train travelling west and not east.

I leapt out of my seat, through the doors and onto the platform. My heart raced. I was going to be late for my appointment. Where was the platform on which to go back? Looking about me, every commuter was cold-eyed, focused only on getting to their destination. God, help!

Then came the thought that maybe the platform on the opposite side was the eastbound train. I wove through the passengers making for the exit, crossed to the other platform and looked up at the LED display.

"Plaistow. 2m."

I checked my map. Yes, Plaistow was one of the last stations to the east and the train was only two minutes away. Phew, thank you!

I made it to TimePlan very flustered but only slightly late. Travelling in the wrong direction was one mistake I would *not* make again.

Despite my initial confusion, I enjoyed train travel. It was efficient, the hypnotic motion relaxing and there were so many opportunities for surreptitious people watching. The names of the stations fascinated me, whether historical ones like Temple or Charing Cross, ones from childhood games of Monopoly such as King's Cross Station and Bond Street, or quirky ones like Angel, Barking and Elephant & Castle. I wondered how many of the approximately 270 stations I would visit before my year in London came to an end.

Gaining experiential knowledge of the London Transport system didn't come without financial expense and neither had the initial setting up purchases of items like bed linen, and ongoing costs of rent and food. My hard-saved New Zealand dollars—which had bought a depressingly low number of pounds—were dwindling at an alarming rate. I urgently needed to be earning.

With this harsh reality in mind, I took the first teaching assignment I was offered—the confidence crushing one I'd discussed with Rieta. Others were not much easier. The students were streetwise and hardened, quick to sense weakness and attack you verbally if you gave them the opportunity. Also difficult was the foreignness of the UK education system: from the way the roll was called, and monies collected for school lunches, to daily assemblies, to the different names of year levels and even art paper. It was confusing.

My days were filled with self-doubt and anxiety, but God was amazingly creative in how He encouraged me. On the way to another inner city assignment I saw a poster that said, 'Take Courage.' I laughed when I discovered later it was an advertisement for beer!

These stresses of day-to-day supply teaching soon made me more amenable to a long-term position. So when TimePlan offered one in May, I reluctantly shouldered the unwanted burden of paperwork in order to obtain some stability with a class of my own and the satisfaction of creating relationships with the pupils.

The job was at an East Ham school on the opposite side of the metropolis that was London. If I needed a lesson in how huge the city was my journey supplied it, although by London standards the travel time was not exceptional. It took approximately one hour and fifteen minutes to make the short walk from my flat to Kilburn tube station, travel to Baker Street where I changed lines from the Jubilee to the Hammersmith and City, travel to East Ham, make a brief bus journey and then a short walk to school.

Most of the children were Asian with exotic names like Hephzibah, Henna and Inderjit, and as there was no school uniform, many wore traditional clothing of tunics and leggings. They were delightful—well behaved and friendly—and the school, although large, was welcoming so the class paperwork was a bearable trade-off.

One Thursday lunchtime in June, rumour flooded the staffroom that the London Underground staff were striking that afternoon. How on earth would I get home? I had no idea what alternatives there were. Was there a British Rail station nearby? Anxious thoughts dulled my usual voracious appetite.

I turned to the middle-aged teacher sitting next to me. 'Does this affect you? Do you take the Tube?'

She stopped eating to answer. 'No, sorry, I drive to school.'

Just then the head teacher walked into the staffroom. 'Excuse me,' she said and the chatter stopped. 'You may have heard the rumours about the tube strike. Well, it's just been confirmed. Because this will make it difficult for those using the Underground to get home, I want all staff affected to leave school as soon as the children have been picked up. Don't stay for meetings, just start making your way home.'

A young woman in a navy pinafore dress spoke up. 'Will buses be running?'

'Thankfully,' answered the Head Teacher with a grin. 'Otherwise, I hope you've got comfortable footwear.'

Her joke met laughter mixed with groans.

As the Head Teacher left, I got up and approached the woman.

'Hi! Would you like to walk down to the high street and catch a bus together? I'm a bit nervous about this and it'd be great to have company.'

'Sounds good,' she smiled.

'Great, let's meet here ASAP after school.'

At 3:35 pm we met, used the toilet as we didn't know how long the journey home would take, then set off. When we had no difficulty finding a bus, I began to think that there'd been an overreaction to the situation. That is until the driver pulled over and called out, 'All change!' Stranded on the side of a busy road, I had no idea where we were.

The other teacher had her bearings however. She wished me well and walked off.

Fumbling in my bag, I pulled out my London A-Z, an invaluable gift from Jill. London sprawled so far and wide that the publication consisted not of a fold-out map but a sizeable book. I found out where I was but still wasn't sure of the right bus to take.

After a lengthy wait I hailed the first bus I saw and jumped on, just happy to be going west. Hopefully it would take me somewhere close to Oxford Street. As soon as we reached Aldgate, the streets became extremely congested and travel through the inner city was so sluggish the streets seemed less like moving lines of traffic and more like a giant two-lane car park.

Almost two hours had passed since I left school. I nibbled a couple of chocolate bars but was too apprehensive to drink more than a mouthful of water at a time. If I got off the bus to find a toilet it might take hours before another bus came that wasn't full.

Eventually we got to Oxford Street. I was halfway home. Buses came at regular intervals but because they were all crammed with passengers, none of them stopped. Those waiting with me scanned the road intently and when their bus approached they sprinted down the street towards it. I didn't join them—not only did it feel undignified and desperate but I didn't want to be caught up in a stampede of panicking people and risk getting hurt.

Almost forty-five minutes later the Number 16 bus arrived with just enough room for me and a few others. It was the last stage of my journey. By now the experience had turned from surreal to simply exhausting and I couldn't wait to get home and collapse into bed. It was just after 8:00 pm when, with the last of my energy, I climbed the three sets of stairs to my flat.

It had taken five hours to travel a mere thirty-two kilometres.

I went to bed shortly after eating but knew that if I'd had a husband, I would have first found the energy to relay my journey. Re-telling stories was something I loved and this one had been exceptional. It stung that I had no-one to share it with.

'I realise it's too soon for a husband,' I said to God—the two years I needed to wait until I could legally divorce Karl still yawning ahead of me like an un-crossable chasm—'but I do need a close girlfriend. One who can comprehend what I've been through and who can share the emotions with me.' The verse sprang to mind, "A friend who sticks closer than a brother." 'Yes, exactly,' I said, and wept because His prompting of the scripture reminded me that He knew my need.

In the morning the Tube was running as normal. Nevertheless, the two and a half hours of daily travel added to the demands of teaching meant that I always arrived home tired and longing for quietness. Unfortunately, my flat was just off the Kilburn High Road and the traffic noise was relentless. Buses, lorries, taxis, cars, and motorcycles thronged the streets. The Metropolitan and Jubilee trains clattered across the over-bridges which ran at eye level with our kitchen and bathrooms. Adding to the din was the clamour of voices rising up from the street—chatter and shouts and sometimes violent arguments.

I found the cacophony seriously distressing and even wondered if it would drive me crazy. After a few weeks it came to a crisis point when I had to deal with my toxic thoughts. I'd been asking God to help me and the idea came that it might simply be a case of mind over matter. So I told myself firmly and repeatedly that I was going to get used to it. Over time, my mind obeyed until the wondrous point where I only noticed if the traffic noise temporarily diminished.

Constant noise wasn't the only aspect of Kilburn to which I needed to adjust. The other was the filth. Kilburn boasted few trees or green spaces, and the streets were dirty. While fruit and vegetable stores were numerous, their wares were displayed on stacked crates on the footpath and covered with a fine film of exhaust and grit. Advertisements, notices, and even graphic handbills for prostitutes were plastered everywhere—not only on walls but lampposts, doorways, and bus stop shelters. The large concrete-tiled pavements were stained and littered with the inevitable cigarette butts, sweet wrappers, crisp packets, and tattered shopping receipts; worse though were objects like syringes, condoms, and—once—human faeces. But what really churned my stomach was the sight and sound of men hawking and spitting cloudy globules onto the pavement.

As I grew accustomed to these assaults to my senses, I was intrigued to see how many diverse people and ethnicities made their home in Kilburn: Irish, Moslems, Asians, Europeans, and Commonwealth imports like myself.

I was stimulated by the different cultures, their dress and language, but there was one person who scared me—a peculiar older woman who frequented the high street. Large stick in hand, she walked along muttering and cursing under her breath. That was disturbing enough but from time to time she'd suddenly explode and turn on a hapless passerby—brandishing her stick at them and screaming dementedly.

Not frightening but still disconcerting were the beggars on the streets. It felt so inhumane to sidestep around them, avoiding eye contact and their appeals for money—the occasional gold coin I gifted didn't alleviate my guilt.

On Kilburn High Street were shops of all descriptions. Liquor outlets jostled with Irish pubs, corner stores with greasy cafes; there were newsagents and pharmacies, cab stations, and cheap clothing stores. LED signs in various languages flashed luridly from their windows. Most businesses shut at night and pulled down graffiti-splattered steel roller-doors on closing but some shops were open 24/7.

One of them advertised itself as a place in which one could make phone calls and soon after moving to Kilburn it was the scene of great embarrassment for me. One summer evening when the payphone in our flat wasn't working, I entered the shop, found a booth and rang a friend in London. When I finished, I went to the counter to pay.

'Three pounds,' said the assistant in a bored voice, not bothering to look up from his magazine.

'What?' I replied. 'Three pounds to call London? Really?' I'd thought it might be a pound or two but not three. I was greatly dismayed as £3 was about NZ$6. I was still converting currencies at that stage and it was an exorbitant amount of money for one short phone call to someone in the same city.

'London?' The man's voice now had an edge to it.

'Yes.'

'You rang *London*?' The man now made eye contact with me and looked incredulous.

I shifted on my feet. 'Is something wrong?' I stammered.

'This shop is for *international* phone calls. Why'd you come here to call London?' he demanded. 'Your phone call went from London, all around the world and back to London again!'

I felt like such an idiot. Mumbling something about being new to the UK, I fumbled in my purse for some gold coins to pay for my "international call" to London, and scuttled out of the shop as fast as I could.

Chapter Five

During the mid-term break in May I went to the Lake District with Rieta, Gwen and another friend called Susan to stay at a cottage in Little Langdale.

I'd come from New Zealand with the parochial notion that it boasted the world's best scenery but I had to relinquish such thinking for here was a different kind of beauty from New Zealand's rugged landscapes. Rocky tors tumbled away to brilliant green pastures intersected by elegantly-crafted dry-stone walls—it was a kind of manicured terrain I'd not encountered before. With it being mid-spring, there was colour everywhere in pale-pink apple blossom, flamboyant red rhododendrons, saffron-coloured daffodils, and scarlet and egg-yolk yellow tulips.

One morning Rieta, Susan, Gwen, and I were going to visit Dove Cottage, Wordsworth's home for several years.

'You ready, Leanne?' Gwen called.

I was in the bathroom, halfway through applying my foundation. I still had to put on my mascara and lipstick and hated being rushed—my mascara might smudge and the outline of my lipstick could end up crooked. 'I've almost finished my make-up. Won't be a minute!'

'It's only us,' Gwen laughed. 'You needn't bother.'

I wished she was right and that I could go sans make-up like her. But leaving the house without it was unthinkable.

Gwen and I differed in several ways. Like Rieta she was matter of fact and spoke as she saw, qualities well suited to her vocation as a nurse. She didn't appear to be as in touch with her emotions as I was and had little to say when she learnt that I had been married for ten years. Then again, no single person I'd met had any idea of the devastation caused by the breakdown of a marriage—and to be fair, how could they?

Despite our differences, the holiday helped consolidate a friendship between Gwen and me. She was good company and we were to go to many concerts and movies together. She had a dry sense of humour which I enjoyed. Gwen was also very practical, generous and wonderfully hospitable—a quality which I would come to value greatly in the future.

The Lake District trip fired my desire to see as much of the UK as I could in my one year. To document this I bought a map of the UK for my bedroom wall. A free magazine called *Time Out* proved very useful. Aimed at southern hemisphere travellers, it detailed upcoming gigs, jobs, accommodation, and cheap travel deals. While looking for day trips by coach, I found an excellent company that offered reasonably priced excursions to famous towns and cities, stately homes and castles, all within two to three hours travel from London.

To celebrate finishing school in late July I journeyed to pretty Hever Castle. It was the childhood home of Anne Boleyn, Henry VIII's second and ill-fated wife, and mother of the brilliant Queen Elizabeth I. Her story intrigued me. Standing in Anne's bedroom, I longed to be able to capture a real sense of the woman. It was wishful thinking of course. Nevertheless, being able to visit Anne's home after decades of reading about her, was a remarkable experience.

On the coach journey home, I pondered my fascination with Anne. Some novels depicted her as heartless but accounts of her behavior and speech were recorded only by men *and* from a time when women were accorded less understanding and appreciation than today. If some of what I'd done and said to Karl was examined years afterwards, with no notion of the emotional cruelty that precipitated them, I doubt they'd be interpreted sympathetically either.

A summer holiday in Europe beckoned but there were six weeks to get through without pay. Another concern was that I wasn't yet brave enough to travel solo. A solution came in the form of a Christian company called Oak Hall Expeditions which provided budget coach holidays to Europe. I booked a trip to Pineda del Mar, a small seaside town about fifty kilometres north of Barcelona in Catalonia, Spain.

While it was true I was excited, there were also negative emotions. From the few pleasant memories of travel with Karl, I knew the comfort and ease of having a companion. You could share your impressions of people and places you were seeing and even poke a little fun at the most absurd. To travel alone would have its unique sadness.

On arrival at Victoria Station from where the coach departed, my nervousness was exacerbated by the now apparent fact that the majority of the forty or fifty others were in their early twenties. At age 33, I hoped I wouldn't be excluded as the granny of the group.

I was relieved when two young women invited me to make up the third person in a hotel room sleeping three.

"What do you do, Leanne?" Jane asked as we were getting ready for bed on the first night.

I paused in putting away my clothes. "I'm a primary school teacher. How about you?"

"I work as a secretary for an accountant."

"And you," I asked her friend, Tracey.

"A sales assistant at Topshop."

"She's so lucky," Jane moaned, "she gets staff discount on all her clothes."

"Don't forget I get some for you too!"

Jane laughed. "You're right, you *are* generous. That reminds me, when we get back can you get me a crop top like Scary Spice wears?"

Lying in bed listening to Jane and Tracey talk, I felt that our life experiences would make closeness impossible. By my mid-twenties I was married, had purchased a house and was budgeting for a mortgage, rates, and insurance.

A few days later I crossed paths with a slightly older girl and guy from our group. They were good friends but not dating, and were open to expanding their friendship to include me.

"Tell us about your impressions of teaching here in the UK," Karen asked as we ate paella one evening in Barcelona. We'd discovered we were all teachers, albeit I taught primary school and they taught secondary. We had endless scope for conversation about teaching and shared an admiration for Gaudi's brilliance, but when it came to relationships the dialogue petered out.

"I'm sorry to hear that," Karen said when I divulged I was separated.

"That can't have been easy," Pete added. Then he changed the topic and asked if we knew anything about the La Font Magica performance our tour group was going to view that evening.

Can't have been easy? No kidding! What an understatement. I felt painfully alone. My experience was that of a married woman and yet I was no longer married; I was single and yet had little knowledge of life as a single person. Feeling I belonged nowhere was a solitary and uncomfortable place to be. I longed for the inbuilt companionship and support of marriage, the ready availability of physical touch. Hugs were so few when you were single. Sometimes I felt I was withering up without them.

But aside from my personal struggles, I loved Spain. As someone who felt the cold, one of the first things I appreciated was the even temperatures from early morning to evening. The unbroken warmth was blissful, as was the freedom from having to carry extra layers of clothing.

The pleasure of visiting ancient cities was immense. My eyes roamed constantly, cataloguing scenes and impressions: medieval cathedrals where leering gargoyles lurked, narrow cobbled passageways that beckoned with intrigue, balconies dripping with bright flowers and sometimes household washing, and niches set into walls filled with decorative carvings or sculptures.

Spain also appealed culturally. Being a lover of afternoon naps I appreciated the practice of siesta, even though it meant some stores were closed when we wanted to shop. And in the balmy evenings there was pleasure in seeing many three-generational family groups strolling together.

During this time I became acutely aware of how monolingual I was, and how small-minded and ignorant that now seemed. It was the first time in my life I felt inclined to overcome a long-held aversion to foreign languages due to an unfortunate experience as a twelve–year–old when I'd moved from a tiny primary school to a high school of 450 students.

In my first French class, our teacher, Mr Walter, told us to turn a certain page in our textbooks. French was a language and culture of which I knew nothing. Nervousness gnawed at me. I found the relevant page. The heading said "Diner au Restaurant."

Presumably it was talking about dining in a restaurant. Maybe French wouldn't be too bad.

'Drew, please read the first section,' said Mr Walter.

Reading out loud? No! Was there to be no instruction, no book work? Then I felt sick remembering that because I'd begun late in the year I'd missed out on three terms of teaching.

A cocky boy with curly blonde hair read the heading, "A la Carte" followed by several sentences. I noted the words sounded nasally but most striking was that they bore little or no resemblance to how they were spelt.

'Thank you, Drew.'

Who would be next? My stomach contracted.

'Leanne, could you read the next part?'

What? My heart thumped hard. The words stared at me, daring me to attempt them. "La Buffet" was the heading.

'Please begin, Leanne.'

My whole body tense, I made myself speak. 'La Buff-it.' Thinking I'd made a reasonable attempt, I was stunned to hear a few snickers behind me. What had I got wrong?

'That's "la buffet,"' corrected Mr Walter.

Tears pricked at my eyes. How was I supposed to know that? This was so unfair.

'Please continue, Leanne.'

The first phrase was utterly indecipherable, as were my pitiful attempts. The words and my classmates' expressions silently mocked me. What a stupid language! And so I blamed French for my humiliation which was easier than facing up to the unkindness of both my teacher and peers.

That self-delusion reminded me of my inability to face up to Karl's emotional cruelty. I had kept making excuses for it, putting it down to his damaged childhood. The price of that was to contort myself and my behavior to avoid giving him any reason to criticize me or be unkind. I'd told myself subconsciously that my only role was to love and forgive him and in doing so God would hopefully soften his heart. I'd been too afraid to acknowledge that if Karl had truly loved me, he wouldn't have continued abusing me. Admitting the truth would have meant giving Karl an ultimatum and I wasn't willing to face the grief and loneliness that might have followed.

After ten years of such treatment, it had become so normal that I had difficulty identifying it. God revealed this in an astonishing way, providing an old friend in whom I could confide. Erica and her husband were a couple Karl and I had known from a church we'd attended in New Zealand and they'd been employed by Oak Hall Expeditions for a position not dissimilar to "camp parents."

One evening after dinner had finished, Erica and I remained behind in the dining room to chat.

'So, Leanne, what are your plans for the future?'

I sat back in my chair and considered for a moment then replied that I'd love to be remarried. My hesitancy had been because many Christians thought that I should simply accept my circumstances and remain unmarried.

Erica, however, was understanding and asked if I'd met anyone.

'Not yet, although I am interested in Vic.'

She frowned slightly.

'You know, one of the few older men on the trip, the one with dark hair. He's divorced,' I added to let her know that he'd had a similar experience to me. I found Vic attractive and he'd intrigued me with his taciturn manner and the challenge that lay in drawing him out.

Erica's response was immediate. 'Leanne, he's not the type for you. There's a ... a coldness, a kind of hardness about him.' She paused to look directly at me with a sweet smile. 'You need a kind man, someone patient.'

Shocked into silence at her directness, I considered her statement. Reluctantly, I conceded that Vic was not warm. I'd been drawn to an elusive personality but why should I be the one making all the effort? Didn't I want to be cherished and pursued? And why was I thinking that patience and kindness were synonymous with tame and boring?

My counsellor in Auckland had advised me not to date for the two years of separation required before I could divorce Karl. He said I needed to give my soul time to heal. The wisdom of what had seemed like a life sentence at the time now revealed itself in full because I was still exercising poor judgement. I could have been persuaded to ignore his advice if Erica hadn't spoken up.

Clearly my relationship with Karl had so depleted my confidence and distorted my expectations that it seemed normal to be treated badly.

When I arrived back in London I saw the city afresh, as you do when absent from your home for a time. I missed Spain's warmth and slower pace of life. The harried hustle of workers on the streets and the Tube, the oppressive grey skies, and the cooler weather were depressing.

I also keenly felt the loss of male company that I'd enjoyed. It was with men that I was more likely to discuss history and architecture—topics of special interest to me now in history-steeped Europe. Men were often ready with a joke and I loved to laugh. And there was no denying the frisson present in talking with an attractive single man.

I pondered how to achieve the regular company of men without dating.

One way to meet them would be to join a sevens rugby team but I'd never been sporty. One of the few forms of exercise I enjoyed was dancing, although it was only the boogying kind as I'd never had formal dance lessons. Having heard good things about a French jive called Ceroc, I decided to try it. Ceroc classes were extremely popular in London, and one of its locations on Friday nights was in stylish South Kensington at St Paul's Onslow Square where I went to church. It gave me confidence to know that at least the journey and venue would be familiar.

For my first evening I selected black trousers and a colourful top. I suffered from flat feet which quickly became sore when I wore heels so I donned comfortable shoes for the journey there, with my low-heeled dancing shoes stored in a backpack—the ubiquitous accessory of car-less Londoners.

When I arrived, I found a far more glamorous event than I'd anticipated. The couple on the stage teaching were stunning, in both looks and execution of their dance moves. Female dancers looked chic and feminine, most wearing short, full skirts. I immediately knew I'd spend the next week after school searching for one. The men weren't quite as well-dressed but most made an effort, and some brought a small towel with which to mop up their sweat, and even a change of shirt. I only had to place my hand once on a man's shoulder and feel a damp, sweat-soaked shirt to appreciate that courtesy.

The evening commenced with a half-hour beginner class, freestyle for the next thirty minutes, then an intermediate level lesson for the next half hour, followed by freestyle for the rest of the evening. One of the many excellent aspects of Ceroc was that you didn't need a partner for the lessons. Couples were placed in rows and after every song the surplus male or female dancers were invited to join in, with the same number of 'tail-end' dancers stepping out to form a new queue. This system meant that everyone got regular dances throughout the lessons as well as changing partners often.

My dance moves were slow and studied. I tried to make up for my low skill level by being extra friendly and chatty—as much as I could with my mind and body desperately struggling to follow the man's lead and master the steps. But in spite of my slowness to learn I immediately felt this was a place in which I could come to feel at home and was determined to persevere. I loved the upbeat music, the fact the event was alcohol free, the opportunity to learn at a basic level each week, and the chance to dress glamorously for an evening. Equally important was the weekly opportunity to be held by a man, although a few of them were boorish and one or two gripped your fingers like you were their last pound.

As I went along week after week, I made several male friends and even though I never dated any, I thoroughly enjoyed their company. One was Augustine, a Singaporean man who was always teasing me and encouraging me to relax, and another was Paul, a friendly, laid-back Cockney who entertained me simply by talking.

'Yer from Australia?' he asked, the first time we were partnered.

'No,' I laughed. 'Next door.'

'Yer 'aving a larf.'

'No, no... sorry, I didn't mean next to South Kensington. I meant the country next to Australia.' So much for my clumsy attempt at humour.

'Ah, Noo Zealand,' he said, lifting my right hand to indicate that I should step forward. 'Beau'iful country I 'ear.'

Before I could answer, he spoke again. 'Looks like yer moving on. Might see yer la'er at the Crown.'

In the following weeks as I became a regular at St Paul's Ceroc, I went with the dancers who poured into the local pub after Ceroc finished at 10 pm. Socialising over a drink was fun and getting to know the men helped me relax with them while dancing. I could better interpret their hand signals, learn the moves and how to spin without losing balance.

After almost six months, there came an evening when I suddenly realised I was focusing on the music and my feet were automatically keeping in time with the beat. It was a glorious moment. With this transition came newfound confidence and I started attending Saturday night dances at the Hammersmith Town Hall where I was frequently asked to dance. Ceroc nights became the highlights of my week, not just for the satisfaction of having mastered the basic moves and the physical pleasure of dancing but the anticipation each evening that I might meet a special man. Although at the back of my mind nagged the thought that if I did, it would be very difficult to keep the relationship at a friendship level until my divorce was processed.

But no-one special materialised and my resolve was not tested. Night after night I made the long journey home alone with my hopes deflated. I tried not to look too enviously at the couples I saw as I walked despondently back to the Tube station with aching feet and equally aching heart. Unable to shake the feeling that my best-by-date was fast approaching, I felt that what remaining youth I had was unappreciated and going to waste.

When I wasn't socialising, I was working assiduously at a Church of England school in which I had a position for the autumn term. Thankfully it was nearby in Camden and I didn't need to add much travel time to the long hours the job entailed. The school was well known for its art and after school in addition to the normal tasks of planning and marking the children's work, I spent hours framing their art. Even once the double-mounting in complementary colours had been completed, it had to be arranged to best advantage on the walls of the school hall.

The most difficult part of this position, however, were several challenging children in my Year 3-4 class who took full advantage of the restrictions that limited a teacher's disciplinary actions. I had several run-ins with a girl called Zoe but one particularly rankled.

It was time for Physical Exercise and the children had just come back to class having changed into their PE kit in the bathrooms.

'Well done for changing quickly, Room 3. Can you please line up and we'll head out to the courts. Jack and Peter, can you take this key and get out one ball and a dozen training bibs from the PE room and meet us on the court?'

'Yes, miss,' said Jack, reaching for the key.

The children made a zig-zag line between the desks. I was about to tell the first child to lead us out of the classroom when I saw Zoe out of the corner of my eye. She was still seated at her desk.

'Zoe, please join the line.'

Her eyes locked with mine. 'No.'

'Zoe, there isn't a choice,' I said, my eyes boring into hers. 'We're all going out for PE and you're coming.'

'You can't make me,' she retorted with a toss of her head. Several boys snickered.

No, *I* can't but the Head Teacher can. Then it hit me. She was away on a course! I stepped up to Zoe's desk, hoping my proximity might make her acquiesce.

'You can't touch me,' she sneered, 'it's against the law.'

As much as I desperately wanted to grab her arm at that point and march her outside, I knew she was correct. Meanwhile the class was getting restless.

'Come on, miss, you're wasting time!' called out a girl and several others muttered their agreement.

'It's not fair!' a boy complained. 'Just leave her here and let's go!'

I was so frustrated—with Zoe, with my impotence as a teacher but also with the rest of the class who couldn't seem to understand that I was powerless.

'I'm sorry Room 3 but the school says that no teacher can leave a student alone in class. As Zoe refuses to come we'll have to remain here. She will be reported to the Head Teacher and I'll make some time for PE tomorrow instead. Now, can you please go and get changed back into your uniforms?'

The students' moans echoed my own silent ones.

The week-long mid-term break in October couldn't come fast enough. With the Oak Hall experience behind me, I felt sufficiently confident to travel on my own and so I booked the train to Holyhead in Wales and the ferry across to Belfast. Alongside my fascination for English history was a similar but very personal interest in Northern Ireland as my dad's mother came from Ballymena in County Antrim. In fact, it was because of this that I was able to attain my UK Patriality Visa. Nearly halfway through my year in London, time was running out to meet my Nana's cousin who lived in Belfast and with whom I'd been in correspondence. It was one of Nana's dearest wishes that I would get to meet Aunty Charlotte, nicknamed Chatty.

I arrived in Belfast on Saturday afternoon and checked into a single room in a youth hostel.

The next afternoon I visited Chatty. After a happy time together, she phoned around her family and so began unexpected but delightful whirlwind visits to several Irish relations. I'd never been so feted. Then Chatty's niece, Irene Brown, generously invited me to go and stay with her for a few nights. She was lovely and we got on very well, both single women enjoying the blessing of company.

Having made a friend as well as met a relative, it was sad saying goodbye to Irene. I missed the lovely lilt of her Northern Irish accent and the sense of being connected to family whilst so far from home. It was back to being alone.

Not long afterwards I had another farewell. Rieta had decided to move back to New Zealand so Gwen, Bridget, and I accompanied her to Heathrow. She'd been such a wonderful gift from God. It gave me a feeling of security knowing that God had gone before me and prepared my way, and it was a big step forward in my journey to learn to trust Him again.

After mid-term break, each class at school began preparations for an evening Christmas service to be held on the last day of term. When the occasion finally arrived, it was more special than I could have dreamed.

The hall was awash with candlelight, making the gorgeous Christmas-themed artwork on the walls come alive. The children's pictures glittered with gold and silver paint, and the ambience was simply magical. My class's flawless performance of Gloria in Excelsis Deo left me with tears in my eyes. Before I left I was given a beautiful bouquet and several lovely gifts from students. The beauty and kindness I experienced that evening displaced the difficulties I'd faced there during the autumn term and left me feeling grateful for the experience.

A few days later I took a train to Ashford, Kent, to spend Christmas with friends from New Zealand. Richard and Sarah were a Kiwi/British couple who had moved to the UK just before me; it was so comforting to be with them for my first ever Christmas away from my immediate family. They were great company and we enjoyed lots of laughter; one of the reasons being that Richard was hilariously outspoken.

In keeping with that fact, he asked me one evening, 'So, when are you divorcing that plonker?'

'Richard!' exclaimed Sarah. She looked at me and rolled her eyes.

'It's okay, I know what he's like!' Although thoughts of Karl were fewer and more fleeting as time went on, it wasn't possible to put a decade of memories to rest in just one and a half years. Occasionally it was a relief to talk with people who had known Karl and knew what I'd been through.

'It can't come soon enough. I just want to have it over and done with and then forget all about him. He left in May '95 so I have about six months to go till the two years are up.' I stopped to give a little grin. 'My sister Wendy's going to serve the papers.'

'Good for her,' replied Richard. 'I hope she rolls them around a baseball bat and hits him with it.'

I snorted with laughter at his outrageous comment—it was immensely gratifying to have a male friend take my side.

After three wonderful days, made even more festive by a light snowfall, I reluctantly said goodbye to Richard and Sarah and took the train back to London.

1997

Chapter Six

The remainder of the two weeks Christmas break sped by and wasn't long enough in which to fully recharge. If it hadn't been for me needing a steady income, I would have gladly tried my hand again at supply teaching. However, in addition to my London living costs, I had New Zealand expenses—the storage of my furniture and a private superannuation scheme. The financial pressure had led me to accept a one term position in another Church of England school, this time south of the River Thames in Lambeth.

The children lived mostly in soulless high-rise apartments or housing estates. I believed the confined conditions and lack of green space in which they could play had a negative impact on them as they seemed to have a pervading tetchiness. This wasn't improved by the school's old, cramped classrooms and small concrete playground devoid of any grass.

Added to the behavioural issues with which I struggled were two other matters. The first was that the school was being inspected by Ofsted, the UK's Office for Standards in Education. I'd heard the assessments were rigorous, entailing meticulous planning and the stress of class inspections. The second was that I had a Year Two class which was one of the two primary school year groups in the UK to undergo yearly standardised testing. The pressures were so immense that I approached the school management and was granted concessions and extra help. In acknowledgement of their support, I agreed to stay to the end of the school year.

To make the workload bearable I needed an overseas holiday to look forward to and God provided a delightful travelling companion. At St Paul's I'd met another friend-of-a-friend from New Zealand, an early childhood education teacher called Margot. Her job was also intense and like most Kiwis working in London, she wanted the recompense of travel. The first trip we booked was to Malaga, Spain in the April holidays.

Our time in the Costa del Sol exceeded my expectations and was memorable for many reasons, my favourite being our day trip to Granada. Overlooking the city was a U-shaped ridge which featured the palace and fortress complex of the Alhambra. It was a gloriously sunny and warm spring day and we spent the afternoon exploring every inch, marvelling at the fecund gardens bursting with flowers and fruit, the fragrant walls of Cyprus trees, sparkling pools, and tiered pathways of warm brick framed with climbing roses. The perfect foil to this colour and life were the Moorish buildings with their adorned arches and intricate geometric shapes.

From a room inside the Alhambra, I looked through a window out across the beauty of the gardens and the Sierra Nevada Mountains in the background.

'If I ever get remarried,' I said, 'I want to honeymoon here. It's sublime.'

'I hope he's well-heeled," replied Margot.

'Yes,' I laughed. 'I guess it would be expensive. Maybe I'd better not limit my options to a rich man—they're not exactly queueing up!'

I jested but it was true. Although I didn't need a queue—just one man of integrity who would value me.

History of another culture was on offer when Margot and I made a day trip to Morocco. A coach took us past Gibraltar to the Port of Tarifa where we were ferried across the Strait of Gibraltar to the coastal city of Tangier.

Our tour guide took us on a walking tour of the Medina, the ancient quarter of the city. We threaded through narrow side streets with buildings painted in faded yellow and dusty cream with small wooden-shuttered windows, overhanging door lintels, metal transoms, and tiny closet-sized second storey rooms jutting out into the walkways above our heads.

We emerged into an open area with markets which exploded with colour, textures, and smells, overflowing with goods ranging from leather and wool to metal and pottery. Trinkets abounded but what I wanted to purchase was something larger, something purposeful that I could enjoy daily. A colourfully-striped cotton throw with tasselled ends caught my eye—I could use it to decorate my rather Spartan bedroom. On checking the price, I was disappointed to discover it was more expensive than I'd budgeted for. I was about to walk away when suddenly I realised how I could pay for it.

It was April 1997, virtually two years since Karl left. My divorce was imminent and there would be no further need to wear my ring. Until then I'd felt I should continue to do so as legally I was still married. I turned to Margot who was contemplating her own purchases.

'Hey, I've just had an idea.'

'Hmm,' she said, twirling a silver necklace in her hands.

'You know how I was talking about throwing my wedding ring into the Strait of Gibraltar on the way home?'

'Oh yeah,' she grinned, looking up, 'your grand gesture!'

'Cheeky! Well, why don't I trade it for something instead? That way I actually make use of it.'

'Maybe. But what about selling it in London?'

I sighed. 'I don't understand why but second hand it's worth almost nothing—astonishing when you consider how much rings cost to buy new.'

'Go for it then,' Margot urged, and so I did.

At the end of the bartering, I slipped the ring—the last physical reminder of my marriage—from my finger. As I placed it in the creased palm of the Moroccan trader, I suppressed a smile at the thought that it had been purchased by a conman for the second time.

And so I went back to the UK minus a wedding ring plus a growing love for Spain.

Back in London I continued to keep in touch with a man from Surrey who I'd met during my first Spanish holiday. I suspected he was younger than me, possibly quite a bit younger, but he wouldn't be drawn on the subject. On his suggestion we attended an opera in London—not an experience I'd care to repeat—and then he invited me to stay with him and his flatmates for a weekend in May.

I went with curiosity, wanting to find a way to casually address the issue of our ages.

I'd taken a train down on Saturday morning and after I arrived we put away my luggage and went to sit in his kitchen. He poured himself a drink of milk, and asked what I'd like.

'Do you have any fruit juice please?' I asked, 'Although I probably *should* be drinking more milk for the calcium now I'm over 30.'

I watched him closely for a reaction. What would he do? There was the merest blink of his eyes and then, as he poured me a glass of orange juice, he said, 'Did I tell you about this girl at church? She's quite sweet and I'm wondering if she's interested in me.'

I was impressed by his adroit sidestepping of the topic but not how—in a matter of seconds—I went from potential girlfriend to agony aunt. Clearly his legal training was paying off handsomely. He was polite for the remainder of the weekend but Sunday afternoon and the train back to London couldn't come fast enough.

On the journey home I reflected on the friendship gone sour. It seemed not only was I interested in men who were aloof but ones who were too young. Karl had been eighteen months younger than me. Maybe I needed to consider older men, although the idea was repellant.

Despite that knockback, my social life was becoming busy and exciting as I added rock concerts to Ceroc. One evening I'd gone with my cousin, Malcolm, to see Sting perform. Enthralled by the live performance and having discovered that the tickets weren't exorbitant, I subsequently kept my eye on upcoming concerts by other artists.

When I phoned my sister, Wendy, later in May to arrange for her to serve the divorce papers, she raised the subject of whether I was coming home as I'd planned. Her question prompted the realisation that the idea held zero appeal. London was beginning to feel like home and there was still far too much to experience and explore of the United Kingdom, let alone Europe, to consider leaving. There was also the fact that the UK held far more single Christian men than New Zealand. And so I decided to stay on for an indefinite period of time.

On the basis of that decision Wendy helpfully arranged to house a few of my favourite pieces of furniture, store several boxes of special things, and then sell the rest of my belongings on my behalf. It was a relief to be released from my monthly storage fees and have some welcome extra funds.

With the arrival of the summer school holidays I set off for my second journey with Oak Hall Expeditions to Tuscany, Italy. Like thousands of tourists before me, Tuscany held me captive to its beauty. There were piazzas, off which were charming narrow streets crisscrossed with high ornate arches, and stunning black-and-white marbled duomos. Then there were the postcard panoramas over sepia-coloured roofs to green lines of grapevines and hazy silver dots of olive trees. The constant warmth was also a boon.

But what really set that holiday apart was the way God had planned for me to meet two sensitive, kind, and fun-loving Christian women who would become lifelong friends, Christy and Alison.

We befriended a few others, including an Irish guy called Alan, and two close friends, Mark and Matt. The latter two loved to clown around and kept our group well entertained. On one occasion they asked each of us two questions. Inexplicably, our answers caused them great hilarity but they wouldn't divulge the reason. Then came my turn.

'What's your favourite animal and why?'

'Horses,' I replied, 'because they're beautiful, graceful and strong.'

This resulted in more laughter. To the question of what was my second favourite animal I said, 'A dog because it's faithful and loyal.'

Knowing looks passed between Mark and Matt but still they said nothing.

When everyone had given their answers, all was made clear—the first answer revealed how you saw yourself and the second answer, the qualities you desired in a partner. Laughing along with everyone else, I felt acutely embarrassed thinking about the immodesty of my first reply. Yet the more I contemplated my answers, the more insightful the second seemed. I'd never put into words the characteristics I was looking for in a future husband but faithfulness and loyalty now held tremendous value for me.

All three guys were kind and thoughtful and genuinely decent young men whose company I thoroughly enjoyed. All far too young though.

Some of the group wanted to pair me up with Alan, but I wasn't drawn to him as more than a friend. He did endear himself to me though by introducing me to the British group, Delirious, whose upbeat and heartfelt Christian songs lifted my spirit. "What is This Thing Called Love?" contained the thought that as we cast away our dreams, maybe they would return in time. Personalising the lyrics instilled hope in my soul that maybe love would come my way again, although I now acknowledged I needed a man of experience and not a youth.

Maybe Erica's advice was taking hold.

Arriving back in London I had less than twenty-four hours in which to wash my clothes, repack and fly to join Margot in Dublin for a minivan tour of the Republic of Ireland. There couldn't have been a more vivid contrast to Tuscany's Mediterranean climate than Ireland's wild, damp, verdant lands.

With my Nana having come from Northern Ireland and Margot claiming some Celtic heritage—and looking the part with her gorgeous curly red locks—we felt some kinship with the country and relished Ireland's misty emerald splendour. The tour visited the lonely round towers at Glendalough, the mysterious phenomenon of the Brownshill portal tomb, and the dramatic Rock of Cashel. We were also taken to Blarney Castle with its terrifying backwards lean over the gaping hole 26 m above the ground to kiss the Blarney Stone.

The sights were splendid but unfortunately, the tour was incompetently run in several regards. In the end the owner paid for those who wanted to, to take the bus back to Dublin and be completely re-funded. Margot and I took up the offer and as we'd already toured much of the eastern and southern parts of Ireland, we took a train north to Londonderry and then made our way down the west coast.

We stayed at a B&B in Salthill, Galway, where the proprietress made delicious Irish soda bread for breakfast. On each of our three nights we enjoyed the foot tapping live Irish music at the nearby O'Connor's Famous Pub.

Of all the highlights of the holiday, the most dramatic was a day excursion from the port of Galway to Inishmore in the Aran Islands. From its cracked carapace of grey rock—water-split and laced with fern—to its imposing rock fortress towering above pounding seas, what could have been bleak I found starkly beautiful.

Margot and I departed Ireland reluctantly.

The holidays were rapidly receding and the new school year loomed. Before the previous one had ended, I'd been persuaded by the Lambeth school to come back for a full school year to teach the upcoming Year Two class. By now I was familiar with its standardised testing regime but there was still plenty of class preparation to do and so for the last week of August I was back at school setting up my classroom, writing long term plans, and gathering resources.

Shattering my focus was an event in Paris on Sunday, 31 August. That morning as I opened my bedroom door to go to the bathroom, my flatmate Dee came out of her room which was next to mine.

'Good morning, Dee!' I smiled.

'It's not,' she said. It wasn't like Dee to be abrupt so I looked at her more closely. She appeared troubled and her eyes were red. 'Princess Diana's dead,' she said brokenly and gestured for me to follow her back into her room.

My mouth went slack with shock. 'No!' I protested but as I sat down on Dee's bed in front of the television, I could see the awful truth in the headlines ticker-taping across the bottom of the screen.

I looked across at Dee, my eyes like hers, spilling over with tears. 'What happened?' I whispered.

'A car accident.'

We sat and watched as the story emerged of how the People's Princess was essentially hounded to her death by the paparazzi. Neither of us would have considered ourselves royalists but this was tragic.

Very quickly it became obvious that people the world over grieved for Princess Diana. The vast majority of us had never met her but we recognised and respected the courage she had displayed in revealing the shameful way she had been treated, and then making a new life for herself. In her endeavours to be a wonderful mother to her two boys and use her influence to make the world a kinder, safer place, millions of us had drawn her into our hearts.

On the Friday night I travelled with Christy to her flat in Reigate to stay for the weekend. Together we watched Diana's funeral the next day. It seemed the whole nation stopped, to either line the kilometres of roadway along which the cortege would drive or to watch at home on television. At the end of the weekend, I went back to London to continue with my life but I knew from my experience with Karl that moving on for Prince William and Prince Harry would be much harder; it brought home to me that while a husband is replaceable, one's mother is not.

The gloom surrounding Diana's death was echoed by the weather. The greyness I'd come to expect from September onwards descended on cue—it seemed that by summer's end London's meagre allocation of sunny days was exhausted and a dull grey curtain fell, blocking out the blue sky until spring.

As an antidote to the drab autumnal weather, God had gifted me with sunshine of another kind in my flourishing friendship with Christy. With Margot soon to move back to New Zealand, I was so grateful. Christy was bright and bubbly and radiated enthusiasm and a sense of fun. Before the summer finished, I accompanied Christy on a spectacular evening picnic and concert at Leeds Castle in one of summer's last warm evenings. Early in autumn we shared a weekend together in Wales with two of her male friends.

One of her many friends that I got to know well was a tall, dark-haired, loquacious man called Daniel. He could be intense but his conversation was engaging and amusing so I didn't mind. He enjoyed the latest adult Britpop and gave me a hard time about not keeping up to date and only listening to music from the 1980s. His good-natured goading caused me to make the effort to engage with and come to enjoy current music on Virgin Radio like Coldplay, Blur, and the Verve.

As well as meeting Daniel with Christy and others, he came up to London one evening alone and we shared a meal together. However, it soon became apparent he was hankering after an ex-girlfriend as conversations always included her.

Any chance I might have had was ruined by a humorous card about farting that I sent to cheer him up when he'd been unwell. Christy told me later that his sensibilities had been offended so I guessed that's why he hadn't been in touch. Once again it seemed my purpose had been as an agony aunt. It was very disappointing and I greatly missed his entertaining company.

It wasn't until much later I had the revelation that like Karl, he was the only one allowed to "shine" in the relationship. If we'd become a couple, I would have been relegated to the back seat once again.

Christy and I met up again at an Oak Hall Reunion weekend in Otford Manor, Kent. During the reunion Christy and Matt gravitated towards one another and no-one was surprised when they began dating soon afterwards. I was so pleased for her, but wondered if I would ever meet anyone. Did love only come to those in their 20s? Was I deluding myself or even being greedy to think I could experience love again when some lovely Christian women I knew hadn't experienced it even once?

Although Christy and I still socialized, it wasn't the same with Matt being her priority. So I was delighted when my friendship with Alison—who'd also been at the reunion—deepened. Alison could also be funny and playful but like me she had a more serious side due to her husband having deserted her. We both knew the pain of being blindsided by our spouses, and during weekends when I'd visit her in Stroud, Gloucestershire or she visited me in London, we drew comfort from one another. It was such welcome solace to talk and compare stories with someone who identified so closely with my experience; to cry and laugh together, and to discuss aspects of our marriages that still puzzled us and needed further exploration before they could be laid to rest.

Also helping me cope with the autumn gloom of 1997 was the anticipation of my first trip back to New Zealand for a two-week summer holiday over the Christmas period. Ironically, the weather turned out to be terrible—cool and overcast. Being with my parents though and basking in their love was very welcome. It was a place where I knew everyone's back stories and all the in-jokes. As much as I was feeling at home in London, I could never capture the same feeling of cultural belonging as I did in New Zealand. In the UK, people's references required clarification, past events needed explaining, and I knew so few famous personalities; sometimes the effort to keep up was frustrating and tiring.

One part of stepping back into my family I did not expect was the sense that it was the old Leanne they welcomed back and related to, not the one I now knew myself to be, the one experienced by my UK friends. That said, it was a wonderful holiday and having my lovely mum cook and care for me was very special.

It was tough saying goodbye to my parents but despite the pain of parting I was drawn back to London by my many friend-ships. With Karl I'd had a small group of friends, now I had dozens and in lieu of a husband they were very valuable to me. They brought love and laughter and the knowledge that my company was desirable, which was a balm to my soul.

1998

Chapter Seven

My new Year Two class seemed even more irritable and argumentative than my last one and I struggled in the first term. My previous classroom had been a prefabricated single-storey building of reasonable size and easy access. This year it was a small room upstairs in the main school block, accessed by walking up steps that curved almost 360°. As I led my students upstairs I could see only the first half a dozen of them. By the time we were all in the classroom, two to three children were in tears, others complained of being pushed or knocked, and a couple of children were arguing or even physically fighting. Dealing fairly but firmly with these situations and in a timely manner so I could actually get to teach, was exhausting. By the time I'd got to term two I was at breaking point.

One week in late January it all came to a head. I broke down and cried every afternoon after school. By Thursday, the acting head teacher—the previous one had resigned—asked me to go and see her.

'Have a seat, Leanne, and maybe a tissue too,' she said kindly, handing me the box from her desk.

'Thank you,' I sniffed, pulling out a tissue and blowing my nose.

'As you know I've spent time in your class and recorded twenty-one strategies that you were implementing to combat the behavioural issues. You've been doing your absolute best.'

I swallowed hard but even so a tear escaped at her welcome acknowledgement of my skill and efforts. 'Thank you.'

The woman smiled. 'But sometimes, Leanne, it's still not enough. These children are difficult and require a certain type of teacher who can impose order simply by their very presence, or force of personality, if you will.' She paused. 'Don't take this the wrong way but you're not one of those teachers. You're warm and compassionate and the children take advantage of that. You and your class are simply not a good fit. This is *no* reflection on your teaching abilities and *nothing* you should feel ashamed about. This is going to come as a shock but my suggestion would be to find a school where the students are easier to manage and you can concentrate your skills on teaching.'

I was stunned. Stunned but feeling like I'd been handed a most precious gift. I wasn't someone to give up when things got hard but here was a legitimate reason to stop. Permission had been granted to quit and the relief was palpable. I felt physically lighter.

However, the thought of escape was almost too good to be true and I sought more assurance from the acting head teacher. She not only provided it but offered to give me a great reference. Bringing the meeting to a close, she stood up and gave me a hug, then told me to leave everything—marking, planning, etc.—and just go home, write my resignation letter to the school board, and then relax for the rest of the evening.

I was never so glad to follow a head teacher's lead and did what she suggested. With my end date being half term, permanent relief was only a few weeks away.

February was to offer much more than release from a job that had become distressing, it was to grant me legal freedom from Karl.

The order dissolving our marriage had finally been made in December, and with no request for hearing made by Karl it was finalised in mid-January 1998, and I was waiting for the papers. One day in February my mail included an envelope from New Zealand. The internet was gaining popularity—I'd created a Hotmail address and was exchanging emails with mum and dad—so it was unlikely to be correspondence from them. Turning the envelope over I saw my sister Wendy's return address. She'd served the papers to Karl, so this must be the sealed order from the courts.

I sat on my bed and tore open the envelope. Having pulled out the papers I slowly unfolded them. "The Registrar of the Family Court, by this order, dissolves the marriage that took place on the … between the applicant and the respondent." The wording was entirely dispassionate and there was nothing personal to recall Karl, only an unknown address.

Taking a deep breath I refolded the papers, slid them back into their envelope and stored them at the bottom of a drawer in my desk. It happened to be my birthday and the marriage dissolution papers were a strange gift—something I'd longed for and were a huge relief to finally hold, yet also a melancholy one. Ten years of marriage—only for the initial love and laughter to submerge and drown in a well of tears.

Dating was finally legitimate.

The irony was there were no contenders at church. It was only at Ceroc that men showed any interest in me but most of them did not have a faith in God. I knew how difficult marriage could be. I needed a man like David in the Old Testament who God described as having a heart after Him; a man whose love for God was as central to his life as it was to mine, someone whose ultimate loyalty lay beyond me. Such a man would seek to please God and in doing so would pray and work with me to make a strong marriage to honour Him.

Although conscious of not having a guaranteed income, I followed through with my plan to go to Edinburgh during the mid-term break in February with Ingrid, my Dutch flatmate. Wanting to watch every pound, I was grateful to Ingrid for obtaining cheap accommodation at a Christian centre through friends she knew.

Edinburgh was cold and drizzly but the weather served to enhance the city's gloomy medieval atmosphere. Edinburgh Castle sat bulwarked by rock, impregnable and stern at the head of the Royal Mile, its cobblestoned streets leading down to the palace of Holyrood House. During a tour of the latter, the group I was with was ushered into a small, windowless, supper room in which Mary of Scots' Italian secretary, David Rizzio, had been murdered in front of her. It would have been a horribly intimate setting in which to experience such savagery.

It occurred to me that violence in the intimacy of one's home is the worst kind. It's the one place you are supposed to be safe. It holds true for violence of an emotional kind too. I should have been protected from verbal abuse in my own home but yet that's where the bulk of it occurred. How sad and ironic that what should be one's haven can turn out to be one's hell.

Edinburgh had a gripping sense of history but I was glad to return to the relative warmth of London. I urgently needed work so I contacted TimePlan Education and let them know of my availability for day-to-day assignments. Now that I was well-established in London and had gained experience within the UK school system, I felt much more capable of handling the supply work.

Of course, children often tried to give me the runaround; some providing false names, others telling me the teacher does things "this way" or lets them do "such and such" and generally trying to lead me in a merry dance. Quickly learning the children's names was key to imposing discipline, for it was a complete joke trying to nip some escalating behaviour in the bud by having to resort to, 'Would the boy with the glasses sitting next to the window stop poking the girl beside him ...' Unfortunately, remembering names was never my strong suit.

What *was* under my control was being organised. I rose very early so I could complete the travel, often an hour or more, and still arrive by 8 am in order to study the teacher's plans, photocopy worksheets, and quickly familiarise myself with the school's lay-out and routine for that day.

Something I could not avoid, however, was the morning roll. It was a task I hated, for I frequently mispronounced children's Muslim and Asian names. Especially difficult were those at Catholic schools where many children had beautiful sounding but impossibly spelt Irish names whose pronunciation bore little or no resemblance to the spelling. I still cringe to remember one particular class's derision when I pronounced 'Padraig' as 'Pad rag.' I later found out it was pronounced Patrick.

Of all the schools at which I taught, there were a few where the teachers were friendly and helpful and the children were pleasant, where the routine was easy to follow, where you felt you actually achieved some quality teaching. Happily, some of these were ones to which I got asked back. However, there was a particular once-a-week job that I absolutely dreaded. I was a fair teacher and, if the class didn't take advantage of it, a fun one, but these particular children never gave me a chance. They had a mean and disgruntled pack mentality and the slightest rebuke or disciplinary action towards one of the class provoked a strong backlash from the rest with cries of, 'Why did you do that?', 'That's not fair!' and 'He didn't do anything!' Their belligerent protests were disheartening and wearying, making me constantly second-guess myself. It seemed that I spent the majority of each morning weighing up every sentence before I spoke.

If I'd been married I could have gone home and unburdened myself. My husband would have empathised and prayed with me. But only God knew if that would ever materialise.

Thankfully, with the majority of teaching work being one-off assignments, knowing that I would leave at the end of the day and possibly never see the class again helped to put things in perspective. Other than the money, there were two aspects of supply teaching that I really enjoyed, one being the lack of paperwork and the second travelling home each day from school. Buoyed with the relief of another battle of wills completed, I could sit back on a bus or overground train like Docklands Light Rail, and enjoy seeing new parts of London.

Some areas were leafy and quiet, others village-like or trendy, still others industrial and commercial, and sometimes they were rundown estates. Each produced emotions in me: in some areas I felt comfortable or even happy, in others intrigued and curious, whereas some places made me feel depressed and miserable. But regardless of the emotion, I found it all fascinating.

Steady supply work enabled me to afford some more travel, the next a long weekend in Paris with Alison at the end of March. Paris reflected the spaciousness and order produced by Haussman under the commission of Napoleon III. It boasted wide boulevards and elegant buildings, as well as pretty little parks scattered here and there. I had to admit it was picturesque in a way London was not.

Alison and I had taken a coach to Dover, a ferry across to Calais, and then boarded the coach again to Paris. One of the travellers was a quiet, well-built Spanish man to whom I was attracted. We chatted while on the coach and when he said goodbye at the end of the weekend, he invited me to go and stay with him, and gave me his address. As I'd barely gotten to know him, I didn't take things any further than sending him an Easter card. But while taking the high-speed Eurostar back to London Victoria, I had fun daydreaming; it was pleasurable to know that a handsome man found me attractive.

The brief acquaintance served another purpose in that it fed a growing interest in the Spanish language. It was inspiring to witness Alison employ her high school French to great effect in Paris and I relied on her to order every meal, whether a croissant or coq au vin. Her ability to successfully negotiate everyday exchanges challenged me, helped me face the reality that I was embarrassingly monolingual. While the idea of learning another language was intimidating, I was nevertheless developing a desire to learn Spanish, for the country appealed to me and its language held no negative connotations.

April saw the much-anticipated arrival in London of my brother Glenn. I found him accommodation with a friend of mine called Steve who I'd met through the church I lived above. Steve loved music—we'd once gone to see the Notting Hillbillies at Ronnie Scott's—so I thought they might get along. Living at Steve's also meant Glenn would be a mere ten minutes away from me by bus and one stop on the Tube.

Although Glenn and I were the youngest and eldest respectively, we were quite close. It was great to have his company and receive regular hugs, and I enjoyed teaching him about various aspects of London living. The best part was having a companion to attend church with because, prior to Glenn arriving, it had been a solitary experience. With three Sunday services required to accommodate everyone, it greatly decreased the chance of seeing someone you knew, and I usually sat by myself. When I added the two hours travel to the one–and–a–half hour service, they were the loneliest three and a half hours of my week. It would have been so easy to stay at home but I knew my soul needed the joy that came with singing praise to God; it was when I felt closest to Him.

Frustratingly I was unable to afford any summer travel. Supply teaching didn't pay holiday pay, or rather it did but it had been added to my weekly pay and I'd not disciplined myself to put money aside. I paid for this profligacy by having to find employment during my summer holidays. Only two positions arose—a carer in an old people's home in Enfield and a worker in a residential care home for children in Dagenham East.

Not only were both jobs draining but each journey involved at least one and a half to two hours travel each way; the only positive was that I was able to use the time to daydream about a man I'd recently met. Jayesh was an Indian who I'd seen at Ceroc one Friday night. Being tall, dark, and well-built I found him attractive so I approached him to chat and learnt he was a Christian. Although he had little interest in Ceroc and never went again, he gave me his phone number and we began a friendship.

Jayesh invited me for dinner at his flat, and we also enjoyed a few meals out. Having developed a tutoring business, we had teaching as a common interest. He had a naughty sense of humour, a trait which had always appealed to me. He was one of those people who said things that I thought but was never brave enough to say *and* he had the ability to get away with it!

My hope for our friendship leading to serious dating became greater than for any other man I'd liked in London. Projecting myself into the future as women do, I envisaged myself in a red wedding sari. I began mentioning him in letters to my family.

I brought up the topic of our friendship with Alison one weekend she came to stay with me.

'Do you have enough in common?' she asked. I'd gone to meet her off the train at Paddington station and we were making our way back to my flat. 'Marriage is hard enough without adding in different cultures. The juxtaposition of your cultural differences alone could cause issues.'

I couldn't help but laugh.

'What's funny?' Alison asked, looking puzzled and a little hurt.

'I'm sorry, Alison,' I said and hurried to reassure her. 'I just love the way you use words that I know but have never heard spoken before. You're the only person I've ever met who's used "juxtaposition." It's one of the many things I like about you.'

Alison smiled. 'Oh well then, I guess you're off the hook! But you know what I mean—you've always said you hated Indian food although you discovered a few weeks ago you actually liked chicken korma. But you can't live on that dish for your entire married life!'

She had a point but I didn't want to think about such obstacles, let alone that Jayesh didn't like to dance and there were facets of his personality that I found disquieting, like the way he could be cynical and couldn't maintain a serious conversation for long.

However, I pushed those doubts aside with the excuse no-one was perfect. Which is, of course, true but doubts should always be faced. That I could not was a dangerous sign that I was still vulnerable to forming a relationship that I might come to regret.

It had been a dispiriting summer with the only bright spots being fun weekends with Alison and meetings with Jayesh. I'd not earned enough to save anything and so my financial situation was precarious and caused me anxiety. All I had going into the autumn term was some weekend tutoring which I'd obtained from Jayesh, teaching mathematics to two motivated primary school aged boys. It was a subject I liked and I enjoyed the interactions. The tutoring at £14 an hour plus £2 to cover travel costs was much more lucrative than my carer roles but due to the travel time and later start time given it was Sunday, I could only tutor two students per morning. The £32 provided for the bulk of my weekly groceries which was very welcome but they weren't my only costs.

During the holidays I'd been in contact with a teaching agency about a job in a special needs school. When it unexpectedly fell through just before school started, I was greatly dismayed. I immediately made myself available for day-to-day supply work but at the beginning of the year teachers are rested and in good health resulting in very few assignments.

It was a constant battle not to be anxious; I kept reminding God I needed work, and tried not to fret. I swung between trusting Him to provide for me then worrying again when I couldn't determine how He was going to do it. It's strange how we think that if, in our limited capacity, we cannot conceive of a way for God to do something, that indeed He *cannot* do it.

In this case he used the aborted job to instill in me a determination to pursue special needs work which produced a most unexpected result.

Mid-September, two weeks after the academic year had started, I went back to the Church of England school in Lambeth where I used to work. I'd lent a book to Hannah, a Christian teacher I'd made friends with, and rather than ask her to post me the book, I thought I'd pick it up in person and have a quick catch up with her and the staff.

During the visit I spoke with the deputy head. I relayed my new interest and asked her what training I'd need to undergo to qualify for special needs positions. To my surprise and immense interest, she said that they were looking for a teacher to work with their special needs students as the previous one had resigned. I'd arrived as school finished for the day and had a warm reception from children, parents, and teachers alike. Heartened by their response, I was keen to go back to the school in this new capacity. It was an added incentive that working with individuals or small groups would pose little to no behavioural issues.

When the new head teacher offered me an interview the following week I was delighted. I was even more thrilled when he gave me the job on a trial basis for the remainder of the autumn term. Amazingly, the offer was based on my reference from the head teacher of the Church of England school in Camden, who happened to be a good friend of his. God was definitely looking after me and weaving together the threads of my various teaching experiences.

I also realised that in God directing me to this line of work He was bringing me full circle in my teaching, for my first job after graduating in New Zealand had been in a small class of children with special needs. It was reassuring to learn my teaching positions in London had not been a series of random events but that God had had a long-term plan in mind.

My position with special needs children was not just confined to Lambeth. A school in Tower Hamlets had offered me a similar job for three days a week which dovetailed beautifully with the two days a week in Lambeth. From having little work, I was now fully employed and thrilled at the prospect of not having to scrimp any longer. I would now have enough money to once again buy clothes, go to movies and concerts, and save for further trips.

Approaching Christmas I was a little anxious, wondering whether anyone would ask me to stay with them over that period. It was the one time I deeply felt the absence of my family. I was very grateful to Gwen when she invited me, along with Lu Ping, another one of the girls in our Kilburn flat, to spend Christmas with her in the flat she'd bought in Hendon.

It was a companionable Christmas and Lu Ping and I greatly appreciated being recipients of Gwen's generous hospitality. She'd made her flat into a very comfortable home, having re-decorated the rooms and outfitted the bathroom. Her ample kitchen was so prized after the cramped space in our Kilburn flat. As for being able to sit together on comfortable couches in an actual lounge—it was unparalleled luxury!

Blessed as I was though with friends and finances, deep down the longings never abated for a husband and a home of my own.

1999

Chapter Eight

Mid-winter was particularly cold that year which discouraged any day trips or other outings. In the remainder of my two-week holiday I had a lot of time to reflect on my friendship with Jayesh. During late autumn our time together had dwindled. By Christmas I'd been relegated once more to an agony aunt as he began confiding to me his interest in a young woman I knew. Our contact now was largely on a business level regarding the tutoring that I did for him, and while he did invite me to his birthday later in spring, the closest we would be was friends.

However, from the beginning of our friendship I'd taken the difficult step of asking God to decide our future, so I worked to graciously accept Jayesh's withdrawal from my life.

As I did this, I came to realise that part of Jayesh's appeal might have been the fact he wasn't English. I was becoming choosy in who I wanted to date and New Zealand men with their strong, silent culture and little appreciation for femininity held zero appeal. Nor did the more urbane men from the United Kingdom embody the manliness I sought.

The only man who had truly impressed me had been a Canadian who was the boyfriend of a friend of Gwen's. He was pleasingly well-mannered and exuded a strong masculinity; I instinctively felt he was someone you could trust to take care of you. It wasn't a quality I'd ever really considered before. However, all I knew about Canada was that it was the land of cold and conifers, both of which I hated, so that train of thought held no future.

And anyway, I was putting down firm roots in the UK, so it was from this pool of men that I needed to find a husband.

The frustration of singleness and the difficulty of finding someone suitable to date, let alone marry, was often the topic of conversation between myself and other single Christian women. I also discussed the situation with a man called Ian Gregory who I met at Ceroc. When I discovered he'd written a book about this issue called, 'No Sex Please, We're Single,' I engaged him in long conversations at The Crown. I was shocked and perplexed to hear him disclose that single Christian men bemoaned that there were few suitable Christian woman. No, it was the other way around!

One evening when I was the only one in the flat, I called mum to tell her yet again of my mounting frustration.

'Leanne,' mum said once I'd finished, 'you probably don't want to hear this but have you thought that as you're not meeting anyone, it's not God's will for you?'

The idea was like a weighty stone dragging me underwater to drown. 'No,' I choked.

'I think maybe you should consider surrendering your desire.'

Mum's tone of voice was kind but the idea of surrendering to 40 or so years of loneliness was abhorrent.

'Look, mum, I need to go,' I said tearfully. 'Give my love to dad.'

'I will.' Mum sounded upset as well. 'Oh, Leanne, I'm sorry.'

'Me too. Bye, mum.'

I hung up and went back to my room. My hurt was giving way to anger that it was always those who were *already* married who gave that advice.

However, as painful as it was to hear and explore, I did talk to God about it because above all I wanted to please Him. Trying to surrender the desire to be married, however, was like trying to wrestle with a snake—it kept slithering out of my grasp.

Alison also hoped for a husband but in lieu of any contenders we planned another trip in mid-February to add some excitement to our lives. I'd enjoyed my day in Tangier and was curious to explore more of North Africa, so we settled on Tunisia. We hoped to get some welcome winter sun and booked on the understanding that it would be warm enough to sunbathe for an hour or two each day. Unfortunately Tunisia had the coldest winter in 20 years and we had to wear every layer we'd packed. Even then we were barely comfortable.

If being noticed by Tunisian men could have warmed us, however, we would have sweltered. On visiting the outdoor market the morning after we arrived, we encountered more male attention in one hour than in our entire lives up to that point. Or at least I did; Alison, with her curves and wavy blond hair, seemed to have much less difficulty. The stallholders were all men and they looked us up and down unashamedly, making entirely inappropriate comments and paying us ridiculous amounts of false compliments. Their promises of 'special prices for the pretty English girls' seemed more like orders than invites and were intimidating.

We took the opportunity to go on two day-excursions by coach, the first to El Jem and Kairouan. El Jem was an enormous, remarkably intact Roman amphitheatre and in Kairouan the two sites of interest were the markets, including a visit to a carpet maker, and the Great Mosque.

A second visit took us to Matmata, where some of the Berber people still lived in troglodyte dwellings. The Berber men were respectful if dour and distant, far different from the urban Tunisian men we encountered, who were very forward and clearly primed for European women tourists looking for holiday romances. I accepted the offer of drinks one night with a man I subsequently dubbed Slimy Sami. It was an absolute waste of time. In retrospect I don't know why I bothered—maybe I was more desperate for male attention than I realized.

The evening wasn't entirely pointless, however, as it raised the issue that despite my many male friends over the years in London, I hadn't actually dated properly and lacked experience. Alison never appeared ill at ease with men. Wishing I was as natural and relaxed as she was, I discussed this with her. Of all her advice, one thing remained with me—the importance of wholesome physical touch with an acquaintance, whether male or female. A light touch on someone's shoulder or arm did not need to indicate you were attracted to them but simply that you were wanting to make a genuine emotional connection, one human to another. Initially I had to force myself to do this but as I practised, the gesture felt more natural and comfortable, and I liked the sense of connecting with someone.

As Alison and I mulled over the holiday on our last evening, we had to admit that, despite the men's lack of integrity, both our egos were still somewhat bruised after our divorces and it was nice to be noticed.

My strong desire for male company kept clamouring to be met and I began scanning the singles pages in local magazines. Advertisements by Christian men were rare but eventually I found a suitable one and we arranged to meet. Hugh was attractive and seemed decent but he never arrived for our third date. When he phoned—by now I'd had a telephone installed in my bedroom as I was fed up with trying to have private conversations on the pay phone in the hallway—he said only that his plans had changed! Hugh then admitted to not obtaining the information on a Monet art exhibition as he'd promised. And to add further insult, he asked *me* to organise tickets to the Chelsea Flower Show when *he'd* been the one who suggested we go! By now I was furious and said that if he wanted to see me, he could organise the events. Of course he didn't bother.

It was yet another disappointment. It seemed that every man I was interested in either disqualified himself or just wanted me to function as a sounding board for their relationship difficulties. Maybe mum was right and God didn't have anyone for me.

The prospect overwhelmed me with loneliness and despair, of decades of only half-living; becoming a husk of a woman who appeared to be functioning on the outside but inside was hollow.

To help fill up my life and provide something to look forward to, I organized another holiday. My travel destination arose from meeting a Croatian woman and her infant son, Filip, in New Zealand in 1995. After experiencing the bloodshed of the Balkan wars in the 1990s, she and her husband, Davor, decided to investigate immigrating to New Zealand. My heart went out to her and so I gave her some assistance and in the process we became friends. Sadly, their idea proved unviable and she returned home a few months later.

We had kept in contact and she asked me to visit them over Easter. They had an apartment in Stolzape, Austria, where Davor worked, and also an apartment in Zagreb, Croatia. Blazenka wanted me to experience both countries and suggested I fly to Vienna and then back from Zagreb.

Blazenka and Filip met me at the Vienna airport and that evening, to gratify the child in us all, she took us to Prater Park. The historical amusement park transported one to older times with its theatrical architecture and gaudy colours. As it was spring, night fell early and the attractions, rides and food stalls were brilliantly lit up with a wealth of red and gold lights that whirled and flashed. Music played, vendors shouted at the passersby, and on the rides, teenagers screamed and children squealed. The entire venue pulsed with excitement and witnessing Filip's enjoyment enhanced my own—it was the perfect antidote to too much introspection.

The next day we had a wonderful time in Vienna, then the following day Blazenka drove us to Stolzalpe in Styria, a mountainous region in southern Austria. We didn't see Davor because he'd gone to Zagreb to look after their younger son, Marko, so that Blazenka could spend time with me. After a day in Stolzalpe, we left for Croatia.

Blazenka and Davor lived on the sixteenth floor of an apartment block which gave a panoramic view of the city. Davor welcomed me warmly which helped me feel comfortable with Blazenka's suggestion that he take Filip and me to Medvednica Mountain the next day while she cooked a traditional Easter meal. Our destination was 15 kilometres from the city; a popular venue for skiing in winter and walking in summer. Arriving at the foot of the hill we took a gondola to the top and walked some of its trails amongst the beech and fir, finishing with lunch at a rustic café.

On my final full day she gave me a walking tour of the old part of the city; it was charming. There were stone clock towers capped with onion domes, extravagant flourishes of wrought iron where something utilitarian could have sufficed, small intimate gardens, and cobbled paths leading under stone walls. On the way home we enjoyed the funicular railway which carried us down to the newer part of Zagreb.

That evening Blazenka suggested we go out to a bar. The lights were dim and with it being our last evening together, it was an atmosphere ripe for emotional intimacy. Blazenka's forthrightness was a quality I admired in her but on that occasion it proved to be uncomfortable when she revealed her sense that I found Davor attractive.

I reddened but met her eye. 'You're right, I do.' Glancing down, I played with my glass for a moment then looked up. 'I feel really embarrassed. I tried hard not to let it show—I hate it when women flirt with other women's husbands.'

Blazenka smiled. 'Davor *is* attractive. But men his age are wrong for you. You need an older man. I think that would best.'

'Hmm,' I replied, sipping my cider. One of the reasons I liked Blazenka was that she was astute and I had a great deal of respect for her opinion. At the same time, I still found the idea of an older man repugnant. I recalled a teaching colleague of mine in New Zealand who, once Karl had left, had invited me out. He was considerably older than me with a comb-over hairstyle and walk shorts with knee-length socks. The very thought of dating him made me shiver with distaste. Then there were the two mature but yawningly dull men that Hannah, my Lambeth colleague, had introduced me to at a birthday party of hers.

'Another friend told me that as well,' I said.

Blazenka nodded in approval. 'She understands you. She sees what I see.'

'But older men are so boring. They have one foot in an old people's home and the other on a banana skin.'

After taking a moment to consider the idiom, Blazenka laughed. 'Then you have met the wrong men. Older men can be exciting.'

It was my turn to laugh. 'I'll have to experience that to believe it.'

'You will,' she said and clinked her glass against mine.

Her advice was unpalatable. But I pondered over it from time to time, and in the future I'd recall her insight with admiration.

One term remained in the school year. I'd worked in multicultural settings ever since I began teaching and my position in Tower Hamlets meant I now had Muslim colleagues and students, as well as an Iranian teacher in whose classroom I assisted. All were friendly and welcoming and I found the children respectful and charming.

A few memories stand out from that time, one being that some of the girls drew a comparison between me and Shania Twain. I'd never heard of her before so I did some research and learnt she was a Canadian country singer. While country music usually left me cold, I had to admit some of her songs had a distinctive pop flavor and were very catchy. Then I saw a photo of her! The comparison was immensely flattering and bewildered me—did my students need glasses?

Despite spending frequent weekends with Alison, I still saw Christy. It was clear that she and Matt were in love and they got engaged in the spring with their wedding set for 31 July. I was delighted to be asked to be one of her bridesmaids. The day dawned sunny and mild and it was a joy to be a part of their very special occasion.

A little later in the summer Alison, Gwen, and I went on a two–week trip to Aghios Stefanos, a small village on the north-eastern coast of Corfu. Our accommodation was a small cottage surrounded by pine and tamarisk trees and we shared a swimming pool with a larger house nearby. We were about 500 m from the town and had a panoramic view across the bay towards Albania, which was a remarkably close distance away across the Straits of Corfu.

On our first morning we walked down to the village; with only one local grocery store there were few choices for lunch. Placing some bread and cheese in a basket, we walked over to the fruit and vegetable display.

'Oh my goodness,' I exclaimed. 'Look at the tomatoes!' They were assorted sizes and all misshapen and marked.

'Shh!' said Gwen, 'the shopkeeper will hear you.'

'I have to agree though,' Alison said, 'they look rubbish.'

'Well, it's either these or nothing,' said Gwen, ever practical.

She gathered up half a dozen tomatoes and we went to pay for our groceries.

At the cottage we cut open the buns and filled them with slabs of cheese and thick slices of tomato.

'Here's looking at you,' grinned Alison as we each bit into our bun.

I hadn't even finished chewing my first mouthful before I realised that the tomatoes had the most intense flavour. 'Wow, I take it all back!'

'Don't do that,' laughed Gwen. 'They're delicious.'

Alison agreed. 'They're sublime.'

There was a lesson here for me—to not make such hasty judgments based purely on outward appearances—but it was one in which I would need more practice.

In the evenings we had the choice of three tavernas. I made the happy discovery that lamb, a favourite of mine, was a traditional Greek meat and I ordered it on twelve out of thirteen evenings, much to Alison and Gwen's dismay who urged me to branch out and try something new. In the end they gave up and just rolled their eyes at one another each time I placed my order.

Initially the weather was scorching, the temperatures on the first few days soaring to an extreme 43°C. It was far too hot to be active outside so we either lounged in the coolness of the pool or relaxed inside the cottage. When the temperatures dropped to the low 30s we hired a car for two days and explored the island, visiting Mt Pantokratoras and the monastery of the same name, the lovely Palaeokastritsa beach and the striated rock faces that rose out of turquoise water at Sidari.

On our last evening we boarded a boat with other tourists and were taken to the capital of Corfu, Kerkyra. In the Old Town were night markets which displayed a wealth of hand-crafted products—a kaleidoscope of colours and textures.

The pleasure I took from that holiday was greatly enhanced by the constant and blissful warmth of mainland European summers. It strengthened a growing notion that I needed to leave the United Kingdom and move to mainland Europe. The idea was taking shape in my mind of learning Spanish with the aim of living in Spain and teaching English. I still doubted my lingual capabilities but I was sure I could learn enough Spanish to get by on initially and more would emerge as I was immersed in the language.

It was a major decision, akin to that of moving to London initially. But facing the fact that meeting and marrying a suitable Christian man seemed less and less likely, I had to create an alternative plan for my future. Contemplating having to work until retirement was an idea I hadn't really considered before—it was a considerable shock, and daunting. When married to Karl I'd held the subconscious belief that, if I wanted to, I could stop working at any point. I'd considered him to be the breadwinner, and that for me working was optional. It diminished the enjoyment of my career when I considered that I wasn't doing it solely for the love of it but because there was no alternative. Another twenty-five years seemed like a prison sentence from which there would be no parole.

Leaving the European mainland to go back to a depressingly cooler and cloudier London strengthened my resolve. If I had to work to retirement age, doing so at a more relaxed pace in a Mediterranean climate called strongly to me.

Not long after we returned, Alison began dating. At Christy and Matt's wedding she'd been seated at the singletons' table next to Peter, a friend of Christy's who I'd met many times before. He was a kind, thoughtful man with a great sense of humour. They'd enjoyed each other's company and it hadn't taken Peter long to ask Alison out.

It was wonderful for Alison but bittersweet for me. I cared deeply about her and wanted her to find love again. But I was fearful that I would never experience that for myself, and to witness what I longed for at such close quarters would be incredibly painful. Our friendship would never quite be the same—I would no longer have my wonderfully fun single girlfriend with who to travel, go dancing, dream and bemoan the lack of men with boyfriend potential.

I had to ask God fervently for the grace to be genuinely pleased for her and not begrudge her happiness. To her immense credit Alison proved to be amazingly sensitive and kind. She still invited me down to stay with her, and Peter was gracious about my presence; I never felt like a third wheel when I was with them.

When the new school year began, I was back in my Lambeth position. Pleased with the special needs work I was doing, they'd asked me to stay for another year and had increased my role from two to three days a week. Unfortunately, it still wasn't sufficient income on which to live comfortably and I was glad to secure an extra day per week at the nearby Christ Church Primary School.

With God continuing to faithfully provide funds for me, my trust in him was building. I was beginning to appreciate the way He wove together events and their timing. His tendency to do things at the "last minute" could be a bit scary if I looked at such situations in the wrong way. The Bible said that God's timing is perfect. Therefore it followed that if I trusted He would provide for me as He promised, the supposed lateness was not late at all but His correct timing. If I stopped entertaining the lie that He wasn't good and might let me down, it would remove the fear that He wasn't going to provide what I needed.

Of course I'd learnt that God would let some things happen to me that weren't good in themselves and which could make me doubt his goodness. But it was also true that if I kept trusting Him, He demonstrated remarkable ability to bring good from whatever bad He allowed.

I was learning first-hand the truth of the verse that God works all things for good to those who love him and are called according to his purpose. My marriage to Karl had been a disaster but it was of my own making. I'd entered into it without seriously checking with God. But through my move to London, I'd made wonderful friends, learnt new teaching and dancing skills, met distant Irish family, travelled to countries that had bought me great pleasure, and in achieving those things I had gained confidence I'd long lacked. My life overflowed with blessings.

I could finally admit that while it lacked the joy of a loving husband, mercifully it also lacked the presence of a critical, mercurial one.

As if to underscore God's ability to weave the timing of

seemingly unrelated events together, one evening as I travelled home during rush-hour I met one of my flatmates on the Tube. At this time trains ran about every two to three minutes; each train had seven carriages and each carriage when full could hold approximately 80 people. That made at least 10,000 people travelling on one Tube line in one hour. The chance of my flatmate and me travelling at the same time but also on the same train and in the same carriage, then noticing one another when packed in nose-to-armpit, was rather remarkable.

It put me in awe of God's ability to bring people together. It was a phenomenon I would have occasion to appreciate in a far greater way in the future.

In order to continue working in the United Kingdom I applied for my Indefinite Leave to Remain status in the United Kingdom, as my UK Ancestry Visa was valid for only four years and would expire in April. As well as that I needed to apply for my Irish Foreign Birth Certificate and then my Irish citizenship and passport so that I could work in the European Union. Bureaucratic paperwork was a pet hate of mine so it was a considerable discipline to get it all completed.

The next stop was to enroll in a Spanish class. I was very happy to find one in Wembley at the end of the Jubilee Line which meant travel was easy.

My new school year was hectic. Friday and Saturday nights I went to Ceroc or with friends to the movies, a restaurant, or a favourite nightclub of mine called Bad Bobs. Sunday evenings I went to the 5 pm church service, Tuesday night I met with a group of single people from church, Wednesday night was Spanish class and Thursday night I now volunteered for Grandma's.

Grandma's was a charity that provided a free service for children affected by HIV/AIDS which included outings during the holidays, special events and weekly visits. I'd been involved for about six months on an occasional basis, helping with excursions and a Christmas party but had resisted committing myself to weekly visits with a designated family. My reason was that Grandma's was staffed mainly by women. A regular commitment would decrease my opportunities to socialize and meet eligible men, a hope to which I clung although it was increasingly unlikely. In my mind, getting involved to that extent was resigning myself to staying single.

But along with my realization that I had to have a focus for my future other than marriage, I felt strongly that God wanted me to invest one evening a week in a family. My growing trust in God's goodness led me to tell Grandma's I was available.

They soon found a family near Kilburn that was easy to travel to, always a bonus after a tiring day at school. There were two lovely children: a girl about ten years and her eight-year-old brother, and I supervised and played with them while their mum left the house and enjoyed some respite.

I began the Spanish class and it turned out to be fun, nothing like the humiliation of my high school French lessons. I got to know two other mature students and we sat together in class and shared lots of mistakes and much laughter; occasionally we'd meet up during the week to practice.

During that autumn term my resolve to not date a non-Christian man was severely tested. One Saturday at Hammersmith Ceroc I met a man called David to whom I was instantly attracted. The feeling was mutual and at the end of the evening he asked to take me out for a late-night meal. Conversation flowed easily and when he walked me from his car to the ground level entrance of my flat, he kissed me. It was like exquisite food I thought I'd never taste again. But as his hands started to wander, I pulled away and told him I was a Christian, and for me sexual intercourse was reserved for marriage. He responded graciously and left but although we had swapped phone numbers, I never heard from him again.

I was sad for weeks but should have been grateful because what future had there really been for us? I didn't need a relationship with a man who had no heart for God. But my longings were becoming so great I might have fallen for it, if God hadn't stopped it progressing.

It was a dispiriting end to 1999. I didn't hold much hope that the new millennium would bring any change to my single status.

2000

Chapter Nine

The new year was a continuation of my drive to learn Español.

I resumed my class in term two after Christmas, and to expedite my progress I searched online for language classes in Spain in the February mid-term break. Pleased to find a small school in Cantabria that offered dormitory accommodation with other students and provided lessons during the day, I sent an email enquiry. The owner replied and his friendly manner led to increasingly flirtatious correspondence as we arranged the details for my week-long language school.

By the time I stepped into the arrival lounge at the Santander airport, I was expecting to meet an appealing Spanish man and was shocked to find an unengaging, rather dour man who reminded me more of Albert Einstein than Antonio Banderas. The shock then took on a slightly sinister aspect as he casually informed me that due to it being off season there weren't any other students and he'd closed the dormitory accommodation. Instead, I'd be staying with him in his own apartment!

Disquiet churned my stomach. This was weird, there was no other word for it. I felt trapped. My Español was so minimal that I couldn't organise other accommodation, and neither did I have the finances to pay for five nights in a hotel. Not wanting to offend my only English-speaking contact, I told him that it would be fine and started praying that God would keep me safe.

I prayed even harder when I arrived at his place to find a compact two-bedroom apartment where we'd be living in extremely close quarters. Then came some relief when Jamaal told me that each weekday morning a housekeeper would come to cook and clean, and also that I'd be having some lessons with a young Spanish woman. With two women to appeal to for help if

I needed it, surely he wouldn't try anything untoward?

As I began lessons the next day, the dual anxiety over my circumstances and the intensity of one-to-one lessons created the ideal environment for my stuttering to re-emerge. It was a condition that had first manifested at high school when I'd moved from a tiny primary school to a comparatively huge and intimidating secondary school, and I'd suffered from it periodically ever since. It had rapidly gone from the most common and minor form of stuttering (the repetition of initial sounds and syllables) to full-blown blocking—being unable to articulate any sound or word at all. The humiliation of this little-known scenario where people thought you were either stupid or rude, compounded the problem.

I rarely told anyone of my affliction and was too embarrassed to explain to Jamaal. By the afternoon session he understandably grew frustrated with me. My shame over the immense physical struggle to choke out words that stuck in my throat, and the emotional toll it took, led me to break down and cry. With me unwilling to explain what was going on because he was such a cold, unfeeling person and I feared his disbelief or scorn, he assumed I was deliberately being difficult and walked away.

It was an impossible situation.

Regardless of his annoyance, it didn't stop him wanting to take advantage of me. In fact, looking back on it he was quite prepared to use my vulnerability against me. After we'd shared the evening meal, he tried to invite me into his bedroom for some 'touch therapy' which he said would help me relax. For over an hour he tried to coerce me and kept insisting that because he wasn't asking for anything more than for me to lie on his bed for a little stroking, what was my problem? Of course, one of his angles was the insulting accusation, "Was I frigid?"

He was clever enough to make no attempt to physically force me but psychologically I was under siege. Here was Karl in another guise using all sorts of psychological games to twist my words against me, confuse my arguments and emotionally manipulate me into doing what he wanted. Except now I was awake to these techniques.

Eventually Jamaal gave up and went to bed—alone.

It was disquieting being unable to call anyone locally. Nor did I have sufficient Spanish to determine how and where to make an international call. It was just God and me. I did what was practical in the circumstances—hauling a chest of drawers across the room and against the door—and then turned to Proverbs where I knew there were verses about God keeping you safe at night and thanked God for what he promised. When I finished reading a book I'd brought with me, I turned off the light and fell asleep quite quickly. I was blessed with a good sleep and a mercifully uninterrupted night.

But I had no stomach for working further with Jamaal who now made my skin crawl, and apparently neither did he wish to work with me, for he disdainfully informed me in the morning that he had arranged for Gabriela to give me the remainder of the week's lessons. Having said that, he left the apartment; a double blessing.

Gabriela arrived mid-morning. She was lovely. I relaxed immediately, my blocking decreased and I finally started to make some progress. The next day she took me out to a market and provided some full immersion in the language where I got a chance to buy some fruit in rudimentary Spanish.

Once my week's lessons had finished, I had Saturday free before Jamaal took me to the airport the next day. Wanting to sightsee as well as avoid being in the close confines of the apartment, I used information Gabriela gave me to take a bus to the charming medieval town of Santillana del Mar. I learnt it was called the "town of the three lies" for there was no saint (Sant), no sea (Mar) and it wasn't flat (llana).

It reminded me of Jamaal and I began to wonder if he'd fabricated the dormitory as a means of taking in lone female students upon which to prey. He repulsed me. It made me wonder if I'd met Karl as a wiser, more confident young woman, would I have seen through his lies? Or did that sort of instinctual knowledge only come through hard experience?

Despite our paths having seldom crossed since Tuesday, I dreaded the thought of the half hour journey with Jamaal to the airport. When his car had engine trouble and he had to ask Gabriela to drive me instead, I wondered whether God had a hand in that. It was a huge relief to leave Jamaal, his apartment and the unsavoury experience behind me.

At the same time as I learned Spanish, I took the expensive but irresistible step of joining the new Christian dating agency set up by Ian Gregory. I applauded his practical approach to the difficulty single Christians found in meeting one another and was pleased to avail myself of the agency's help. But paying the fee turned out to be the easy part. In order to ensure women were free from any predatory behaviour, the men's phone numbers were given to the women. While it made sense from a safety point of view, it was nerve-racking ringing the men.

The first one whose details I was given seemed agreeable. He was friendly and easy to arrange a date with for an evening meal. Physically, I found him reasonably attractive; he was tall and well-built. Unfortunately, he lacked verve and the conversation was desultory, nor did he appear to have a ready sense of humour. It would have been an evening entirely devoid of fun had I not found something to make a joke about. It made me realise just how much I valued a sense of humour in a man, in fact I realised it was an absolute must. As we said goodbye, he indicated he'd like to go out a second time, but I couldn't bear thinking about another evening bereft of laughter's sparkle so I never called him again.

The man who I contacted next never seemed to be home and because I didn't want to leave my phone number, I finally gave up.

Initially, my third attempt held more promise as I did get to talk to the man over the phone a few times. However, he repeatedly stalled in arranging a date as he was frequently in Europe for work. Finally, one weekend we spoke at some length; he asked several questions and I was pleased to be able to tell him about myself. He agreed to meet that Friday but with the proviso that I would call him on Thursday night to confirm it. That should have served as a warning, and sure enough, when I rang, he seemed to recall nothing at all about me or our planned date! Disappointed and hurt, I politely but firmly told him so. No doubt feeling guilty he assured me he'd honour his agreement and we arranged a place and time to meet.

After hanging up it hit me that I felt no anticipation or excitement, just sadness at how he'd found me so forgettable. On impulse I rang Jayesh for a man's opinion. He was disgusted and told me to stand him up! I had a much-needed belly laugh at that, and felt empathised with and supported. However, I couldn't bring myself to be so rude, so I summoned my courage and rang the man once more to withdraw from our date.

As I contemplated my lack of success, I recalled hearing the rumour that the service was made up of roughly 75% women and 25% men. That may have been an exaggeration but my experience supported a not dissimilar ratio. Reading between the lines of what the last man had said, I think he was fielding so many phone calls and invites that he couldn't distinguish one woman from the other. Realising that helped diminish my frustration and gave me some empathy for him but the fact remained that I'd invested several hundred pounds for only dismal results.

The dating service had been the means for me to connect with Christian men and the death of that dream really stung.

Seeking some motherly comfort, I made a long-distance call home and this time mum didn't suggest that I should surrender my desire to be married. Instead, to my immense surprise and interest, she put forward the idea of joining an *online* Christian dating agency. The internet was still new and I'd not even considered it. Unconsciously I think I'd dismissed it as unsafe. But with it being my mum's suggestion I gave it serious consideration. Discussing the idea with Gwen, she invited me over on a Sunday afternoon to use her computer. Being technologically savvy, she'd already bought her first device.

Our search revealed no online UK dating agency, the only one was international. It seemed a ridiculously large ocean from which to fish but by now I was ready to try anything so I continued. After the hour or so it took to thoughtfully answer their myriad of questions to compile my profile, I finally pressed "Submit."

Then came the wait.

How many responses would I get? Would I get any? From who? Would there be any men from the United Kingdom?

Over the next couple of days I received three responses. The first two were utterly useless—a Buddhist, and a universe–conscious man. I deleted those with a punch of my finger, frustrated at them wasting my time when I'd talked about my faith in Jesus and stated explicitly that I wanted the same in a man. By now I expected very little from the third response.

This man, however, declared himself to be a Christian so I read a bit further. Richard, a business trainer, lived in Edmonton. Even better, I thought. Edmonton was a North London suburb—this was promising. I read on.

But no, this Edmonton was half a world away in Canada! The country had never interested me. It lacked the long, fascinating history of Europe and was a cold land of ugly conifers. Did I even want to be bothered? Then again, he was the only passable respondent. It seemed pointless but curiosity got the better of me and so I replied.

Emailing back, he asked some questions and told me more about himself. A scout leader in his spare time, it seemed we had a connection via our joint interest in children. I was becoming interested to learn more about him until he spoilt things by emailing a photo of himself. He was of average build with the dark hair I liked. What was so off-putting was the stuffy way he wore his shirt buttoned up to his neck (who did that unless they were wearing a tie?) and over his shirt he sported a huge cross. I didn't know if the latter was to emphasize the fact he had a Christian faith or whether he always dressed in such a manner; either way it was all too much for my liking.

After school the next day I showed the photo to Hannah.

'Take a look at what he's wearing,' I giggled. 'He's such a stuffed-shirt.'

I expected Hannah to laugh along with me. She did nothing of the sort. 'Leanne, I think you're being really judgmental. You know God doesn't look on the outside, He looks on the heart.' Leaving me to consider what she'd said, she went back to marking her students' spelling.

I did indeed know that. On the way home on the Tube I mulled over what she'd said. I'd intended on bringing my correspondence with Richard to an end but now I felt that I was basing my decision on wrong motives and should give him a chance. Accordingly, I emailed back and we progressed from emails to phone calls, and during Easter, he asked me to visit.

Somewhat naively, I hadn't expected that—I'd thought he'd come to me—and I weighed it up for about a week. Having never held any appeal for me, Canada was one country I'd decided never to visit. However, during the next week I was aware of Canada like never before: the Tube, shop displays and magazines bombarded me with advertisements, music, articles, and people with links to Canada. It was as if the country was shouting to get my attention.

On the Saturday following Richard's invite it was time to make a decision about whether to go or not. I'd discussed it with Alison and Christy but I wanted someone to talk with one last time and as my flatmate, Rachel, was in the kitchen, I brought up the subject with her.

'What've you got to lose if you go?' asked Rachel, sipping a cup of tea.

'A few hundred pounds if he's a plonker!'

Rachel grinned. 'True,' she agreed, 'but even if you don't like Richard, you might enjoy visiting Edmonton.'

I rolled my eyes. 'Hardly. I've done some research and it's smack dab in the middle of the prairies without a hill or mountain in sight, and the only thing to recommend it is that it boasts the world's largest mall. If I wanted shopping, I've already got the world's best here in London!'

Rachel snorted at my rudeness. 'Sounds like you've made your mind up then.'

I sighed, leaning back on one of the two wooden fold-up chairs that "graced" our kitchen table. 'Well, sort of but then I think, what if I didn't go? What if I never meet anyone and end up an old maid sitting in my rocking chair going back and forth and wondering what would have happened if I'd gone?'

Rachel laughed. 'A double minded woman, eh?' she said, referring to a verse in the New Testament.

'I know, I know. I guess I should just do it. I don't want to live with regrets or "what–ifs." And the strange thing is that all week I've been seeing Canada everywhere. But it's so far away ...'

I deliberated further until I realised how long I'd kept Rachel talking. 'Sorry, you probably need to go.'

'I do actually,' she said, standing up and putting her cup in the sink, 'I need some groceries. But for what it's worth—and I know it's not my money—it sounds like maybe you're meant to go.'

'You might be right. Thanks, Rachel.'

I went back to my bedroom, again asking God what to do, but of course there weren't any verses about Canada in the Bible. It seemed a gamble, but I couldn't overlook the startling proliferation during the week of things associated with Canada. Decision made, I grabbed my handbag and headed down Kilburn High Road to a travel agency. Thirty minutes later I was greatly pleased with my bargain priced flights of about £300; unconcerned I'd achieved it by choosing non-refundable fares.

Until I rang Richard, that is.

'Hi, Richard. It's Leanne here. Sorry to call you at your work but I've got some good news.'

'Ah, yes ...' He sounded distracted but after all he was at work.

I plunged right in to keep the conversation short. 'I've booked flights and I arrive in Edmonton on Monday, 29 May.'

'Oh ... right ... Look, I can't talk now. It's very busy. I'll call you tonight, okay?'

My excitement drained away like spilt good wine. 'Okay. Goodbye.'

'Bye,' he said and hung up immediately.

I put down the handset and exhaled. That hadn't gone according to plan. Why wasn't he happy? He'd invited me, after all! What could be wrong? Maybe I was over-reacting and he was having a stressful day but he still should have been glad. The time difference meant I'd have to wait until the morning to hear from him. With questions like these milling around in my mind it was difficult getting to sleep.

At 6 am the next morning the phone shrilled. I leapt out of bed, willing myself to wake up quickly. I answered the phone, it was Richard.

'Hi Leanne. Hope you slept well. Look, sorry to put a damper on things but I talked to my secretary about your dates and she reminded me that I'm going to be out of town that week doing training in Vancouver.'

I said nothing as my early-morning brain struggled to process this most unwelcome news.

'Leanne ...?'

'Yes, I'm here,' I said, giving my head a quick shake and

thinking quickly. 'I guess I could extend my flights to Vancouver. I could sightsee during the day and we could meet up in the evenings.'

'Ah ... unfortunately I have to dine with clients then. My boss expects it.'

I recalled how Karl had to entertain clients and so I was familiar with this work expectation. I sidestepped this added complication with a last-ditch suggestion. 'Okay. Well, I'm not leaving until Sunday night so we'd at least have the weekend in Edmonton to meet up.'

Again, Richard hesitated. Suddenly his absence of enthusiasm and total lack of solution-finding seemed very suspicious.

'I'm sorry,' he said, 'but I have to spend the weekend in Vancouver too—you know, golf games and the like with clients.'

I'd had enough of his nonsense. 'No, I don't know!' I said angrily. 'All I know is that *you* invited *me* and I've just booked flights in response and now you can't even be bothered trying to find a way to make it work! What's going on?'

'Look, it's late and I'm tired,' Richard responded. 'I'll call you tomorrow, eh?' and he hung up.

But he didn't call. It was the last time we ever spoke.

When Richard didn't ring the next day and wouldn't pick up when I rang him at home, I emailed to demand that he tell me the truth. He finally responded, saying he was sorry but he'd met someone in Edmonton and I shouldn't come.

He was sorry? That was it? I was seething! Three hundred precious pounds wasted!

The non-refundable status of my tickets now seemed a terrible mistake. The trip to Canada was by default of the fact Richard lived there, not because I'd chosen to visit for its own sake. Regretfully I decided it was pointless to go. I'd have to accept the financial loss and not engage in such a foolhardy venture again. Oh my goodness, how stupid I'd been.

Being a verbal processor, I told the story to my fellow teachers and various other people. As I did, a curious thing happened. The first time was when I talked with the educational psychologist assigned to my Lambeth school. Sympathetic to my decision, he nevertheless encouraged me to not squander my ticket but go to

Edmonton and then travel west to Jasper, a pretty little town in the Rockies that he and his wife had visited a year or two ago. How beautiful could it be, I thought scathingly, with all those hideous conifers?

I thanked him for his recommendation but brushed it off. I found it odd, however, when I visited my dentist a day later to find her receptionist had recently visited Jasper. She also told me to go. On the way home that evening I marvelled over the likelihood that two people would make the same recommendation independent of one another but still wasn't persuaded.

That Friday evening I met up with Andrea, a new friend I'd made through Christy. As we sat in a pub waiting for our meal, I told her what had happened with Richard. I was increasingly able to joke about it and was finding it an entertaining story to tell.

'So,' I concluded, 'he simply said he'd met someone else and don't come.' I sat back and took a sip of my lemon, lime and bitters.

Andrea looked shocked. 'Oh, Leanne, that's awful. You must be really disappointed,' she sympathised. 'But at least you get to visit Canada!'

I shook my head. 'No, I'm not going. Edmonton looks boring ... it's in the middle of the prairies with nothing much to recommend it.'

Andrea put down her drink and grew animated. 'Yes, I agree. But don't stay there—take the Greyhound to Jasper—it's a cute little mountain town. I went there last year. You'll love it!'

I was flabbergasted and it must have showed.

'What have I said?' Andrea asked, looking puzzled.

'You're the third person to tell me that.'

Andrea laughed. 'Ah ha ... see! You're meant to go. Let's meet up again when you get back and we can swap notes!'

I still wasn't entirely convinced despite her enthusiasm. But by the end of the weekend I'd come around to the notion that as I hadn't travelled for several months and had already spent the money, I might as well go and have something to show for it. And at least Jasper was in the mountains and not stuck out in the middle of nowhere.

By now there was only about a week to go and I needed to

quickly book accommodation. The first reasonably priced B&B was the home of Joe and Sheila Couture. I emailed them and asked about the nights of Tuesday, 30 May to Friday, 2 June. Sheila replied that they were free and she'd book them for me.

And so it was all organised. I would soon be off to Canada, the one country I'd decided I'd never visit. Maybe one day I'd be able to laugh at the irony.

Chapter Ten

As I stepped out onto the tarmac at Edmonton airport, the first thing I noticed was the lack of humidity. After hours of recycled air on the plane, my eyes felt gritty and the dry air didn't help. They looked as bloodshot as if I'd spent the entire flight imbibing every free drink I could get my hands on.

I was glad I wasn't meeting a man I wanted to impress.

After retrieving my baggage, I left the terminal and hired a taxi. It was mid-morning and sunny as we drove to the city. The highways were another sign I was no longer in the UK. They were wide and unclogged with traffic, and had intriguing North American names like Calgary Trail, and Whitemud Drive. Thinking it behoved me to glean some knowledge of Edmonton, I called out to the driver from the back seat. 'Excuse me. What's the story behind the name, Whitemud?'

'It's the name of the clay found on the banks of the North Saskatchewan River, the one that flows through Edmonton.'

'Okay. Thanks.' Saskatchewan. I tried saying it under my breath; it was unusual but felt good as it rolled around my mouth.

'You're on holiday?'

'Yes. From London.'

'You don't sound Canadian. You mean London, UK?'

'Yes,' I answered shortly, with the unspoken riposte, "What other London is there?" It was only afterwards I discovered the heresy that there was a London in Ontario.

Thinking I'd been a bit curt, I tried to make amends, although my observation was somewhat critical. 'It's very flat. There's not a mountain in sight.'

The driver chuckled. 'They say it's so flat here you can see your dog run away for a week.'

I laughed out loud. The analogy was entirely appropriate.

He dropped me at the B&B I'd chosen which was located close to the West Edmonton Mall (WEM). The bus to Jasper didn't leave until the next morning so I figured I might as well visit the mall. My host gave me directions but you couldn't miss it; it seemed all roads pointed to WEM. It was an unprepossessing concrete behemoth and inside it seemed even larger. Not only was it a retail complex but it boasted a movie theatre, an indoor skating rink, a mock pirate ship surrounded by water, and themed accommodation. It thronged with people and I enjoyed watching them as I ate lunch.

Hours later with my senses on overload and jetlag starting to take its toll, I bought a takeaway dish for tea and walked back to my B&B. While I waited for my meal to reheat in the microwave, I asked the owner for information about how to reach the bus depot the next morning. Once I'd eaten, I retired to my room for the night.

The Greyhound left early and we headed due west out of Edmonton. From my window seat I was astonished to see that commercial and retail areas did little to beautify themselves—there were just a few conifers and occasional ragged plants providing patchy groundcover. Brand names I'd never heard of before flashed past: Canadian Tire, ESSO, A&W, and Tim Hortons.

We drove through the satellite towns of Spruce Grove and Stony Plain, and then farmland stretched as far as I could see with only occasional undulations. There were more place names of interest: Wababum, Entwistle, Wildwood, Nojack, Niton Junction, and Edson. At the latter, we made a short stop to have a bite to eat and visit the loo, although I was learning that Canadians were very polite and called it the bathroom. Very discreet.

Over the next hour or so, the landscape changed from farmland to forest, although it was glacially slow compared to the way scenery in the UK and New Zealand altered significantly within a short space of time. Of course, it reflected the fact I was now on a huge continent, and the sense of space was monumental and somewhat intimidating.

After three hours on the Greyhound, the land began to rise noticeably. At Obed Summit, which the driver said was the highest point on the unusually named Yellowhead Highway, the Rockies suddenly made their presence felt. Beyond the conifers hedging the highway was an imposing range of hazy blue mountains. The association with the hills and mountains of my childhood memories caused my spirits to lift. I felt adrift on the prairies but to me mountains served as boundaries imparting a sense of protection and safety.

The Greyhound made one further stop at a town called Hinton. Leaving there to enter the Athabasca River valley, the divided highway merged into a two-lane road lined by aspen and spires of spruce, and closely surrounded by mountains. Driving through the park gate with its chalet-like ticketing kiosks, we were officially in Jasper National Park.

The road no longer stretched out straight ahead to the horizon but curved around the feet of mountains, expanses of water and the river. I felt much more at home on these winding roads.

About an hour later we passed a sign for Jasper and turned right off the main highway and under a rail overpass. The township opened up with the railroad to the left and the town to the right. The Greyhound drove down the main street, passing numerous hotels, a supermarket and retail stores, then slowed at an intersection to turn left, cross the road and pull up outside the train station, an attractive roughcast building with its lower reaches overlaid in river-stone.

The driver turned off the engine. I made my way down the aisle and stepped down from the bus.

Here I was—Jasper's most reluctant tourist.

Some of my fellow teachers had joked that I'd meet someone here. But I wasn't one of those people who win competitions or raffles, so what were the chances of that happening? If the weather was good, I'd explore as much as I could on my limited budget and take some photos to send home to mum and dad. That was as much as I expected—a pleasant break from teaching before I embarked on the final half term of the year.

Retrieving my pack, I strapped it on and crossed the road—making a mental note to first look left into the oncoming traffic. I didn't want to remember the holiday as one in which I was run over. I entered a shop and chatted to a sales assistant and learnt that this was Connaught Drive and the B&B was only two blocks away in the 700s section. The numbering system seemed regimented although I appreciated it made it easy to find your way around. It was a mild, sunny afternoon and I was keen to get to my accommodation, rid myself of the backpack and go for a walk.

Arriving at the Couture's house, I saw it had wooden siding like many in New Zealand. It was two-storeyed and had three cute

Dormer windows. I walked up several steps to a gate set into a high hedge. Closing the gate behind me, I walked around the side of the house as I had a hunch the back door was used more often than the front. In the back yard I saw a well-tended vegetable plot with long rows of young plants that reminded me of my mum and dad's garden.

I knocked at the screen door. Almost immediately a woman who looked to be in her 50s stepped down from the kitchen onto the landing and opened the back door. She had short blonde-white hair and an open, friendly face lit up by a glorious, beaming smile. I warmed to her immediately.

'Sheila?'

'Yes, you must be Leanne. Welcome! Let's get you settled. Your room's in the basement.' She walked down the stairs before me. I followed her and at the bottom I struggled out of my pack and set it down gratefully, rolling my aching shoulders.

'This looks lovely, Sheila,' I said, glancing around at the open room. It had a small kitchen area, a table and chairs, a sofa with an occasional table and lamp, and a high, fully stocked bookcase which also functioned to divide the space and lend some privacy to the double bed behind it. There was also a bathroom and another bedroom. It was tastefully decorated and cosy, and I knew I'd be very comfortable.

'So, you've come from London.'

'Yes,' I chuckled. 'The trip I never intended making.'

'Oh, she said, her voice piqued with interest. 'Sounds like there's a story there.'

'There is,' I replied and because she genuinely seemed interested, I told her how it had come about.

'Well,' Sheila laughed when I finished. 'We'll have to see you have a good time and change your perception, not only of Canada but of Canadians after what that man did to you.'

I thanked Sheila for her kind sentiments but never gave them another thought. I assumed she was just being polite because in the few interactions I'd had with Canadians politeness seemed a defining feature.

'I'll let you get unpacked. Let me know if there's anything you need,' she said, and then left, shutting the door behind her.

Never one to fully unpack—I couldn't see the point for such a short time, or maybe I was just lazy—I took out my toiletries and then freshened up. Walking back into the heart of town, I passed houses with more siding, others with stucco walls, and many that appeared to have basements. Flower gardens were few although some houses were graced by hanging flower baskets. I entered the Visitors' Centre, a gorgeous building built of chunky river stone with wooden-framed windows and a cedar-shake roof. To help me decide what to do during my four-night stay I picked up some tourist brochures. Beside a display of coffee table books with stunning photographs of the Rockies I saw a stand with bear bells.

What on earth was a bear bell?

I'd heard of Swiss cowbells that herders placed on free ranging livestock but the same principle was unlikely to apply to a bear. I turned over the price tag to read the blurb. "Attach this attractive bear bell to your pack or clothing and it will ring steadily and warn any bears of your presence." Putting aside the ridiculous notion that popped into my mind that this was so the bears would stay put and pose for a photo, I guessed the unwritten message was that once a bear heard the bell it would run off. The thought of a bear encounter chilled me so I bought one in the hope it would keep me safe.

It was nearing time for tea. I walked back down Patricia Street—parallel to Connaught Drive and the main shopping street—to try out a Greek restaurant I'd seen with the odd name of Something Else.

As I ate my lamb chops, I thought of my Corfu holiday with Gwen and Alison. How I'd love for them to be with me, even if they teased me for my choice of meat. I hated eating out alone—I'd had more than enough of it in Cantabria. I felt conspicuous and never knew where to direct my gaze, and it was so boring without a book to read which was my habit at home.

As I swung open the back screen door at the B&B, it squeaked a little and I heard footsteps. Sheila came to the kitchen door as I stepped onto the landing. 'Hi, Leanne, how was your supper?'

I puzzled for a moment and then understood. 'Oh, you mean "tea"?'

'Yes.'

'Oh, good thanks. Something Else serves great lamb chops.'

'They do. Jasper has several Greek restaurants if you like Greek food.' Sheila paused to turn and put down the tea towel she'd been holding. 'Changing the topic, while you were out, I got to thinking. You don't know anyone here, and Joe and I have a good friend who's in a situation similar to you—his wife left him. And he's a Christian too. I thought you might like someone to show you around. He's a park warden so he's very knowledgeable about the park.'

I was gobsmacked. If my school colleagues were here, they'd be squealing, "We told you so!" However, the odds of me meeting someone I really clicked with were miniscule.

'Mmm ... ah ... sure. Why not?' I said, sounding as stunned as I felt.

Sheila grinned. 'Don't worry, I won't charge extra.'

I laughed.

'Right, I'll ring him and let you know what he says.'

I eased off my shoes then tucked my legs under me as I sat on the easy chair to read one of the tourist brochures. Sometime later footsteps sounded on the stairs and then came a light rap on the door. 'It's me, Sheila.'

'Come in,' I called, putting down the brochure.

Sheila entered, smiling. 'I've just talked to Phil and he'll be here tomorrow night at 7 pm to pick you up.'

'Wow,' I said. 'I can't quite believe it. Thank you.'

'You're welcome, and even if he's not your type, he's a lovely man and will be good company for an evening. Well, I'll let you get back to your reading.'

I got up and followed Sheila to the door.

'Thanks again, Sheila. I'll see you tomorrow.'

Closing the door and sitting back down, my imagination went into overdrive. Would he be my dream man—tall and dark—or short and balding? Would he flood me with endless information on the local flora and fauna or be quiet and yawn-inducing? After all my disappointing experiences with men I could hardly bring myself to hope for much.

It was just as well I hadn't got too excited.

The next evening after I'd had tea downtown and came back to my room, Sheila called down the stairs that Phil had arrived. I went to the bathroom one more time. I was wearing one of the new tops I'd bought in WEM, jeans and hiking boots. With it being warm, I'd put my hair up in a ponytail to keep it off the back of my neck. My red lipstick—which I loved for both its colour and the way it deflected attention from my less than perfect skin—was fine.

I walked up from the basement to join them in the backyard. Phil was slim and dressed in jeans and a T-shirt. But he was only a few inches taller than me, had blond hair and was, I guessed, significantly older than me. Damn.

Oh well, at least Sheila said that he was pleasant company, so I endeavoured to shelve my disappointment and greet him with a smile.

Sheila introduced us. 'Phil's been a friend of ours for about 15 years and lives not far from here.' She turned to him. 'Did you walk around, Phil?'

'No, I've got the truck as we're heading up to Cottonwood Slough. We'll see if there's any beavers there.'

I brightened up. 'That would be fantastic,' I said. 'I've been wanting to see one.'

'I won't hold you up then,' Sheila said. 'Plus I've got the supper dishes waiting for me.'

'Isn't that Joe's job?' joked Phil.

Sheila laughed. 'I wish.'

We bade her goodbye and I shouldered my rucksack with my camera and drink bottle, and followed Phil. At the gate he opened it and then stepped back to let me go through before him. I thanked him and walked through.

'My truck's just here,' he said.

It was large, as all Canadian vehicles seemed to be; this one dark blue with a stylish white flame along the side. Instead of walking around to the driver's side, Phil stopped and opened the passenger's door for me. 'Thank you,' I said again. He may not be my type, I thought, but he has amazing old-fashioned manners.

I buckled up my seatbelt as Phil started the truck and pulled out onto the right–hand side of the road.

'Gosh, I thought I was starting to get used to being on the wrong side of the road after my trip from Edmonton on the Greyhound but driving in a truck is a different experience altogether.'

'Don't you mean the *right* side of the road?'

I paused. 'Well, yes, I guess strictly speaking it is,' and had to chuckle. 'You've got me there. So, we're going to a slough, you said. What's that?'

'A slough? A marshy pond. I spotted a beaver lodge there last week and thought it might be something you'd enjoy. I don't suppose, being English, you've ever seen one before.'

'What makes you think I'm English?' I said curiously.

'Sheila told me.'

'Oh, okay. I do live in London but I'm a Kiwi. I thought she'd have picked that up from my accent.'

'She probably didn't notice much difference,' Phil replied, waving to someone as we passed a large complex called the Jasper Activity Centre.

'My English friends would be insulted to hear that. Although to be fair many can't tell the difference between the Kiwi and Australian accents.'

'There *is* a difference?'

I snorted. 'Yes! Of course. Actually, there's an odd relationship between our two countries. If we play against one another in sport for example, we're arch enemies, but if there's any crisis like a bad fire season in Aussie, then we pitch in and help out like best mates. It's kind of a love-hate relationship.'

'Sounds kind of like things between Canada and the US. I don't have a problem with Americans, but some Canadians do.'

'Yes, I've seen some differences already. Kiwis tend to think Aussies are brash and loud, sort of like some Americans. And I can see that Canadians, like Kiwis, are quieter and more reserved. Interesting.'

We left the town and Phil turned up a winding road surrounded by forest. Shortly afterwards there was a break in the trees to our left and the open view looked out over a sizeable body of water which presumably was the slough. Surrounding it were bushes and tufts of tall sedge-grass. Behind the slough were low grassy rises and a timbered ridge beyond. Overlooking it all was a sharp-sided mountain range, in which Phil said the tallest peak was Pyramid Mountain.

Phil parked on an area of shingle. We each grabbed our rucksacks and opened our doors. 'I was coming around to open your door,' Phil said.

'Oh, thank you! I'm not used to such great manners.'

'Then you don't know the right men.'

I smiled. 'Apparently not.'

Phil led me through the bushes and grasses and up a high sloping bank to the right of the water. 'Let's go for a short walk and then come back and see if there's any beavers about.'

Once back at the ridge above the slough, Phil sat down on the grass-and-lichen-covered ground. I did the same, placing my pack between us and taking out my water. Phil eyed my bottle as I unscrewed the cap.

'Volvic, with a touch of lemon,' he read from the label. 'Looks fancy.'

'I never used to drink bottled water,' I said, swallowing several mouthfuls before refastening the cap. 'But you can't drink the London water—it's terrible. They say it's passed through at least seven people before it gets to you.'

Phil guffawed then grew serious. 'We need to quiet down if we want a beaver to come out.'

I glanced around. Beyond the water's edge were the bristly conifers I disliked so much. To my pleasure I noticed some deciduous trees with white trunks scored with black markings and delicate, light green leaves. Lurking at the back of this peaceful scene was the potential for bears to make an appearance. This unwelcome knowledge prickled at the base of my neck. It was a reality I'd never experienced before. I didn't feel entirely at ease.

Breaking into my musings, Phil whispered, 'There's one. Can you see him?' and pointed to the right of the slough.

'Not very well.'

'Hang on, I've got binoculars.' He took them out of his pack, looked through and adjusted them, then passed them to me. Our hands accidentally touched. I was embarrassed but the moment lost its awkwardness when Phil exclaimed at my cold fingers.

'Yep,' I laughed. 'I'm afraid so. But as my grandad used to say, "cold hands and a warm heart."'

'I haven't heard that one. I've got gloves if you'd like them?'

Gosh, I thought, this man comes prepared. Probably a better boy scout than Richard would ever be. 'Yes, thanks, that would be great.'

I pulled on the blue fleece gloves then scanned the slough below me with the binoculars. Locating the beaver, I pulled up my knees so I could rest my elbows on them and still my view. Water glistened on the sleek dark coat of the beaver as it gripped a leafy branch in its mouth and rippled through the water. I watched until the beaver dove under the water to its lodge in the centre of the slough.

'Wow,' I exclaimed, lowering the binoculars and handing them back to Phil. 'That was magical. I've loved beavers ever since reading *The Lion, the Witch and the Wardrobe*.'

He looked puzzled. '*The Lion ...*?'

I repeated the title.

'Never heard of it.'

'Sorry, I assumed everyone had. It's the first book in the Narnia series—fantasy books for children by CS Lewis.'

'That explains it then,' Phil said, 'I know of CS Lewis but I don't like fantasy. Are you a keen reader?'

'I love reading,' I said, thinking that he probably wasn't a fan of Tolkien's either. 'How about you?'

'Mostly cowboy books ... Louis L'Amour.'

Now it was my turn to admit ignorance. As I did so I gave a little shiver. By now the sun had dropped below the ridge at our backs and the slough was in shadow.

'Are you cold?' Phil asked.

'Yes, that's me—perpetually cold and hungry!' I admitted. 'It's about the only true thing my ex-husband said about me—that I was a human thermometer.'

Phil didn't seem to know what to do with my last comment. It fitted the occasion but it also served to introduce what Sheila had said was a common thread for us both—being deserted by our spouses. Instead, he took the easy option and focused on my physical well-being.

'If you wanted to, we could have a late supper. That way you'll get full *and* warm.'

'Sure! Tea, I mean supper, does seem a long time ago.'

As Phil drove back into town, he asked me where I'd like to go. When I mentioned enjoying the food at Something Else last night, he suggested going there. We were shown to a table and each given a menu.

'So,' asked Phil, after the waiter left, 'what does a Kiwi eat?'

'Grubs and insects?'

'Pardon me?'

'Sorry,' I grinned. 'Bad joke. Lamb usually. On a Greek holiday with friends last summer I ordered lamb for all but one meal, much to their amusement at first and then their dismay. But this late I'll just have something light, maybe the hummus and pitta bread. You?'

'Their Caesar salad is good. I had spaghetti Bolognese for supper so I don't need much more.'

Phil must have seen me pull a face. 'You don't like spaghetti?'

I shook my head. 'No, yuk! My brother loved canned spaghetti but the rest of us kids hated it. We called it worms in blood.'

He laughed. 'I love spaghetti but not canned. I make it fresh with a meat sauce.'

'You like to cook?'

The waiter interrupted our conversation to take our order. Afterwards I repeated my question.

'Yes, I do,' Phil answered, 'when I have the time and space. Working in a small kitchen is too frustrating.'

'I know exactly what you mean! The kitchen in my London flat is tiny. There's five of us girls and hardly any bench space. And I only have one shelf in a pint-sized fridge and two shelves in the cupboard.'

'I couldn't handle that.'

'I didn't think so either—after being married and having a whole kitchen to myself—but now I don't have a choice.'

This time Phil seemed prepared to follow up on the topic of our past marriages.

'So you were married before?'

'Yes. Almost ten years to a man who turned out to be a

compulsive liar. I still don't know how much of our life together was real.'

Phil didn't say anything. However, he made a sympathetic murmur to show he was listening and he hadn't jumped in to change the topic, so I took his behaviour as a sign to continue.

'He left me twice, the second time for another woman.'

'Second time lucky,' Phil commented.

'What?' I frowned. 'Do you mean Karl got lucky with the second woman?'

'No, no,' Phil hastened to reassure me, 'not at all! I meant you were lucky to get rid of him the second time.'

'Oh, I see.' I realised his comment was actually a roundabout way of supporting me which felt good. 'I probably would have felt like slapping you if you'd said that at the time but five years on I agree with you. He was very destructive verbally and the worst part was that I let him. I'd never let a man do that now.'

'Good for you,' Phil smiled. When he did so, laughter lines on either side of his mouth creased deeply. He wasn't my type but he did have a lovely smile.

Our meals arrived and we set about eating. The hummus was satisfyingly garlicky.

Phil then shared it was after he took up a temporary post on Banks Island in the Western Arctic that his wife of 27 years phoned to tell him she was leaving.

'Oh, that must've been terribly hard,' I said. 'I'm so sorry.'

Phil acknowledged my empathy then moved on from our marriages to ask me what I'd done that day.

'Canyons fascinate me so I hired a bike and cycled up to Maligne Canyon.'

Phil looked suitably impressed. 'How long did it take you?'

'Too long! I hadn't been on a bike for years so I must admit I walked some of it.'

'What did you think?'

'It was magnificent!' Thinking to impress Phil further, I added, 'I even scrambled over the fence at the top in order to get a closer photograph of the water.' My dad would have applauded me for such a harmless breaking of the rules but not Phil. He looked very serious.

'You know how many people I've pulled out of places like that? Foolish tourists who put their lives—and ours—at risk, all for a photo.'

'No…'

'Far too many. The signs are there for a reason.'

I felt foolish, for in my haste to boast of my daring I'd forgotten he was a warden. In my defense I said that, honestly, I hadn't got too close and was being careful.

'That's what they all say,' he said. I wasn't going to win this one.

'So what else does your job entail other than rescuing witless tourists?'

'Chasing bears out of town,' he answered, his good humour restored and his mouth tugging at the corners like he was restraining himself from laughing.

'You're winding me up?'

'There's no key in your back that I can see.'

I rolled my eyes, although I couldn't deny his quip had been exceptionally quick. 'No, that's UK slang for were you kidding me?'

'Nope. Sometimes bears wander into town, and it's the job of the duty warden to chase them out.'

'They scare me. I saw the "Be aware of bears" sign on the way to Maligne Canyon. It said to stay in your vehicle if you encounter one. How the heck do you do that on a bicycle?' I grumbled.

'Pedal faster?'

'Ha ha … very funny. Seriously though, what *should* you do?'

'As a general rule,' Phil explained, 'don't make eye contact and back away slowly.'

'Okay, thanks.' As I ate, I remembered my purple bell. 'What about the bear bell I bought? Are they useful?'

Phil nodded. 'Yes, they let the bears know lunch is coming.'

I gawped at Phil, who'd kept a remarkably straight face. 'You're impossible!' I said, trying to suppress a grin. 'Seriously, are they useful?'

'It'd depend on how far the sound carries and what the bears associate the ringing with. You're probably better off to sing.'

I snorted. 'I'd feel a right plonker doing that. I'll just pray I don't encounter one, as there doesn't seem to be a foolproof deterrent.'

'With animals, never.'

We finished eating, talked some more and then I yawned.

'Time to get you back to Sheila's,' Phil said.

We left the restaurant, having gone Dutch on the cost of the meals. It was about 10:45 pm and just becoming dark. The evenings were long here.

He pulled up at the Couture's. Having come round to open my door he asked what I was doing the next evening.

'Nothing. I don't know anyone other than Sheila, Joe, and now you.'

'Would you be interested in me showing you some more of the park tomorrow?'

I was surprised but pleased as the evening had progressed easily and with lots of laughter. It was great to have company after being alone all day. 'Sure, sounds good.'

'Pick you up at seven tomorrow then. Don't forget to check for ticks,' he added, as he walked around to the driver's side. 'Night.'

'Good night. Thanks again.' I turned and walked up the steps and through the gate. What did he mean by "check for ticks?" What were ticks? Maybe it was some weird Canadian saying. I yawned as I opened the screen door. I was too tired to figure it out—it was time for bed.

I awoke to sunshine, grateful for another sunny day in which to explore.

As I ate a breakfast of toast and fruit, I looked at the brochures again. By the time I finished eating I'd decided that I'd ride the Jasper Sky Tram to the top of Whistlers Mountain in the morning and then rent a bike again for the afternoon.

I walked downtown to Sundog Tours who ran a shuttle service to the base of the mountain from where the Sky Tram ascended. At the summit the tram shuddered to a halt with a disconcerting series of metallic clunks. I got out with relief. I'd planned to walk some of the hiking trails but had no idea there would still be snow at that elevation. As I hadn't dressed for it, it was too cold to venture outside. Instead, I browsed in the gift shop and then sat in the restaurant to have lunch and enjoy the expansive view.

Back in town I once again hired a bicycle. With my bear bell—for better or for worse—attached to my rucksack, I followed Connaught Drive around to where it joined the highway south called the Icefields Parkway. I'd ridden about 2 km when I came to Alpine Village. It provided log cabin accommodation, each enchanting cabin a dark honey colour with stone foundations and chimneys.

Across the road from the village was a river. I'd lived close to one as a child and loved walking alongside its banks looking for unusual stones, throwing in the occasional stone or stick, or simply being lulled by the murmuring of the water. I propped my bike against a tree and took the chance to explore the river bank. Afterwards I sat on a Muskoka chair which felt a bit cheeky as it was presumably provided by Alpine Village for their guests. The sky was cloudless and the sun strong so I reapplied my sunscreen, then closed my eyes and basked like a contented cat in the warmth.

I returned the bike later in the afternoon, chose a new restaurant in which to eat my evening meal, then walked back to the B&B to rest before tea.

Phil arrived at 7 pm. He chatted with Sheila and me for a while then he bade Sheila goodbye, and he and I walked out to his truck.

'Did you find any ticks?' he asked.

'What? I thought that was some joke. What do you mean?'

Phil opened the gate for me. 'No, they're no joke. They're small parasites that suck your blood. They like warm, moist areas like your armpits and groin.'

'Charming.'

I climbed into the truck as Phil held the door open for me. Once he got into the driver's seat I continued.

'That's so gross. Why didn't you tell me?'

Phil shrugged. 'I guess I figured you knew about them.'

'We don't have them in New Zealand. I had no idea.'

'Just check yourself out tonight then.' He turned the key in the ignition and pulled out into Connaught Drive. 'If you do find one, just tweeze it off. As close to the skin as you can. You don't want to leave any part behind.'

I gave an involuntary shudder. 'This is freaking me out.'

'Don't be. It's not that common to get them and only rarely does someone contract Lyme disease.'

'You're not reassuring me! I'm starting to feel itchy now.'

'Leanne, you're probably fine. Don't worry.'

Phil drove down the Icefields Parkway; as we passed Alpine Village I told him about my afternoon. We continued for about half an hour before we saw the sign announcing Athabasca Falls and Phil turned right into the car park.

'No climbing over the railing!' he instructed as he opened the door for me.

'Yes sir,' I saluted.

We walked first to a lookout. In the background was Mt Kerkeslin, clothed in forest green up to its tree line, above which rain and ice had tooled long gouges down its rocky face. Upstream of the falls, the Athabasca flowed wide and rippling over river stones. As it neared, it curved abruptly to the left then dived down over broad and broken steps of stratified rock, the water foaming white as it plummeted.

To follow the river's path after the falls we left the lookout and walked along a concreted path with railings. Bridges crossed over the canyon, allowing multiple views of the river as it pumped through a narrow passage of zig-zagging rock, spray rising high, until it eased out into a large quiet pool of turquoise water.

Descending steep steps to where the water pooled, we saw that the riverbank was cluttered with chunks of grey rock which had presumably broken away from the cliff sides where the waterfall exited the canyon. They ranged from small cubes to thin oblong slabs to huge pieces the size of a man's torso. Here and there rocks had been arranged in the shape of a person: two short stacks of rocks for legs, some wider pieces for a squat body, two longer ones for arms, and a smaller stone for a head.

'What are those rock structures?' I asked Phil.

'Inuksuk's.'

'Inuk ...?'

'Inuksuks. Inuit people make them as a landmark or to commemorate something.'

'They're cool.'

In reply Phil scrambled nimbly over the rock field, located a flat square-shaped rock, knelt down, balanced it on his head and stretched out his arms. 'Photo opportunity,' he called.

I took out my camera and quickly snapped a shot before the rock fell off his head.

'That should be good,' I said, putting my camera away. 'Isn't there some saying about rocks on your head?'

'That's rocks *in* your head. Close, but no cigar.'

Another of the many Canadian sayings I'd never heard before. I enjoyed word play and discovering word origins and I was keeping a mental inventory of these new idioms.

It was still warm and a long way from twilight. Back in the truck, Phil suggested going for a short hike into Buffalo Prairie which was just off the Icefields Parkway on the way back to Jasper. A few kilometres from town, using knowledge only a local would have, Phil pulled over to park on the side of the highway. We crossed the road and followed what Phil surmised was an old game trail through the trees and quickly came out into a long, grassed prairie with trees along either side. Sunlight was still flooding over the surrounding mountains turning them a soft rose colour.

'Stop,' said Phil suddenly. 'Look over there.' I followed the line of his arm as he pointed to his left where a startled deer was bounding away into the trees.

'Thanks! I wish it had been a coyote though.' I was familiar with deer as dad had hunted them when I was young and now ran a red deer farm. It was my hope to see something more thrilling before I left.

We walked to the far side of the prairie which sloped up into the trees. Scattered about were a few enormous, lichen-encrusted boulders.

'They're quite different to the rocks at Athabasca Falls, aren't they?' I commented. 'Those were smaller and slab-sided, whereas these are huge and rounded, a kind of conglomerate. Funny how I'm interested in geology now but wasn't at school.'

'Real life beats textbooks,' Phil commented.

'I have to agree. Have you studied geology?'

'I did one paper when I was young but I'm more of a flora and fauna guy.'

Heading back to the truck we passed a few young conifers about a metre tall. They were pleasingly uniform in shape with supple branches, and lush with new needles. I stopped to stroke the end of a branch; the bright green growth looked like spread fingers. 'I can't believe how soft they are, they're quite lovely.'

'You sound surprised.'

I pulled a face. 'I guess I should confess—I don't like conifers.'

'You might as well dislike all of Canada, then,' was Phil's perceptive response.

'That's true and I did. I find old conifers ugly, they get so straggly-looking. Plus, as you might have guessed, I hate the cold and to me that's all Canada was—a land full of nothing but snow and conifers.' I looked with embarrassment at Phil.

'Then why did you come?' he asked.

'It's a long story. I'll tell you on the way back in the truck.'

When we were back on the highway, Phil proposed that as it was hard to hear with all the vehicle and road noise, why didn't we have another meal together? It would give me ample time to explain and as I hated rushing stories I agreed. With that sorted, Phil pushed a cassette into the truck's player and I heard the distinctive voice of Van Morrison.

'Van, the Man,' I exclaimed.

'You know him?'

'Yes. I have his greatest hits. I don't know *this* song though.'

'It's from his Skiffle Session with Lonnie Donegan and Chris Barber.'

It was my turn to admit ignorance.

After we ordered at the restaurant, I explained how I came to be in Jasper. He listened well in the sense he didn't interrupt, but I was disappointed. He didn't make any encouraging noises that assured me he was listening thoughtfully or make any comments to express his feelings about what I was saying.

'But Canada is redeeming itself,' I said in conclusion, eager to offset my rude admission earlier. 'I love the warmth, the people have been very kind and the mountains are stunning. And two canyons in two days is pretty amazing!'

'Looks like our food's coming. You can grovel some more after we eat,' he grinned.

I guessed by his cheeky comment I was forgiven. While I still didn't appreciate aging conifers, and the thought of the flat, featureless land between Edmonton and Hinton depressed me, the Canadian Rockies were making a favourable impression.

As Phil dropped me back to Sheila's he asked if I'd like to go for a hike the following evening. I accepted—it was wonderful to see parts of the park I couldn't get to without a vehicle, as well as being able to pick Phil's brain for information about the park. And I had to admit I was also enjoying our banter.

In the morning after breakfast, I climbed the stairs to the landing to get my shoes. Canadians didn't wear them inside and Sheila had asked that I keep my footwear there. I saw her through the screen door, crouching in the garden and pulling weeds.

'Morning, Sheila,' I called as I pushed open the door and sat down on the front steps to lace up my shoes.

'Hey, Leanne.' She stood up, wiping her hands on her shorts. 'Another beautiful Jasper day!'

'Yes, the weather has been very kind.'

'Changing your impression of Canada?' she teased.

'Definitely!'

'And Canadian men?' she asked with a twinkle in her eye.

'Well, I can't speak for all of them and Phil's not the type I go for, but I'm liking his company. He's got a terrific sense of humour and we are finding heaps to talk and laugh about.'

'I'm pleased.'

'Thanks, Sheila. So am I. In fact Phil's coming around tonight as well. He's taking me to the Five Valleys or someplace.'

Sheila chuckled, whether about us meeting up for the third consecutive night or the fact I had the name wrong, I didn't know. 'It's the Valley of the Five Lakes.'

'Oh, right. Thanks.'

'What are you doing today?' Sheila enquired.

'Phil suggested I go for a walk along The Bench and he said you'd be able to direct me. Then I'll probably have a relaxing afternoon looking through the shops. Is there an internet café I can use?'

'Yes to both your questions. I can point you to the trail and there's an internet café in a walkway just off Connaught.'

Sheila went inside and brought out a map. She showed me where we were and pointed out a spot that would be a good place from which to begin. I thanked Sheila and let myself out of her yard through the back gate into one of the alleyways that bisected every block. They were unpaved and acted as service roads, housing the town's bear-proof metal rubbish containers. It was a clever idea to hide the services away and not visually spoil the street frontages.

Following Sheila's instructions, I found the trail which traversed the low wooded ridge that ran along Jasper's west side and was locally known as The Bench. I climbed for about 10 m to join the trail and then set off to follow it northwards. It was another warm day so it was pleasant to be in the shade beneath the trees; the walking was easy as long as you kept an eye out for stones and roots. Crossing over Pyramid Lake Road, I continued until I reached the end of the town where I made my way down off the ridge on a side trail. It came out near the Sawridge Hotel and I walked back into town.

After lunch I found the shop that provided internet services as well as stationery supplies and souvenirs. Paying for half an hour I logged onto my Hotmail account and emailed mum and dad, and then Dee to let her know the Couture's B&B I'd booked was working out well. I also bought thank you cards for Sheila and Phil.

Next I looked through the town's clothing stores. There were only a few, mostly boutiques offering gorgeous items, priced accordingly of course. I had to content myself with the purchase of postcards and handmade chocolates, my favourite being bear paws—oval-shaped milk chocolate with caramel centres and cashew claws.

Figuring Phil and I would probably go out to eat again this evening, I got a small takeaway meal to reheat in the microwave in my room, then walked back to Sheila's with sufficient time to indulge in an afternoon's sleep.

At 7 pm there was a knock on the screen door. I checked my hair and lipstick in the mirror, grabbed my rucksack and walked up the stairs. Sheila and Joe had stepped out of the house to chat with Phil. As I laced up my shoes I heard them talking.

'I thought you might've had enough of the park during your working day,' Joe said with the hint of a smile in his voice.

'Not when there's a fair maiden to escort,' said Sheila.

Phil laughed.

It was embarrassing but well meant. Exiting the house to join them, I thought I might as well meet their teasing head on. 'This fair maiden is ready, thanks.'

'Duty calls,' quipped Phil, then bade goodnight to Joe and Sheila and we walked out to the truck.

The Valley of the Five Lakes was clearly a popular hiking spot because there was a well-established trailhead with sealed parking and signage. The trail curved through the forest, beneath which were buffalo berry bushes and grasses, and then dropped down into a valley and crossed a narrow boardwalk over a stream. Soon afterwards we reached the first lake. Skirting between the bushes we approached the water's edge. The lake was so clear, I could glimpse the smooth round stones on the bottom—it was like gazing at a cobbled street under water. The calm surface reflected the light green vegetation that fringed the lake's far side, behind which darker pines stood shoulder to shoulder.

We walked on to the second lake, and then the third. On a ridge overlooking the latter, I suggested we sit and enjoy the view as the evening was sunny and mild and ideal for contemplation.

Phil agreed, yawning as he sat down. 'I'm not used to going out evening after evening so excuse me if I fall asleep,' he said, lying back with his hands clasped behind his head. 'I can do so fairly quickly.'

'Okay, thanks for the warning.'

I studied the lake and marvelled at its gem-like hue that was so typical of the waterways in and around Jasper. 'What causes the water to be that gorgeous turquoise?' I asked.

I'd learnt that Phil often took a while to answer, so while I waited I continued to enjoy the view. The sun's evening rays kissed the tops of the mountain opposite, and they flushed red in response. There was an occasional cry of a bird and the rustle of a squirrel going about its business.

Phil still hadn't replied so I turned to look at him.

He was fast asleep.

He'd warned me but I'd thought he'd exaggerated. Oh well, if you can't beat them, I thought, so I reclined on the grass. With my rucksack under my head, I studied the puffy clouds gliding overhead and gave a sigh of contentment. I'd grown up in the countryside and being in the wilderness was second nature to me. I missed its tranquility. Even the threat of a bear encounter diminished with Phil beside me, as my instinct was that he would protect me. It contrasted so strongly with Karl. After a motorcycle accident we'd had, then Karl's deliberate fooling around on a raft on a river causing me to fall in and need rescuing, I realized I'd never felt even physically safe with him.

But with Phil I felt secure. Somehow his age—which I didn't know but was certain to be greater than mine—was ceasing to be an issue, if anything it made him reliable and steady. I sensed strongly that I was in good hands. To my surprise I realised this man was starting to strongly appeal to me.

Phil woke up with a snort. 'That was a good little forty winks.'

I laughed. 'You weren't joking, were you?'

'No,' he said, sitting up. 'I never joke about sleep. It's a serious business.'

'Sometimes I'm not sure whether *you're* being serious or not.'

Phil never got to answer as there came a piercing cry; it was a two-note call that rose in pitch upon the second. It was a lonely sound, nothing like the inane twittering of backyard birds—more a call to make you stop and listen, and feel a little melancholy.

'What's making that sound?' I asked.

'A loon.'

'And that's a bird presumably?'

'Yes, a diving bird.'

I smiled at that—me wondering before I'd met Phil whether he would gush with information and bore me, whereas the irony was that I had to practically drag it out of him.

The loon uttered another few poignant cries which carried across the water, then was silent. We stood up, shouldered our rucksacks and walked down to the lake where Phil asked if I'd pose for a photograph. I had the one of him with the rock on his head, apparently he wanted one of me too. It was warming to know that he might miss my company and want a photograph by which to remember me.

My hunch about an evening meal had been correct and we ate out again—this time at Jasper Pizza Place on Connaught Drive. We'd just been shown to a table when someone called out Phil's name. We looked up to see a stocky young man with a beard walking over to us.

'Hi Matt,' Phil said. He turned to me, 'Leanne, this is Matt, another warden. Matt, Leanne. She's over from London and I've been giving her a guided tour of the park.'

Matt and I greeted one another. He had a friendly smile and an open face. I listened in amusement as he and Phil launched into a discussion of his new boots; I'd never heard men discuss the merits of footwear before.

'... so I'm breaking them in,' Matt said, 'before heading out into the Brazeau as soon as the snowmelt goes down.'

'Are they W. M. Moorbys?' Phil asked.

'How'd you guess?'

'I've got a pair. Great ankle support, eh?'

'With the lace ups? Yeah. Not bad looking either.'

The boots were a rich chestnut leather and sported a feature I'd never seen before, an extended fringed flap over the vamp. Another unusual feature was the high, wedged heels.

'The heels look higher than ones I wear!' I teased.

The men weren't at all fazed by me poking fun at them. 'Saves you getting hung up in the stirrups if you pile off,' said Phil.

'Fair enough,' I conceded, a little disappointed to not get a rise out of them.

'I'll let you get back to your meal,' Matt offered. 'I need to buy a drink and rejoin my group. Nice to meet you,' he said to me. 'Have a good evening.'

I thanked him and we said goodbye.

I wondered what would be said in the Parks Canada office on Monday morning but if Phil thought the same thing he didn't mention it. He picked up his menu, scanned it quickly and said he'd have the pepperoni and mushroom.

'Call me boring but I'll just have a Hawaiian,' I said.

Phil went and placed our orders and when he was seated

again, I quizzed him. 'So what's the Brazeau and what's the snow melting got to do with it?'

'The Brazeau's a backcountry district in the south of the park. Matt's—'

'Hang on! What's the backcountry?'

'It's the area beyond the front country.' Seeing me frown, Phil added that the front country was the area immediately surrounding the town and accessible by vehicle. 'There are no roads in the backcountry; it can only be used by hikers and horse groups.'

'Okay ... thanks,' I said, processing that information. 'And the snow?'

'A backcountry warden like Matt patrols his district in two-week blocks, riding in on horseback. So he's got to wait until the river levels have dropped a bit more, so it's safer to cross.'

'Wow! What an amazing job!'

'You think so?'

'Yes! I used to ride as a kid. What an adventure that would be.'

'There's no electricity or running water ...'

'That's no problem. My dad loved all things Western and a few years ago he bought some land and built a small log cabin on it. I've stayed there a few times. There's no power or plumbing. The only thing that bothers me are the spiders that lurk there,' I said, giving a shiver. 'Ugh.'

Phil grinned. 'Well then, you might be interested to learn that I've been given a district in the north of the park and I'm heading there for the first time in a week or two. It's been my dream for years.'

'Oh, Phil, that's wonderful.'

'Yes, God's blessed me alright.'

A waiter delivered our pizzas and between bites Phil fielded more of my queries. I relished finding out how others lived—putting myself in their place I'd wonder how they performed certain tasks or overcame various problems. I could never understand people who had no curiosity.

The evening went by too quickly and as we walked back to Phil's truck I wondered if this was going to be goodbye, for I was leaving the next day. I felt sad as he was good company. But Phil asked if I'd be interested in a canoe ride on Pyramid Lake tomorrow morning. My heart smiled along with my face.

'Sounds wonderful. What time were you thinking?'

'How about 8 am? I know it's early but it'll have to be in order for you to get to the train station on time.'

Canoeing was an activity I'd done as a child and I didn't want to miss out on the chance to do so again in such a setting. But that wasn't the real reason I agreed. I could no longer deny that I wanted more of Phil's company.

'That's fine,' I said.

Phil nosed his truck into the parking area at Pyramid Lake and shut off the engine.

'What a gorgeous day,' I said, relishing the mild sunny weather with no wind.

'Mornings are the best part of day, I reckon.' He came around to the passenger's door and opened it for me.

'UK men have got a lot to live up to.'

'You'd better believe it!'

Once Phil had hefted his wooden canoe off the back of the truck and placed it on the sandy beach, we buckled on the lifejackets he'd brought. Sliding the prow of the canoe into the water he asked me to get in. I placed my rucksack in first and then climbed in gently, holding onto the sides of the canoe. It didn't rock too much. Phil pushed the canoe forward a little more and stepped in at the same time, placing his own pack into the space between our two seats.

'You remember how to do this?' he asked from where he sat behind me.

'Pretty much,' I answered, taking one of the paddles in my hands and finding the familiar grasp by memory.

'Right, let's go.'

The wet slop of the paddles in the water was the only sound in the stillness. We headed north following the half-moon shape of the lake then made for the far shore where Phil recalled there was a loon's nest. In front of us was Pyramid Mountain and the early morning light tinged the rock with pink.

Upon reaching the shore, we paddled up and down a little before finding the nest. Huddled into the bank, the miry mess of sticks was well camouflaged. Although we didn't see the mother loon, we studied it from a distance so as not to disturb the site. Moving a little further away, Phil said to ship our oars and just drift for a while. He unzipped his rucksack, and searched inside. I glanced back and saw him take out some chocolate.

'Would you like some? Or is it too soon after breakfast?'

'Are you kidding? Never!'

As I munched on a few squares of chocolate, Phil fossicked some more and produced a bunch of grapes.

'Oh yum,' I said as he broke off a cluster and handed it to me. 'Thank you!'

I felt touched that Phil had gone to so much trouble for me. The grocery store wouldn't have been open before he picked me up so he must have planned this and bought the snacks the previous night. Also, the canoe was heavy and took considerable effort to load and unload. It seemed undeniable. Not only did I like Phil—his easy-going nature, his boyish charm, his ability to make me laugh—but he seemed to like me. However, he hadn't said anything. I longed for him to do so.

Having finished our snack, we took up our paddles. In front of us was Pyramid Island which Phil said we'd circuit before heading back. We'd almost paddled full-circle when we came to the footbridge that ran from the island to the shore. It wasn't high enough above the water for us to glide underneath and I was momentarily disconcerted.

'Now comes the fun part if you're up for it,' Phil said. 'Just recline as far as you can and we'll go underneath.'

I agreed to the challenge and did as he said; there were a few centimetres clearance above our heads and then we were away.

'Well done, girl!' Phil said.

I was pleased at his praise, while thinking it didn't take much to impress him.

Once back at our starting point we drove onto the sand. I got out and Phil dragged the canoe out of the water, turned it over and then crouched down underneath it. He stood up with it on his shoulders and carried it to the truck where he loaded it onto the box. When the paddles, lifejackets and rucksacks were packed away, we stood silently at the lake's edge. I was acutely aware that time had almost trickled through our hour glass and there was little left in which to speak of our feelings.

Anxious for Phil to speak, I waited quietly.

I was almost thinking he was not going to when he broke the silence. 'So you're heading back to life in London. What does that hold for you?'

It was a serious question and I paused to consider.

'London's been good to me. I've made lots of great friends, been able to travel to many wonderful countries, I've got a job I enjoy, but if that's all there is for the rest of my life, it's not enough.' I paused then decided I had nothing to lose in baring my soul. 'I long to be married once more. Sometimes I think I'll shrivel up inside and die if I'm not held by a man again.'

Phil met my eyes. 'I miss the physical side of marriage too.'

'It's so tough when you know what you're missing.'

'Yes, it is.' He broke eye contact and turned toward the truck. 'Okay, I can't have you missing the Greyhound. This old truck mightn't be able to catch up with it if we have to chase it.'

I laughed. The intense moment had passed. Both of us had expressed our desire for remarriage but neither of us had said anything to further our friendship. I felt sad but then as we climbed into the truck, Phil asked if he could email me.

'I'd love you to,' I said, joy bubbling inside me that this wasn't the end. I opened the small pocket on my rucksack and took out the thank you card I'd written. 'Here,' I said, handing it to him. 'Inside is my contact info.'

As Phil brought the truck to a stop outside Sheila's, he offered to drive me to the train station. 'It's a long way to carry your pack,' he said.

I'd just assumed I'd have to trudge down to the station with my miserably heavy backpack. How wonderful! But even better than that, Phil would be there to say goodbye.

'Thank you,' I beamed. 'I'd really appreciate that.'

'I'll pick you up at 10:45 then,' Phil said and drove off.

When I swung open the screen door, Sheila came and stood in the kitchen doorway. 'How was the canoe ride?' she asked.

'It was great, thanks. Pyramid Lake's beautiful.'

'It is.' Then Sheila got to the point. 'Phil's spent all his spare time with you since your first blind date.'

'He has. He's been very generous with his time and shown me places I'd never have gotten to by myself. Thank you so much for introducing us.'

'You're welcome,' she smiled. 'So what are your thoughts now about Canada and Canadian men?'

'Well I can only speak about Jasper but the Rockies have won me over. And Phil has erased all frustration at Richard. In fact Richard did me a favour. If it hadn't been for him—and you!—I wouldn't have met Phil. He's a lovely man.'

'I'm glad. I hope you two keep in touch.'

'We're planning to.'

'We'd love to see you again,' Sheila said. 'Well, I'd better let you get ready.'

Phil parked in the train station car park and turned off the engine. Reaching into the glove box, he pulled out a medium-sized brown paper bag with the top folded over and held fast by a Bear Paw Bakery sticker. He handed it to me. 'Here's some chocolates. You'll find a little note inside.'

I was feeling sad that goodbye was imminent but the promise of a note to read lifted my heart and gave me hope ... of what exactly I was almost too afraid to put into words.

'Thank you.'

'Well, we'd better get you onto that Greyhound.' He got out and came around to the passenger's side. He opened the door for me one last time and lifted out my backpack from the box of the truck. I threw my rucksack over my shoulder and shut the passenger door.

'Thank you so much,' I said, 'for everything.'

Finally Phil opened his arms to me for a farewell hug. It felt so good to be held, I wanted to stay there in the warmth of his arms.

'You'd better get on board,' he said and released me. 'I'll make sure your luggage gets stowed.'

'Thanks. Goodbye, Phil,' I said and turned away to step up into the bus, squeezing down the narrow aisle and choosing a seat on the right-hand side so I could see him.

The door closed with a hiss and the engine started. Phil stood there: in jeans and a T-shirt that displayed his slim build and broad shoulders, a baseball cap over his blond hair. As he saw me wave, his tanned face broke into the stunning smile, bracketed by generous creases either side of his mouth, that had so captured my heart. He was so unlike the man I'd had in my mind that I wanted, yet now I wondered why I'd not found him handsome from the very beginning. And more importantly than that, he was kind, fun and he valued me.

Phil waved back and then turned towards his truck. As he did so, the bus pulled away from the station and I could no longer see him.

Chapter Eleven

It was Tuesday morning, the day after I arrived back in London. I stepped out of the elevator and exited the Tube station, beginning the ten–minute journey to my Lambeth school. I walked along minor roads with little traffic, then a pedestrian lane skirting the bleak grey apartment blocks that reared an ugly twenty stories into the sky.

Would there be an email from Phil?

His note in the paper bag with the chocolates hinted at him wanting to continue our friendship and I desired that too. Despite my past disappointments and the fact that Phil wasn't at all who I thought I was looking for, we'd connected so easily, banter flowing back and forward, and laughter never far away. I felt safe with him and discovered I liked that, needed that. But how realistic was it when we were continents apart? Had I just been a pleasant interlude who Phil was already forgetting?

My thoughts ricocheted back and forth as I walked to school. I pushed open the gate and went inside. It was early, 7:30 am, but a couple of teachers were already there. I slipped past their classrooms as I didn't want to talk to anyone until I checked my Hotmail account. What was the point of excitedly sharing my time with Phil if he failed to follow through on his promise of an email?

My downstairs workroom didn't receive the internet very well so I walked up the stairs and into Hannah's class. She hadn't arrived yet but was happy for me to use her computer. I turned it on and took off my jacket. The screen lit up and I searched for Hotmail. Seeing the blue and white of the Hotmail login page, I entered my email address and password and waited nervously for the inbox to open.

Phil_Minton...

He'd emailed! I released the breath I hadn't known I'd been holding.

I looked for the time and saw that he'd written on the Saturday night; after three consecutive nights of my company, it had been his first evening without me. I felt a thrill of pleasure and hope—maybe he missed me. I clicked on his email. It was short but he said it was just a test as he was checking he had my email address correct before he wrote more in depth. It also seemed he intended to send me something in the mail because he was checking my postal address as well.

Overjoyed to have heard from Phil in such a promising way, I hurriedly typed a response and then began work, my heart lighter than it had been for years.

At morning tea I told the staff about the success of the blind date Sheila had set up for me with Phil. They were all excited and there was a chorus of good-natured, 'I told you so's!'

I didn't get the same response from my friends and flatmates. They were more sceptical; probably with good cause as they'd heard all about the stream of guys I'd been interested in over the last four years.

However, I knew this was different.

Because I hadn't been initially attracted to Phil, a friendship had developed as we hiked and ate together. I'd been completely myself with him; I hadn't been trying to impress him or show myself in the best light. Our connection was the truest I'd ever made with a man. I thought fondly of Erica's wisdom in saying I needed a kind man. Likewise, I recalled Blazenka saying I needed an older man. Phil fulfilled both qualities.

I was so indebted to Sheila for had I met Phil in other circumstances I wouldn't have been interested in striking up an acquaintance. My narrow search for specifics like hair colour, height and age would have disqualified him.

The admission revealed how shallow I'd been.

Things moved very quickly, with Phil and me exchanging two to three emails per day. Later on the Tuesday he invited me to go back and visit him during the summer and I eagerly accepted. He then asked for time to sort out his available dates as he needed to coordinate them with his backcountry schedule.

That Friday I took the train to Stroud to visit Alison. We'd spoken briefly on the phone but I was looking forward to face-to-face conversation. I wanted the chance to explain why, although such a long–distance relationship seemed outlandish, I had a deep peace about it.

Alison was waiting for me on the platform as I alighted, wearing her gorgeous purple cord jacket that I tried not to covet.

'So what's this Canadian man got that our English men don't?' she asked after we'd said hello and hugged.

'Where do I start?'

Alison laughed as she led the way to where she'd parked her car. 'Let's wait until we get home as Peter wants to know too.'

She zipped through the narrow streets and parked effortlessly in the tiny space above her two-storied home in a row of terraced houses. I grabbed my luggage and followed her inside.

Peter stood up from his easy chair in the lounge. 'Hi Leanne. So, you scored yourself a lumberjack. I hope he's good enough for you,' he said, giving me a hug.

'Well, more a cowboy than a lumberjack! He opens the truck door for me so I think you'll be impressed with his manners.'

'Don't give Alison ideas,' he grinned.

'You can start tomorrow,' Alison replied. 'Leanne, we waited to have tea so I'll go and heat it up. It won't take long.'

'Thank you! Can I help?'

'No, you just laze around with Peter in the lounge and I'll do all the work.'

Peter and I laughed. It was wonderful how well they got on. Now I could be even happier for them, for although Phil wasn't here with me, I felt warm inside knowing that in Jasper there was a very special man who missed me and wanted me to return.

Over the meal I caught up with their news, then after the dishes had been cleared away, we sat in the lounge, each with a cup of tea.

'This was something I missed. Everyone kept offering me coffee,' I said, screwing up my face in disgust.

Alison sympathised for she loved her tea.

'Well, tell us about Phil,' Peter asked.

'How about I show you my photos?' I placed my tea on the occasional table beside me and ran up the stairs to the spare bedroom to get them. Coming back down, I showed them the ones of Maligne Canyon, Valley of the Five Lakes, Pyramid Lake, and Athabasca Falls, ending with the photo of Phil impersonating an inuksuk.

'He looks like he knows how to have fun,' Alison commented. 'But he does seem older than us. What's his age?'

'I'm not sure. I'm hopeless with ages. I assumed maybe five to eight years older.'

Alison looked concerned. 'It's not who you usually go for, Leanne. And I'm not doubting he's nice—he has a kind face—but are you sure about pursuing a relationship with a man in Canada? I mean he lives in a remote place and you're a city girl.'

I suddenly realised that my friends knew only the London me—the one who loved to dress up and go out dancing, meet with friends at a café, go out to the movies and concerts, and shop in Oxford Street. They had little idea of my rural childhood. How I rode ponies, accompanied dad as he trapped possums and fished, explored the bush and crafted shelters, built fires and cooked outdoors. The sense of adventure these activities provided had been long neglected but was part of me still. The desire for them had reawakened in Jasper.

'Well, I wasn't always a city girl,' I said, and tried to explain my childhood and the connection this gave me with the Canadian Rockies. It was clear Alison and Peter wanted to empathise but I realised it was difficult when they hadn't had such experiences themselves.

'Well it's early days yet,' Alison said. 'Let's see what comes from your correspondence.'

She must've seen my face for she reached over and squeezed my hand. 'I'm so pleased you had a good time with Phil and he treated you well.' She paused. 'It just seems like such a leap and of course I don't want to lose you.'

I made myself smile while inside I hurt. It was so hard to try and explain what I had felt with Phil. As unlikely as it seemed that our relationship would succeed, I desperately wanted my closest friend to understand and support me. Yet I couldn't deny she only wanted my best. Like me, she'd been badly hurt by her first husband.

'Ballykissangel is on soon. Let's watch it,' she said, and got up to turn on the television.

'Fancy some chocolate?' Peter asked with a wink.

Oh, bless him. 'Yes, please!'

On Saturday Peter had some work to do so he stayed home while Alison and I went out. Gloucestershire was a county with a myriad of beautiful and historical places to visit and that afternoon Alison opted for both, in taking me to Berkeley Castle. I doubted I could ever see a surfeit of stately homes, manor houses, and castles, and Berkeley was yet another gem in England's treasury: the oak beams that ribbed the ceilings, the stone mantelpieces delicately carved as from a soft grey wood, the mullioned windows, and the rook-like towers in the castle's walls. Outside were terraced gardens where climbing ivy clung to stone, a rectangular pool flaunted yellow lily pads and spiky red flowers, and walkways with low, lichened stone walls. English country gardens were always lush and a feast for the eyes.

With the knowledge that Phil would appreciate a picture of me, I overcame my reluctance to be photographed and asked Alison to take one. I always felt awkward about how to hold myself when I stood and so I chose a more relaxed pose by sitting on some stone steps.

That evening we ordered Indian takeaways so Alison didn't have to cook. She brought out a printed menu and sat on the couch beside Peter to look at it.

'I'd give you the menu but I'd be wasting my time,' she grinned. 'Chicken korma, I presume?'

'Yes, thanks.'

Peter suggested a tikka masala with which Alison was happy. After our meal we watched television together before I excused myself to go to bed—not to sleep but to write at length to Phil.

The next morning after breakfast we went to get some exercise. Stroud was situated in a steep sided valley through which ran the River Frome and there were many pretty walks nearby.

Going back to Alison's, we had lunch of sandwiches paired with Walkers crisps. Before living in the UK, I'd never combined the crunch and saltiness of crisps with the softness of bread before but I'd come to relish it.

'I'll have to share this habit with Phil, see if I can convert him,' I said. I realised that like an infatuated teenager, I was trying to edge Phil into as many conversations as possible.

'Do Canadians even eat crisps?' Alison asked, placing her half-eaten sandwich on a plate to pick up her mug of tea. 'Maybe it's just corn chips.'

'You're wrong *and* right,' I said. 'They do eat crisps but they call them chips like we do in New Zealand. Talking about different names, they also have dollars and cents like back home but they call their one cent pieces, pennies! It took me ages to stop saying dollars and cents and use pounds and pence, then Canada combines the terms!'

'One of the downsides of being a world traveller,' teased Peter.

I rolled my eyes. 'Very funny.'

After lunch we stayed chatting in Alison's lounge, the sun streaming in through her window. It was so relaxing there among good friends. I loved spending weekends with them and it was usually a little depressing to think of having to say goodbye and travel by myself back to London. The journey took a tedious two hours and forty–five minutes. Now, however, I was quite happy to have the opportunity to daydream about my time with Phil.

My three days a week position in Lambeth was going well. I loved being able to assist children who were struggling—to equip them with skills and knowledge and see their confidence lift as they made progress. Also rewarding was being able to do so individually and in small groups; to be able to teach for the entire lesson and not waste time and energy on behaviour management.

In contrast, supply teaching on the Thursdays and Fridays was taxing and unsatisfying. I was usually at a new school each day and had to meticulously plan out my journey the night before, figuring out the right transport combination of bus, Underground and British Rail. Journeys often took an hour or more which necessitated getting up ridiculously early to allow for any delays and still be at school with ample time in which to prepare.

Sometimes I was asked back to a school in which I enjoyed working, which significantly reduced the strain. Not only was I familiar with the travel route but more importantly I had some idea of the layout of the school and things like its break times, assemblies, lunch ordering, and use of the photocopier, not to mention the students.

One school, St Agnes Roman Catholic Primary, where I'd worked a couple of days in April, called me for an interview. It was for a year's work of two days a week starting in September. I was excited by the prospect of steady work, and leaving behind the pressures of day-to-day supply teaching. It was also a mere two short bus journeys from Kilburn.

There was just one problem which I mentioned to Phil in an email. He'd been talking about phoning me for the first time and this was the prompt he needed.

It was 11.40 pm when the phone rang. Phil finished work at 4.30 pm. It was the same time difference as when I'd spoken to Richard, but in all other respects the situation was so different.

'Hi Leanne!'

'Oh Phil, it's so good to hear your voice. Thanks so much for calling.'

'The pleasure's all mine, Leanne.'

I closed my eyes to focus on his pleasing Canadian accent and the deep timbre of his voice. It made him seem so immediate and I could imagine him with me.

We discussed how our days had gone; I was able to imagine Phil's fairly well but he had little concept of city life, let alone in London.

'Well, it's late for you,' Phil said after a while, 'and I've got to get supper ready soon so tell me about your dilemma.'

I shared again how I'd come to be offered the job.

'You must have made quite the impression!' he said when I'd finished.

'Thank you! The problem is that if they tell my agency the school has to pay a £500 fee, which is *so* much money. And if I get the position, I won't start until September and it will have been six months since I worked there which would mean a fee no longer needs to be paid. However, my contract says I must inform the agency of any job offers and there seems to be no time limit on that.'

'Hmm, that's difficult,' Phil agreed.

'Yes, very. Either way I'm upsetting someone. I want to be

honest before God and fulfil my contract. I'm with a new agency called Teachers'R'Us. The owners are a Kiwi/Australian couple—they're lovely and they've become like friends. But if I do tell them, then the school needs to pay them hundreds of pounds and they'll either be upset with me—which is an awful way to start a new job—or maybe not give me the job at all.'

'Damned if you do, damned if you don't.'

'Exactly! The only thing I can think of is to offer to have the fee taken from my pay but, gosh, that would hurt.'

Phil gave a low whistle. 'I'm not sure about the exchange rate but it sounds like a lot.'

'It is,' I sighed. 'It seems there's no easy solution but I really appreciate you listening and understanding. Would you please pray about the situation with me?'

'I was going to do so even if you hadn't asked.'

I felt myself relax and my shoulders drop. 'Thank you.'

'Yep.'

Unable to help myself, I yawned.

'You're tired. I don't want us to stop talking but you need your beauty sleep,' Phil said. 'Well, actually you don't,' he laughed, 'but you know what I mean.'

I giggled and agreed reluctantly to hang up, Phil promising to call again soon. I replaced the handset in its cradle. From the immediacy of Phil 'being there with me' he was now back to being more than 7,000 km away. Yet this lovely man was interested in what I was facing and had my back; it was more than I'd dared dream a month ago, before I'd met him.

God had given me such a precious gift.

Then he blessed me with two more. The first was that the "interview" hadn't been an interview at all. This was remarkable as I hate them. I can articulate well what I want to convey in writing but in the time-pressured situation of an interview I'm pretty hopeless. I have a tendency to go blank under pressure. The lack of requirement for a formal interview was because the deputy head at my Lambeth school had given me such an excellent reference that the head teacher at St Agnes simply offered me the position. I was thrilled to accept.

The second gift related to the issue of the fee. To put the

school's mind at rest, I said that once I'd received the job offer in writing I would contact my agency and offer to pay the £500. When I did so, the agency owners were so appreciative that I was frank with them that they kindly decided to waive the fee. I was extremely grateful.

The weekend after I left Jasper, Phil had been due to head to Calgary to stay with his cousin, Kathy. However, he got sick and didn't go. In an email on the Monday he sang the praises of his two "ministering angels," writing that, "Finally, I think you would have to share."

My mind exploded with questions. Share him with the two ministering angels? Become just one of many women friends? After all Phil had intimated, was I no more special than the others? Was he subtly telling me to back off?

Insecurity ambushed me, leaving me confused and anxious. Determined to directly combat these feelings, I emailed Phil explaining that I felt he was sending mixed mess-ages, saying I couldn't help comparing our current situation with what happened with Richard. I also addressed the issue that Phil had been very vague about the dates which I needed as soon as possible in order to book the cheapest flights.

It felt scary but also absolutely right; if Phil was going to falter and there wasn't a serious future for us, the sooner I knew that, the better.

Phil's reassurance that I was special, more special than his two friends, came quickly. He sent me an e-card, left me a phone message, and sent two sets of dates for the summer holidays from which I could choose.

But his gratifying response was tempered with a startling revelation. In passing he mentioned he was under stress finalizing separation and divorce procedures! *He wasn't divorced?* My newly constructed, happy world was knocked sideways. That he was still legally married came as an awful shock and caused me great consternation. I had assumed it had been completed and Phil was free to pursue me.

Phil went on to write, "It has been a long drawn–out thing and my lawyer tends to take his own sweet time doing things." A myriad of questions clamoured to be answered and so Phil and I arranged another phone call. In it I learned that his wife had left him in July 1998, almost two years ago.

I pondered our situation long and hard. I didn't want to be dating a legally married man, but yet I couldn't deny that God had brought us together. The long series of events that it took could have broken down at so many points, yet it hadn't. The circumstances were extraordinary and had God's imprint on them. Maybe it was just as well we were so far apart while the divorce was realised.

Regarding its timing I took heart from the fact that Karl, having been the one who had left me, had not contested the separation agreement I'd presented him with, nor our divorce. Surely Phil's wife would do the same. With me now in Phil's life I felt confident that he would put pressure on his lawyer and speed things up. I wasn't due to arrive until late July so surely resolution would be achieved by then.

How wrong our suppositions can be.

Phil's two options for me were to spend a fortnight with him in Jasper between his backcountry trips, or two weeks in which we'd travel to his home town of Amaranth in Manitoba. Jasper's mountain ruggedness had endeared itself to me, whereas the prairies didn't enthuse me at all. And yet the trip across Canada had one major aspect in its favour—it would enable me to discover if there were any proverbial skeletons in Phil's family closet.

The reason for him going to Manitoba was for the Amaranth homecoming—an event whereby people who had shifted away from their home town came back for a weekend reunion. Attending would provide me with an unparalleled opportunity to meet his family and school friends. It was a rare shortcut to finding out about Phil and so I seized it.

Chapter Twelve

Friday, 21 July found me taking my seat on the plane. All my preparations were complete: my rent had been paid in advance, the cleaning roster in the flat reorganised, I'd made the painstaking decisions of what clothes to take, I'd visited the beauticians for a leg wax, eyelash and eyebrow tints, and struggled with my luggage all the stages from Kilburn to Gatwick airport.

Resting my head back, I took a deep breath. I could feel my shoulders lower and I began to relax; it was thrilling to be seeing Phil again so soon. I opened my handbag to check my diary. I was staying overnight in Edmonton and catching the Greyhound to Jasper early the next morning, arriving at lunchtime. Phil and I would enjoy a few days there and then set off on Wednesday for the two-day trip to Amaranth. We would stay with his brother and sister-in-law on the family farm where Phil had grown up and attend the homecoming event with his family over the weekend. The following Wednesday we'd leave, Phil taking me directly to the airport in Edmonton for a Thursday night flight, getting me back to London on Friday, 4 August.

I knew what to expect in Jasper. But driving almost halfway across a huge continent from Alberta, through Saskatchewan and into Manitoba was a complete unknown. Such a road trip was in the realm of movies—that *I* was going to make one was surreal.

The Greyhound pulled into the train station and I spotted Phil's blue truck. There he was standing beside it—wearing shorts, a T-shirt and a beaming smile. I straightened my blue floral Laura Ashley dress—it was sleeveless and knee length and I was grateful the weather was warm enough for me to wear it. During my first visit I'd worn only jeans and tops and I wanted to wow Phil by wearing a dress. I was a little nervous though; Karl had once made a derogatory comment about my legs and I was still somewhat self-conscious about them.

The instant the driver turned off the engine I was on my feet. I grabbed my rucksack and moved into the aisle. My usual habit was to exit after all the other passengers as I disliked jostling for position. But this time I had a special man waiting for me and couldn't get to him fast enough.

I stepped down from the bus and in a few strides was in Phil's arms. There was no hesitancy between us now and being hugged felt so good. I wondered when Phil would first kiss me. He collected my luggage and carried it to his truck. For the first time I noticed his number plate.

'LPX? Your number plate has my initials on it,' I laughed. 'But what's the X for?'

'Extra special?'

'Sounds good to me,' I said, feeling warm inside.

Phil opened my door as he had on the first trip. Starting the truck he turned into Connaught Drive.

'How *is* Sheila?' I asked as we drove past her house.

'She's great. Busy as usual, and exploring every inch of the park.'

'Good for her.'

Phil parked in his garage that was reached from the back alley behind Patricia Street.

'Jason's home so I'll be able to introduce you.' Jason was Phil's eighteen-year-old son. Of the three of us, he was the only one of typical dating age—it felt slightly weird for Phil and I as mature adults to be the ones dating.

Phil's home was single storey and rectangular. The property was elevated about a metre above the street so there were steps leading up from the sidewalk to the front door. There was a small strip of grass and garden in front; at the back there was an area of lawn, a vegetable garden, and garage. Phil rented his home from Parks Canada and there was a wooden plaque to the right of the front door that proclaimed, "Warden Residence/Residence du Gardien."

Phil opened the screen door, then the back door and stood aside to let me enter. As at Sheila's, there was a small landing, steps on the left leading down to the basement, and a short flight to the right up to the main living area. I took off my shoes and walked up the stairs to find a small kitchen immediately to the right. Ahead was the front entrance; connecting this space with the kitchen was an L-shaped area containing the lounge and dining room. To the left was a hallway down which Phil directed me. There was a bathroom to the left and a bedroom opposite, then at the end of the hall, the master bedroom was on the left with a third bedroom to the right.

I entered the master bedroom as Phil had kindly offered it to me; he was going to use the bedroom opposite. Phil followed with my luggage. Looking around my eyes fell on an object on the bedside table.

'Oh Phil, is that wee stone from Blue Creek?' I'd asked him to bring me back a memento from one of his trips. Laying down my rucksack, I reached for the stone, it was smooth and heart-shaped.

I turned to Phil. 'Thank you,' I exclaimed, 'it's lovely.'

'It took a long time to find that stone but you were worth it.'

'I'll treasure it. And you've put flowers on the bedside table, too. How kind.'

'I had to feminise it somehow,' Phil explained. 'After my wife left, I bought this Aztec themed duvet and bed linen—it fits my cowboy style—but I wanted something pretty for you.'

'Thank you.' I suddenly felt shy being there with Phil in his bedroom. 'I must use your loo.'

'When you've freshened up, we'll have lunch,' Phil said and left for the kitchen.

Having closed the toilet door behind me, I fiddled with the handle trying to figure out how to lock it—the last thing I wanted was to meet Jason with him standing in the doorway and me sitting on the toilet. I flipped on the light switch—remembering that you pushed Canadian switches up to turn them on which had seemed so strange during my first visit in May.

When I joined Phil in the kitchen, I saw that he'd made some sandwiches which he took through and put on the kitchen table.

'I hope you like ham and cheese,' he said.

'Yes, thanks. Oh great, I see you like whole wheat bread.'

'Yes, I gave up white years ago.'

Just then we heard footsteps pound up the stairs from the basement.

'Jason,' Phil called. 'Come into the dining room for a moment.'

A tall, fair-haired young man walked through from the kitchen and stood at the end of the table. He wore board shorts, a T-shirt and a Chicago Blackhawks cap.

'Jason,' Phil said, 'this is Leanne. Leanne, this is my son, Jason.'

'Hey, Leanne,' Jason said. 'Dad said you'd be coming.'

'Hi Jason,' I said with a warm smile, 'nice to meet you.' I felt for him, it must be so hard for him to see his dad with a woman other than his mum. 'Yes, I'm lucky to be back in beautiful Jasper. Your dad knows the park so well, he's the perfect guide.'

'Do you want to join us, Jas?' Phil asked.

'No, I've just come up to take a shower, then I'm meeting Chris.'

'Okay then, you two have fun,' Phil said.

'See you later, Jason,' I added.

'Sure,' he said and headed for the bathroom.

We chatted throughout lunch and then Phil told me to take a seat on the Chesterfield while he made us hot drinks.

'Chesterfield? Do you mean the couch?'

'Yes,' Phil laughed. 'Don't you call it that?'

'I've never heard of the word before,' I replied as I sat down on the blue striped three-seater. 'Where'd the name come from?'

'A Mr Chester Field?'

I groaned. 'Come on, Phil, you can do better than that!'

Phil chuckled. 'What do you want to drink?'

'Tea, thanks,' I replied. 'But please—not Earl Grey!'

'What's that?'

'Well, if you don't know, you probably don't have it. It's terrible stuff—tastes kind of soapy.'

'The packet says black tea.'

'That'll be great.'

I looked around as Phil boiled the jug and busied himself in the kitchen. 'Your lounge doesn't have a ceiling light. Is that normal in Canada?'

'Not that I know of.'

'I guess that's why you've got a few floor lamps. I love lots of light—muted light makes me feel sleepy.'

'Here, this will wake you up,' said Phil. He handed me my cup of tea, then went back to get his own.

It was my first for the day and I was looking forward to it. When I stayed with Alison we drank tea so often that I'd developed quite the habit. But I almost spat out my first sip.

'What's this?' I spluttered. It was foul, tasting like someone had grated soap into it.

Phil came into the lounge with his own cup and sat down. 'What do you mean? It's the black tea you asked for,' said, he looking flummoxed.

'Sorry, Phil, I don't mean to be rude but this *isn't* plain black tea. It must be Earl Grey.'

'But the packet said it *was* black tea.'

'Can I see it please?' I didn't want to be argumentative but something was wrong.

'Sure.' Phil got up, brought back the Red Rose cardboard packet and handed it to me.

I scanned the description. 'Well, you're right, it isn't Earl Grey but it *is* flavoured. Look! *Orange Pekoe.*'

'But *all* our black tea is Orange Pekoe,' Phil explained.

'Really?' I felt hugely disappointed. No drinkable tea in the whole time I was in Canada?

'Don't worry, Leanne,' Phil said taking the packet from me. 'Let's take a look in the supermarket this afternoon. They might have some.'

'Yes, please!'

We talked some more, me sipping on warm water while Phil drank his nasty Orange Pekoe brew, then he invited me to unpack while he did some washing in the basement. Jason had finished showering so Phil could use the machine.

In my bedroom, I took out my toiletries and pyjamas but couldn't be bothered doing anymore, deciding instead to join Phil. I walked down the two flights of steps and stopped at the bottom. In front was an open area and to the left was a washing machine, dryer and large sink against the wall with a large, cylindrical contraption nearby that must have been the central heating system. Jason's bedroom must be to the right.

Phil stood at the washing machine.

'There you are!'

'Spying on me, are you?'

I laughed, moving to stand beside him. 'Just checking up on you. Making sure you're doing the washing properly.'

Phil put down the jeans he was holding and turned to face me. 'Checking *up* on me or checking me *out*?' he teased softly, the creases on either side of his mouth pulling into deep grooves that were so very attractive.

'What do you think?' I replied, my eyes not leaving his and feeling like a nervous schoolgirl.

Phil leaned forward, placed his hands lightly on my shoulders, and lowered his mouth to mine in a gentle kiss. I closed my eyes and savoured the firm pressure and taste of his lips and the wonderful feeling of mutual desire.

Jason's bedroom door handle turned. We immediately stood apart and I took hold of Phil's jeans. 'Were you going to wash them without turning them inside out?' I asked.

As I spoke, Jason walked from his bedroom and up the stairs. 'See you, Jas,' Phil called out, then turned and winked at me. 'Right, what were you saying?'

'Well, jeans wear better and keep their colour longer if you turn them inside out before washing.'

'Seems you can teach an old dog new tricks after all,' Phil said as he followed my suggestion. He loaded the rest of his clothes into the machine, added the powder and turned on the machine.

With the washing taken care of, Phil suggested we walk downtown to Super A on Patricia Street, the closest of the two grocery stores in Jasper. I changed from my dress, which I felt had served its purpose well, and into shorts and a T-shirt.

'Oh bother,' I exclaimed as I sat on the steps leading down from the kitchen and laced up a pair of comfortable walking shoes.

'Did you forget something?' Phil asked as he stood on the landing putting on his sandals.

'Yes, a hat.'

Phil gestured towards his sartorial collection. 'Take your pick or should I say cap?'

I stepped past him to see what was on offer. There were caps advertising sports teams, some with business logos and then I saw a plain blue one. 'Are you happy if I use this?'

'Sure. There'll be a fee though,' Phil grinned.

I placed the cap on my head and walked up to Phil to stand on the step below him. 'Such as?' I challenged.

In answer, he bent his head and brought his lips close to mine, gazing intently into my eyes. 'A kiss,' he said softly.

At Super A, Phil directed us to the aisle with the coffee and teas.

'I'll let you choose so I don't get the blame for another soapy one.'

'Yes, if the service doesn't improve I might have to check out the availability at Sheila's.'

Phil laughed.

'Right, what do we have?' I asked, looking at the packets of tea one by one. 'Red Rose, no! Tetley? No, it's Orange Pekoe too. Lipton's? No, it's Darjeeling, whatever that is.' One brand remained. 'Blue Ribbon ...' I turned the packet every which way looking for a description. Black tea was all that it said, no mention of any flavour. 'Let's try this.'

Phil held his hands up in a gesture of surrender. 'Okay but don't hold me responsible if it's flavoured. Now, let's get a bagged salad to have with the chicken for supper.'

Here we go again, I thought, another Canadian-ism to learn. 'What's a bagged salad?'

'A very tired one,' Phil said with a straight face. I wouldn't have understood his joke if I hadn't learnt last trip that 'bagged' meant tired.

'You're such a tease!' I said. 'Seriously, what's a bagged salad?'

'A salad in a bag.'

'Oh dear, I probably should have guessed that.'

'I reckon ... maybe Kiwis aren't quite as smart as Canadians.'

I opened my eyes wide in mock horror and elbowed Phil in the ribs, or at least I tried to but he stepped adroitly out of the way, backing straight into a middle-aged woman.

'Excuse me, ma'am,' he said, as I covered my mouth with my hand and turned my head away to disguise my laughter.

The lady muttered something then headed into the next aisle. Phil turned to me with a grin. 'I'll have to leave you behind next time, you're getting me into trouble.'

Selecting a salad, Phil paid for the items and we exited the store. Then, for the first time, his hand sought mine. I found it wonderfully intimate, not in the same manner as a kiss but it connected us in a different way and relaxed me deep inside. Phil's hands were dry and warm, lightly callused and capable, in which my own felt safe and protected.

In fact my whole being felt like that with Phil.

I awoke early, whether from jetlag or excitement, I didn't know. Curious about the day I got out of bed and crossed to the window. I opened the curtain and pulled up the blind—blue sky!

Giving my hair a quick comb, I put on my dressing gown and opened the door. Stepping into the hallway I saw that the door to Phil's room was closed; I figured he must still be asleep.

As I left the bathroom, Phil was just coming out of his room. He wore a navy-blue dressing gown; his hair was a little spiky where he'd slept on it but he still looked handsome. Without foundation on to disguise the reddened, acne-damaged skin on my chin, I felt I didn't measure up to him. My fear was that Phil would recoil and revise his appraisal that I was beautiful. It was hard to look him in the eye and smile naturally.

'Good morning, Leanne,' Phil said, wrapping me in a bear hug.

'Oh,' I sighed, nestling into him. 'I could stay here all day.'

'I'd like that too but this bladder needs the bathroom. See you in a minute.'

I released him and went up to the kitchen and put some water on to boil. The kitchen window looked out over the backyard, across the unsealed alleyway and onto a two storey apartment block. Remembering there was an outside temperature gauge attached to the window frame in the dining room, I went through the open doorway and pulled back the net curtain to take a look. As a lover of warmth, the temperature was always important to me—22° C already!

I went back to the kitchen and glanced around. There were several magnets on Phil's fridge so I casually perused them. Suddenly my attention was riveted. "Life begins at 50!" What? Phil was 50? I'd thought he was maybe five to eight years older than me, but twelve?

Just then Phil walked into the kitchen. 'How'd you sleep?'

'Ah ... fine, thanks,' I replied, still a little shocked by my discovery. However, there was something more pressing to discuss.

'Phil ...' I paused again, wondering how to start.

'Spit it out. You didn't get up at midnight and eat all my chocolate, did you?'

'No,' I laughed. 'It's something really personal that I need you to be very sensitive about. No joking please.'

Phil's face took on a serious demeanour. 'Go ahead.'

I explained how self-conscious I felt about my facial skin and how fearful I was of being judged ugly if people saw the real me. Phil's response was crucial. I waited apprehensively.

He reached out to cup my face with his hands. 'Thanks for telling me. But if you'd said nothing I don't think I would have noticed. You're beautiful, Leanne, from the inside out. Some red skin doesn't change that.'

I wiped away a tear that had formed. 'Really?'

'Really!' he said, kissing me to prove it. 'Now, church starts at 10 am so let's get breakfast.'

Once back home I looked again at the temperature gauge—26° C. Due to the heat, Phil had suggested a walk around Lake Anette which would keep us mostly in the shade.

After lunch I changed from my dress and got ready for the hike. It struck me how relaxed and patient Phil was as he waited, alerting me to how impatient Karl must have been. I was able to take my time without a curt command to hurry up.

Anette Lake was only ten minutes' drive away. To get to it, we went north and crossed a truss bridge over the Athabasca River. At the lake there was ample parking in a large grassed meadow dotted with a few trees. Parks Canada had provided a toilet block, and across the other side of the meadow was a roofed shelter with seating and a central table on which you could spread a picnic.

'Do you have anything you want me to take in my rucksack?' Phil asked.

'Oh yes, please. My drink bottle. And my sunglasses case, thanks.' I handed them to Phil then waited while he came around to open my door. I snapped my clip-on sunglasses over my prescription glasses, grabbed my borrowed cap and climbed down from the truck.

'Gosh, it's hot,' I said.

'Not as much as Manitoba. This is just practice!' He locked the truck. 'We'll head over to the lake, go past the quicksand and then we'll be in the shade.'

'Quicksand!' I said, taking Phil's outstretched hand. 'It sounds like something you'd find in a desert.'

'We've got it all in Canada,' he grinned.

Reaching the lake, we walked alongside the stretch of sandy beach. There was a family with young children and few groups of young people sunning themselves, throwing a Frisbee and splashing in the lake.

Turning away from the lake onto the trail, we saw a yellow sign. "Danger, quicksand. Sables mouvants." Ochre Lake was an area of dark water with bushes and tall grasses to the fore and trees down to the waterline at its rear. It looked deceptively harmless. The trail passed it by and rose slightly as it entered the trees. As it catered for those in wheelchairs, the surface was smooth and reasonably level, and even paved in places. Some mature spruces and saplings grew between the trail and the lake. The sun fell in a shining beam across the water, reflecting the light and making it glint like silver.

The overcrowded concrete and metal world of London felt a galaxy away from this natural world of water and wildlife, valleys and vegetation. Sometimes it seemed absurd they could exist simultaneously and I could flourish in both. Although flourish was probably too sanguine a word, suggesting my cup was full and it wasn't. No matter how rewarding a session with a student, how skilfully I danced at Ceroc, how much laughter and good food I enjoyed with friends, I still went home alone to an empty room. The companionship that had led to romance with Phil was like God was pouring nectar into my cup and it was nearing the brim.

'You're quiet,' commented Phil.

'Just contrasting London and Jasper,' I said.

'Who's winning?'

'Well, London's exciting but it can be exhausting. Being in Jasper is so relaxing.'

'But might get boring after a while ...' Phil let his sentence hang.

Was he trying to gauge if we had a future here? Could I live here? The thought was not unwelcome which was incredible given that three months ago I would have dismissed out of hand the idea of visiting, let alone living in Canada. My family had moved frequently when I was a child as Dad sought new rural teaching positions. I was used to starting again in different places. But despite the newfound appeal of the Rockies, it all rested on Phil being at its centre.

I stopped and turned my head to look at him. It was the classic time to glance coquettishly through my eyelashes, but I was never one for playing games. I looked at him directly. 'Not if you're with me,' I said.

Phil squeezed my hand. 'Let's sit over there,' he said, indicating a fallen tree near the lake's edge. We sat down beside one another. Phil opened his rucksack and took out our drinks, handing me mine. I thanked him and unscrewed the top to take several long draughts.

'I've got chocolate bars if you'd like one,' he offered.

'Yes please.' I was happy to snack but was Phil not going to continue with the topic?

He passed me one, then took one for himself, tearing the packet open and taking a large bite. 'I could get used to this,' he said.

'What? The chocolate or the view?' I asked, a little frustrated. If Phil wanted to make references to my company, he needed to be more obvious.

He looked at me. 'No, Leanne, being with you. I'm just worried that there's no future for a city girl here in Jasper.'

My heart which had felt so buoyant now plummeted. Was Phil deciding for me, for us, that our relationship couldn't work?

'I think it's time I told you more about my childhood,' I said. 'It wasn't until I left high school that I moved to the city, because the small town in which I lived had very limited job prospects. Before that I always lived in the country as dad taught mostly in small country schools. From when I was six to twelve years old I lived on the West Coast of the South Island. It's isolated and rugged, and covered in temperate rainforest. The place was remote, and the nearest grocery store was an hour's drive away.'

I stopped to take another drink. Phil had been listening intently and so I was encouraged to continue. 'As kids we had so much freedom. When my sister and I and our two friends weren't riding their pony or picking blackberries in autumn, we'd be in the bush with a pocket knife, a small axe and matches. Exploring, building huts, damming creeks, fishing for crawlies—that's freshwater crayfish—or making a fire and frying potatoes, which we usually ended up eating half raw! On the weekends we'd spend the mornings or afternoons away from home. Sometimes the whole day so we'd have to drink from the creeks and make sure we had a roll of toilet paper with us.'

'Maybe we've got more in common than I thought,' Phil said, adjusting his cap. 'I must admit being impressed when you went to the bathroom in the bushes when you got caught short in the Valley of the Five.'

I snorted with laughter. 'What a way to impress a man! Well, we had to as kids. There weren't outhouses in the bush.'

With the issue of our differences at least partially addressed, my mind turned to the discovery I'd made that morning.

'Phil ...' I began tentatively, 'there's something I'd like to discuss with you.'

'Oh well, why stop now!'

'It's about your age, or should I say *our* ages.'

Phil shifted his position on the log, turning his body towards me. 'I'd wondered about that.'

'So why didn't you say something?'

'It didn't bother me, I guess.'

'I suppose not. After all, it's in your favour!'

Phil gave a loud guffaw. 'By how many years?'

I paused, waiting until he looked at me. 'Twelve.'

'Lucky me! Does it bother you, Leanne?'

I pondered a moment, brushing away a mosquito. 'How can I put this? The number does but not you, if that makes sense?'

Phil looked puzzled.

'I mean, the idea of the age difference seems huge but with you it doesn't seem of significance. You're in good shape physically and if I hadn't have known, I wouldn't have guessed.'

'How'd you find out then? Having worked in special investigations I'm supposed to be the one with detective skills.'

'Really? You'll have to tell me about that some time. No, it was when I saw your fridge magnet.'

It was good to have the subject out in the open and we talked about it for a while. Then we stowed our bottles and plastic wrappers in Phil's rucksack and continued on around the perimeter of the lake. In the comfortable silence I pondered our conversation. With it being so early in our relationship it was understandable we were skirting around the weighty topic of marriage. However, it seemed clear that it was in our minds. We both seemed to be thinking long term. As living together was not an option for us as Christians, marriage was the inevitable end point.

Monday was another sunny day but this time it was a more pleasant 24°C. After a leisurely morning Phil suggested a hike into an unnamed meadow, just off Highway 93 and south of the bridge over the Athabasca River.

Parking on the hard shoulder we set off parallel to the river and then turned away through a stand of trees and came out into a large meadow. It was lush with tall grasses and flowers, and partially encircled by low wooded ridges. I quizzed Phil about the different wildflowers that graced the grass like jewellery. There were white pussytoes, blue-eyed grass and harebells—the names as pretty as the flowers themselves.

We chose a place near the middle of the meadow. I'd brought a jacket just in case and spread it out to sit on. But with the sun streaming warmly on my body I couldn't resist reclining on my back, cushioned by the thick grass. I raised my arms to shield my face from the sun and gazed at the hazy sky that looked as sleepy as I felt.

Phil had done the same and we were quiet for a while, closing our eyes and basking like lizards. Eventually he rolled over and raised himself onto his elbows. I opened my eyes to look into his. The intimacy was intense. He bent closer and kissed me. Such powerful feelings of love for Phil overwhelmed me that it was all I could do to refrain from whispering "I love you" for I wanted him to be the one to declare it first.

It was Phil who broke the silence. 'It's so hard being single again after being married,' he said.

My body felt stirred by his kiss; I knew exactly to what he was referring. 'Yes, it is—you know what you're missing out on.'

For both of us it was unspoken that because we loved and honoured God we wanted to reserve sexual intercourse for its rightful place in marriage. But it didn't mean our desires were diminished.

Phil's admission prompted a frank discussion as we lay side by side in the meadow. I wished Phil liked Sting's music because he would have agreed that 'Fields of Gold' was the perfect soundtrack to our afternoon—a song set in similar surroundings that simply ached with sexual desire.

Near the end of the conversation Phil reached over and curled a strand of my long hair around his finger. He looked intently into my eyes. 'I love you, Leanne.'

Joy so strong I almost wanted to cry with it, exploded in my heart. Thank you, God! 'I love you too, Phil. I've been holding myself back from saying it all afternoon.' We sat up and hugged each other, both knowing it would be too dangerous to do so while lying down.

Tuesday was our last day in Jasper before driving to Amaranth. Warm and sunny, it was perfect for a hike but Phil had things to organise before he left.

As we relaxed on the couch after lunch I asked Phil about the painting he had in his bedroom. Entitled "Healer" by Joy Caros, it featured the face of a distraught woman in whose eyes two large tears had formed. Above her was a bearded man representing Jesus. He was looking down at her with great love and holding out his hands.

'Tell me about the painting,' I asked. 'Where'd you get it from?'

'That's quite the story,' Phil answered. 'After my wife left I started seeing a Christian counsellor from an organization called Burden Bearers. The counsellor had it on his wall.' Phil went on to say that it resonated with him and he wanted to get his own copy. With the counsellor's help he traced it to 100 Huntly Street, a Canadian Christian television programme. They had a couple of prints left and after hearing Phil's story they generously sent him a print free of charge which he had framed.

'That's amazing,' I said. 'And what I really love is that you don't shy away from tears, you actually want a picture of someone crying. Karl would always make me feel bad when I cried.'

'I'll never do that, Leanne. Tears are cleansing, they help release the stuff that causes us to cry.'

We talked some more and then I asked what he'd learnt from the counselling, keen to know about Phil's emotional journey to wholeness after the desertion of a spouse.

He thought for a moment or two. 'That we all bring things to the table that aren't healthy. My wife may be the one that left me but it would have been stuff I did that we never discussed that caused her to leave.'

Chapter Thirteen

Wednesday dawned overcast but mild.

We'd said goodbye to Jason the previous night as Phil thought we'd probably leave before he rose. We drove south down the Columbia Icefields Parkway on Highway 93. Once past Athabasca Falls it was new territory for me.

The highway was wide and sweeping as it made its way through the Canadian Rockies. Initially it followed the river flats of the Athabasca River until Sunwapta Falls where it exchanged them for those of the Sunwapta River instead. Further on, the highway hugged rocky bluffs; down one of these fell a creek aptly named Tangle Falls as it zigzagged steeply in white ribbons of water. Sombre conifers dominated the landscape, brightened occasionally by aspens, winsome in their soft green.

But what drew my eyes the most were the mountain peaks. Devoid of timber, their bones were laid bare. Laceration by wind and rain, ice and snow, produced profiles as individual as people, their faces split by horizontal lines and intersected by vertical clefts. No two were the same and I rarely tired of studying them. The highway showcased the grandeur of the Rockies and I saw why the Parkway was considered one of the world's premier drives.

About two hours after leaving Jasper we reached a small settlement called Saskatchewan River Crossing where we pulled in for morning tea.

Once back on the highway it divided into two. The southbound one continued on to Banff and Calgary; we took the eastbound one beside the North Saskatchewan River. The mountains continued to unscroll along both sides of Highway 11. Every now and then we'd swing closer to the river and gain glimpses of it through the trees that lined the road. Further on was Abraham Lake where the roadside abounded with wildflowers. I asked Phil to stop so I could take some photographs. He left the truck to join me and named the cheerful yellow flowers with fuzzy red-domed centres as gaillardias, and the exquisite flame-coloured flowers as Indian paintbrushes.

Leaving the lake we bade goodbye to the Rockies and entered

the foothills, coming to Nordegg and later on to Rocky Mountain House. I was desperate for lunch but Phil convinced me to wait until we got to Red Deer.

After a meal there we made our way out of the city and into big sky country. There was more sky than I'd ever seen before; in the Rockies it had been a sideshow to the glorious mountains, here it was the main event. On either side of the highway, grassy farmland flowed as level as water all the way to the horizon. The sheer scope was daunting. Mountains and hills gave me my bearings as well as beauty and I felt lost without them.

After the glory of nature, I was disappointed by the farm houses I saw. They were plain and utilitarian—unadorned by fences and flowerbeds, bushes or trees—I found them soulless and depressing.

The only aspect of interest were the place names. Best of all was a town called Biggar. Its sign read, “Biggar, Saskatchewan” and around the perimeter it boasted, “New York is big, but this is Biggar.” It was rather corny but you had to admire their audacity.

Walking back to the truck after taking a photo, I opened the passenger door.

‘Oh, it's so good to stretch my legs,’ I said to Phil as I clambered in. I checked my wristwatch and did a quick calculation. It was about 6 pm. ‘We've been on the road about nine hours.’ I returned my camera to its case and buckled up.

‘It's a big country,’ Phil stated.

‘No kidding. And so's my appetite.’

‘Can you wait until we get to Saskatoon?’

‘I could probably manage if it's about half an hour away.’

‘More like two hours.’

Phil hadn't yet grasped that I had a fast metabolism and needed to eat regularly to avoid grumpiness. ‘Sorry, but it's feeding time at the zoo. I need something substantial before then.’

He thought for a minute. ‘Up ahead is Perdue. Let's stop there for some fast food, and then get going as soon as we can.’

‘Thank you, Phil, I really appreciate that.’ I put my hand on his leg and gave it a squeeze. ‘I'm sorry, you must be getting tired and just want to get there.’

Phil grinned. ‘Nothing a Coke and peanuts can't fix!’ he said, turning the key in the ignition, signaling and turning back onto the highway.

The road trip wasn't quite living up to expectations. The truck wasn't as comfortable as a car and with it being a bench seat without a head rest, I couldn't recline to sleep. And the road noise meant it wasn't easy to talk to Phil, especially as he was still getting used to my accent. Quite content to pass my time in the Rockies by studying the scenery, the prairies did nothing to fire my imagination. I felt no affinity for the land—to my eyes it was empty and featureless. Again, I struggled to relinquish my desire for the landscape to change every thirty minutes.

We came to Perdue and stopped at a gas station. While Phil fueled up I bought a sandwich and a small carton of flavoured milk. Phil bought a Coke and bag of salted, roasted peanuts. Buckling up, he took the cap off his drink, opened the bag of peanuts and began to pour them into his Coke.

'What on earth are you doing? You'll choke!'

Phil just laughed and tipped the remainder of the peanuts into the Coke. To my consternation he then drank—or was it ate?—the contents over the rest of the journey.

Almost two hours later we approached signs of a city: roadside advertising, light industry, farming equipment stores, vehicle dealerships. On the outskirts of Saskatoon the highway leaned to the right and we were soon at a motel. After checking in and taking our luggage to our room, we headed out to get an overdue supper, then were very glad to get an early night.

'It'll be a shorter drive today,' Phil said, lifting our luggage into the open box on the back of his truck.

'Good. Road trips are a little overrated.'

'Where's your staying power?' teased Phil, opening the passenger door for me.

'The same place as my breakfast—absent,' I moaned. 'Honestly, fancy having the cheek to call two pieces of thin white bread, breakfast.'

'The coffee was okay.' Phil said as he backed out of the car parking space.

'Not my tea!' As there'd been no electric kettle I had to resort to using the glass jug from the filtered drip-coffee maker. After Phil had made his coffee, I rinsed the jug thoroughly then refilled it with water. Once it boiled I made a cup of tea but despite my precautions it was tainted with coffee. I'd not been impressed.

From Saskatoon we joined Highway 16. From the two-lane divided road stretched vast prairie pastures of hay, canola and sunflowers, and cereal crops of wheat, barley and oats. Occasionally we passed massive grain elevators where the sun glinted from the shiny silver silos.

We ate lunch at Yorkton then continued on, leaving the Yellowhead for Highway 10.

Three hours later and after 600 km of level land, the road suddenly sloped downwards. It was almost disconcerting.

'We're nearly at the border,' Phil said.

The road curved to the left over the Assiniboine River, up through farmland and some woods then levelled out again, the landscape reverting back to expansive pastures and fields. The traffic was sporadic, made up mostly of trucks, petrol tankers and semis.

Roughly 15 km later, we entered the first small town in Manitoba. I caught a glimpse of its name and glanced back to check but it was too late.

'Did that say Goblin?'

Phil chuckled. 'No, Roblin!'

About an hour later we entered the city of Dauphin then travelled on Highway 5 to McCreary where we turned east onto Highway 50. This took us to a gravel road called South Leifur down which we drove about one and a half kilometres.

'We're almost there,' Phil said as he turned left. Half a kilometre further, he pointed to a house set in from the road. 'Here we are.'

It was where Phil had grown up. His parents had farmed there from 1932. In 1951-52, Phil's dad had upgraded the family from the log house in which Phil had spent his babyhood, to a modern home. His dad had built it with his own hands and the help of his older sons and neighbours. Phil's parents had retired from the farm and were living in a retirement complex in Portage la Prairie when his dad died in 1989. The farm was now owned by the eldest son, Bill, and his wife, Marge, and consisted of a house, outbuildings and grazing land for cattle as well as a few acres of cultivated land for supplemental cattle feed.

The two-storey white house had stucco walls and the upstairs Dormer window surrounds were covered in wooden siding. Behind the house was a line of trees. I was pleased to see lots of flowers in the yard, some spilling out of old toilet bowls and baths, and even disused farming equipment.

Phil parked in front of the house and turned to me. 'Well,' he said, stifling a yawn, 'how are you doing?'

'Feeling a bit nervous.' I wondered how Phil's family would react to me. Would they compare me to Phil's wife—I supposed that was inevitable—and what would they think about me not being Canadian? At least with Phil being the youngest of six children, they were all older than him, which gave me some reassurance. Being the eldest in my family I often felt more at ease with those of the generation above me than I did with my peers.

'You'll be fine,' Phil smiled. 'I'll keep you close.'

'Thank you.'

We saw some people in a gazebo in the back yard but Phil couldn't see Marge there. 'She's probably in the house,' he said. 'Let's leave our bags and say hello to her first.'

Phil came around and opened my door. As I stepped down from the truck toward him, he made the most of our closeness to give me a quick kiss.

'Careful,' I giggled, 'they'll see us.'

'Let them.' He took my hand and led me to the house, calling out hello in response to greetings from those in the gazebo. Pulling back the screen door to the house, we stepped inside into the back entrance.

'Hello,' Phil called out, as we slipped off our shoes.

'I'm in the kitchen, Phillip,' a woman's voice answered. 'Come on in!'

We walked up the few steps from the back entrance into the main living area. The compact dining room-cum-kitchen was to the left and Marge was drying her hands on a towel. Putting it down she gave us a lovely smile.

'Just in time for afternoon tea,' she said, giving Phil a big hug.

Releasing him, she turned to me.

'This is Leanne,' Phil said, 'who I told you about.'

She also gathered me in a motherly hug. 'We're pleased to have you, Leanne.'

'Thanks, Marge,' I said. She was a plump woman with short hair, and her warm and cheerful personality made me feel at ease.

'Bill's just digging some spuds. He'll be back in a minute. Head out to the gazebo and say hello to everyone. I'll be out soon.'

We thanked her, put our shoes back on and crossed to the gazebo. It was roofed with asphalt shingles and screened in with mosquito netting.

'Any room for two more?' Phil grinned, opening the door.

'Of course, Phillip!' said a slim, older man who stood up to get two folding chairs and set them up for us. 'Come and sit down,' he said, reaching out to shake Phil's hand.

Phil then stepped towards an older woman with white hair and a kind expression who I imagined was his mum. He stooped slightly to give her a kiss on the cheek. 'Oh, Phillip,' she beamed, 'it's so nice to see you.'

A woman who looked very much like Phil with short blonde hair and similar bone structure, stood up and embraced him, followed by two older women. Another man stood to shake hands with Phil. After we sat down, Phil made the introductions. The man who got out our chairs was Phil's Uncle Art; the woman Phil kissed was indeed his mum; the other man was Phil's brother, also called Art. The woman who resembled him was indeed his sister named Vivian, and the other two women were Phil's Aunt Emily and Uncle Art's wife, Aunty Betty.

'Would you like some pop?' Vivian offered.

From the cans I saw in people's hands, I guessed she meant soda pop. Phil took a root beer and I accepted a lemonade.

'How's things in the mountains?' Art asked Phil. 'You still chasing bears?'

Phil laughed. 'It's mostly elk and mule deer that come into town. Although bears will come onto the tracks near town if there's been a grain spill.'

'A good season for grain, this year,' Art commented.

'It looked that way from the highway.'

Vivian kindly turned the conversation to me. 'How'd you find the road trip, Leanne?'

'Long! In New Zealand we consider it a day's journey to travel five hours.'

'Oh, you're from New Zealand,' said Emily. 'What do they call you again? It's the same name as those fuzzy green fruits.'

'A Kiwi.'

'Yes,' she said, 'that's it.'

Further conversation about New Zealand was halted due to Marge coming into the gazebo with a plate of cookies. She put them on a small wooden table in the centre and sat down. Just as she did so an older, rangy man wearing jeans, a checked shirt and Pith helmet carried a bucket up to the back door.

'Bill,' Marge called, 'leave them there and come and join us.'

Phil's eldest brother walked over and entered the gazebo. 'Hello, Phillip. Ronnie's truck still running well?'

Ronnie was their brother who had died of cancer ten years ago and the truck was one of his possessions he'd left to Phil.

'Despite what Jason thinks about Fords, I haven't had any problems. It runs well,' replied Phil, then gestured to me. 'Bill, this is Leanne. She's a Kiwi but lives in England.'

Bill said hello in a matter-of-fact way but he had a twinkle in his eye and his face looked like it was ready to break into a smile at any moment. 'I hear there's lots of sheep in New Zealand.'

'Yes, the ratio used to be twenty sheep for every New Zealander,' I said, offering a fact that many people found amusing.

'Goodness,' said Aunty Betty.

'They wouldn't last long here, the coyotes would get them,' said Bill, causing many chuckles.

'I see you brought in some spuds,' Phil said. 'How's your garden doing?'

'I guess you'll find out tonight when you get it on your plate,' Bill said with a grin tugging hard at the corners of his mouth. I soon learnt it was a typical Bill response to give an indirect answer. I liked his sense of humour and anticipated some amusing exchanges over the weekend.

The conversation turned to family members and local farming families. With me not knowing a single one it was hard to keep focused on the exchanges and look interested. As much as I could without being rude I let my eyes wander, taking in the farmhouse surrounds. There was pasture on the far side of the drive and some modern buildings in the south-eastern corner.

Sometime later Phil stood up and stretched. 'Well, Leanne and I have done a lot of sitting today, I think we'll go for a bit of a walk.'

'Well, don't be late for supper, Phillip,' Marge said.

'Or you'll find it in your bed,' added Bill.

I turned to Phil in puzzlement and he explained that their Dad used to say that if they didn't eat their supper, they'd find it in their bed. Phil's mum laughed at the memory.

'See you soon,' I said to Phil's family as I followed him through the door of the gazebo.

Phil took my hand as we walked to the truck. 'That wasn't so bad, was it?'

'No, they're lovely. I feel quite at home.'

'Good.'

'Bill's a hard case.'

Phil looked at me. 'A what?'

'Oh, sorry, another Kiwi-ism!' I paused. Sometimes, explaining the idioms you were so familiar with required some thought. 'Someone with a quirky, dry sense of humour.'

'That fits Bill.'

Phil led me around outbuildings and showed me Bill and Marge's garden. It was huge, about half the area of a football field and filled with lushly growing vegetables—potatoes, carrots and lettuces to mention just a few. Pumpkin plants spread out in abundance, bursting with golden star-shaped flowers; beneath their umbrella-like leaves, jointed runners ran like miniature plumbing pipes along the rich, dark earth.

On the way back we went to the truck to collect our bags. The women had gone inside but the men were still talking in the gazebo. Once inside the house Marge told us where to put our luggage—mine in the bedroom nearby beside the bathroom, and Phil's in the upstairs bedroom.

'What can I do to help?' I asked Marge as we came back into the kitchen.

'Nothing at the minute, thanks, I've got a good team here.'

Aunty Emily and Aunty Betty were sitting at the dining table shelling peas and Vivian was drying the dishes that Marge was washing. Phil's mum was resting as was her due at age eighty-seven. Phil said that she'd been a prolific cook, baking everything from bread to doughnuts, as well as canning chickens and fish, vegetables and fruit.

'Sit down and tell us about Jason,' Marge said to Phil.

It had been years since Marge had seen Jason. Having travelled the distance myself I could understand that visiting family as far away as Jasper wasn't something done very often.

Supper was at 6 pm and Marge called for everyone to come and help themselves. She had an impressive variety of dishes on the kitchen table: cold meats, potatoes, buns, lettuce salad, pickled beetroot, carrots, an array of relishes and something I'd never seen before that looked suspiciously like jelly. What was a dessert doing with the main courses?

'What's that?' I whispered to Phil who standing next to me.

'Jellied salad.'

'Which is ...?'

'Cooked peas in lime Jell-O.'

'You mean *sweet jelly*?'

'Yep.'

Sweet'n'sour pork was one thing but the thought of sweet'n'sour vegetables did not appeal. 'Hmm, no thanks.'

'All the more for me then,' chuckled Bill who, to my embarrassment, had overheard our exchange.

There wasn't enough room for us all to sit around the table so once our plates were full we took them into the lounge, where the kitchen chairs were scattered amongst the lounge furniture. As we ate, there was more talk about local people and events. After a while Aunty Betty interrupted the flow.

'I'm sure Leanne would enjoy a story about Phil.'

'Definitely!' After all, my over-riding reason for choosing this trip was to find out more about his family. If they proved dysfunctional, I knew I'd be wise to seriously consider the future of our relationship—although now that I'd fallen in love with Phil, I had to admit that I didn't know if I'd have the strength.

'Phillip must have been about four or five years old,' Aunty

Betty began. 'Art and I came to visit one day and Phil took me out to the barn to see the bull. It looked rather fierce and I must have said so because Phillip said, "Don't worry, Aunty Betty, I won't let him hurt you."'

The men laughed and the women aahed.

'He was only knee-high to a grasshopper,' said Phil's mum, 'so I don't know how he thought he could protect you.'

'He was so cute,' said Aunty Betty.

'Leanne thinks he still is,' teased Marge.

My blush was more than adequate confirmation.

After the meal and the dishes were done, the family settled down with cups of tea and coffee and home-baked cookies. Someone casually commented that there were fireflies outside.

'Fireflies!' I exclaimed. 'Really?'

The family seemed amused by my child-like excitement. 'You've never seen them before?' asked Marge.

When I said no, she told Phil to take me outside for a walk.

'Just wear some long pants and a jacket,' she advised. 'Fireflies won't be the only bugs out tonight.'

With me thus attired, Phil and I walked down the driveway and onto the road. The night sky was clear and stars were out in brilliant abundance. Sadly, there were almost as many mosquitoes. I had to keep swiping them away from my face.

Suddenly I saw a firefly. 'Oh, look!' A metre off the ground a yellow dot flashed on and off then reappeared a short distance away. Then more lit up and soon circles of light sparked here and there like luminous bursting bubbles.

'They're so pretty. I want to chase and catch one!'

'You'd be disappointed. They're just beetles.'

Phil's pragmatic comment wasn't the only damper on my mood. Suddenly I felt a sting on my wrist. A mosquito bite. 'Blast!' I sighed. 'Sorry, Phil, but we'll have to go back inside. I've just been bitten and I tend to swell up badly. If I get bitten on my face I'd be too embarrassed to go to the dance.'

'Well, Cinderella must go to the ball,' Phil said and took my hand to walk back to the farmhouse.

By the end of the evening I was weary. I'd had to remember to slow down my speech as the family seemed to struggle with my accent. To my embarrassment, at one point I heard someone ask quietly, 'What did she say?' But more tiring was the effort to remember names and stories and local history. It was an important part of Phil's background but I was already fatigued from the journey and glad to say goodnight.

I'd learnt late in life that being an introvert meant that while I might enjoy social interactions and even play an active role in them, afterwards I needed time to myself to recharge. Lying in bed, I mulled over the evening. Phil's family seemed welcoming, friendly and kind. I couldn't feel any undercurrents. However, this was only my first night with them and people were inclined to give their best impressions initially. I would wait and see what the rest of the weekend revealed.

Usually I was a later riser but I woke early the next morning. My longing to see Phil and have some time alone with him overcame desire for further sleep. I rose, pulled a cardigan on over my nightie and went to the bathroom to freshen up a little. The eyelash tint meant my eyes didn't need mascara.

Exiting the bathroom I quickly opened the door at the base of the stairs. It was right next to my bedroom so I hoped I could slip through it before anyone saw me and teased me about it.

Closing the door, I walked up the stairs which made a ninety degree turn halfway up. At the top Phil's bed was just to the right. He lay with his eyes closed and one arm outstretched on top of the duvet.

'Are you awake?' I whispered.

Phil's eyes opened and his hand shot out to grab my leg.

I gave a start and then giggled. 'You gave me a fright! Just as well I've been to the toilet!' I sat down on the bed and leaned over to kiss him good morning. 'Good morning, Phil.'

Phil removed his hand to stretch and yawn. 'Morning, beautiful.'

'Thank you.' It was years since I'd heard those words and my heart sang. 'The day looks gorgeous.'

'Of course, it's summer time in Manitoba.'

We chatted for a while then I left so he could get up and dress.

'I'll see you downstairs for breakfast.'

Taking one last lingering look at the handsome man with the tousled blond hair, I went downstairs to shower.

Only Marge and Bill, Phil and I were at the house. Everyone else had departed last night to Portage la Prairie. With the homecoming not starting until that evening and the extended family not expected back until the afternoon, Phil and I had the morning free.

'What do you two have planned?' Marge asked Phil as the four of us sat around the table eating breakfast.

'A swim at the beach, I think,' replied Phil.

'Best beach this side of Hawaii,' said Bill, reaching for the milk to pour over his porridge. 'But people don't go there like we used to. Every Sunday afternoon the whole district used to show up for a picnic, a swim, and ball games.'

Phil nodded. 'I remember Fred Mayor saying that there was nothing like a good cup of tea made from Lake Manitoba water boiled over the bonfire.'

'Yeah, especially after everybody peed in it,' Bill said.

Marge and I looked at each other and groaned.

During the pause in the conversation I took the opportunity to ask what was going to happen that evening. I wasn't very spontaneous and preferred to know beforehand what to expect of a new situation.

'It's really just a social time,' Marge said. 'You register for the weekend and then have a chance to visit.' She turned to Phil. 'Are you and Leanne going? If so, could you register the rest of us as well, as we'd rather stay home this evening?'

'I'd like to go and see who's there,' Phil said. 'Sure, I can do that.'

Borrowing towels from Marge, we set off for McLeod Beach on Lake Manitoba. I'd expected a pretty aspect and was disappointed. The beach was a lacklustre stretch of grey sand and stones bordered by straggly bushes and patchy grass.

'Not quite the image I had in my head,' I said to Phil, pulling off my shorts and T-shirt so I could sunbathe in my swimsuit.

'Oh, I don't know, it pretty much matches mine!' grinned Phil.

'What?' I frowned, initially not understanding. 'Oh, you mean me?' I blushed. 'Thank you. To tell the truth I was feeling a bit self-conscious. It was so hard to find a nice pair of togs.'

'Togs?'

'It's Kiwi slang for a swimsuit.' I'd been hoping for something pretty but this plain black one-piece was the best I could find: it was modest and went some way to flattering me. Other than bra fittings, I found searching for togs the most demoralising shopping of all, my every flaw seemed magnified.

'It's not the wrapping that's most important, it's what's inside,' Phil said, having taken off his T-shirt.

'That's actually quite poetic,' I smiled. 'By the way, I like what I see too,' admiring Phil's broad shoulders and chest, and his muscled arms. Being alone and semi-clothed only enhanced the strong sexual tension between us.

'What's that scar on your left shoulder?' I asked, sitting down on my towel, glad to have found a distraction.

'I had rotator cuff surgery,' replied Phil, sitting down beside me.

'Why? What happened?'

'My shoulder had a history of dislocation—it started with a baseball game—and I got fed up with it.'

We talked for a while longer until we had baked sufficiently to feel like cooling off. We made our way down to the lake.

'Brr!' I said, halting when I was up to my knees. 'This is freezing,'

'Nah,' said Phil. He waded in up to his waist and then plunged under the water. Standing up a few seconds later he shook his head and upper body, water droplets spraying in all directions.

'You'd make a good dog,' I said.

'Your turn now,' challenged Phil, moving towards me.

'No,' I shrieked, turning to splash through the water, then run up the beach. Phil followed and grabbed me in a wet hug.

'Get off!' I laughed. But my protest was half-hearted and ceased altogether as Phil turned me around and kissed me.

After lunch I helped Marge with supper preparation, then the family arrived in time for afternoon tea. We squeezed around the kitchen table to eat and drink, and remained there to chat until Marge shooed everyone into the lounge so she could lay the table and put the final touches to supper. Following the meal Phil and I drove into Amaranth to the community hall and registered us all.

The next day after breakfast, Phil went with Bill to dig some potatoes for the evening meal and I helped Marge prepare a picnic. Mid-morning we left for Amaranth to watch the parade. Phil and I travelled separately and met up with Marge and Bill and the rest of the family on the main street, joining groups of people dotted along the roadside in the warm, sun-drenched weather.

Leading the parade was a lone bagpiper in Scottish dress and behind him marched an RCMP officer. Following them were a variety of cars, a Bombardier, trucks with people sitting in the back sporting balloons and fluttering ribbons, tractors and four wheelers towing trailers with displays, one holding three generations of a family called the Bergsons, and several horse-drawn vehicles: wagons, flat decks and buggies. Lastly came riders on horseback.

At the conclusion of the parade, people made the short journey to the grassy area surrounding the local curling rink. They threw down rugs, set up deck chairs and opened up hampers. Our family group claimed one of the few wooden tables and once Bill had carried the basket from where we'd parked the truck, Marge set out the food. She'd brought sandwiches, cookies and beverages. Inside the rink, hot dogs and hamburgers with ketchup and mustard were being served.

While we ate, some locals came up to chat with Bill and Marge. Phil knew a few of them and joined in the conversation. As people finished their visiting we made ready to leave. Phil thanked Marge and said he and I would go for a walk and we'd see them all at the farm later on.

'Where are we going?' I asked as Phil took my hand and we left the others.

'Nowhere that exciting, just a piece of history. There's an old railway spur close to here.'

We soon reached the spur. The railway ties had been

removed, and grasses and flowers thrust through the gravel. Phil bent down to pick some wildflowers, made a small posy and handed it to me.

'Oh thank you, Phil, that's so sweet.' Holding the flowers in one hand I reached with the other to place it behind Phil's neck, gently drawing his mouth down to mine.

'I'll have to give you flowers more often,' he said, when we stepped apart.

I smiled and then paused a moment to change the topic. 'I feel like I'm living another life. Canada's so removed from either London or New Zealand.'

'It's all pretty ordinary to me.'

'Of course. But then again the weird thing is that in some ways it *is* familiar because most of the Western world is steeped in North American culture. It feels like I've walked into a book or a movie.'

'Well, I'm sure glad you're in my book,' Phil said, squeezing my hand. 'It's lonely by myself. But tonight I get to go to the dance with the best-looking girl in town. Lucky me!'

'Thank you! But I won't be the best dancer,' I laughed, absently kicking at a stone. 'I've gotten good at Ceroc but that's not what you'll be doing tonight I imagine—is it line dancing?'

'No! That's more a city thing. Tonight it'll be waltzes, two-steps and polkas.'

'How do you two-step and polka?'

'Two-stepping's easy but polkas have a four-four time with a bit of a shuffle step.'

I felt my confidence deflate. 'I don't even know what that means! It took me a long time to get the hang of Ceroc, and even then it's mainly about upper body moves, not fancy footwork.'

'I'm keen to polka so I hope you don't mind if I dance with some girlfriends from school—just for old time's sake. But we could two-step together. It's much easier.'

The thought of Phil holding other women unsettled me. Despite forgiving Karl, painful twists of jealousy were easily triggered. I wanted Phil to understand my struggle but it was a scary subject to broach. If I exposed my deepest fears and Phil downplayed them or disregarded them, I'd be devastated. Yet how could he take my feelings into account if he didn't know what they were?

I made the decision to be vulnerable.

'Can we sit down for a moment?' I asked, and we made ourselves comfortable, Phil's muscled brown legs touching my pale ones as we stretched them out in front of us.

'Actually, Phil, I *would* struggle with you dancing with other women. I'm not saying don't but please realise it'll probably make me feel jealous and inadequate. Your wife never cheated on you, so you can't imagine the hurt involved and the fear I have of it happening again. I'll need you to pay me a lot of attention when you're not dancing so I'll be in no doubt as to who you want to be with.' I locked eyes with Phil. 'Does that make sense?'

Would he brush my concerns aside? Tell me not to be silly?

'I think so ...' Phil paused and thought for a moment before speaking slowly. 'I love you, Leanne. Just because another woman can polka wonderfully doesn't mean I want to be with her. It's just a bit of fun. It's you I want.'

I gave a deep exhalation. 'Thank you.'

Phil's unhurried and considered answer helped emphasise its sincerity. He had not dismissed or exploited my vulnerability but responded to it with kindness. I felt reassured and safe.

'Well,' Phil said, standing up, 'we'd better get back. They'll think we've gone off the rails.'

'You're crazy!' I laughed and gave him a playful shove as I got to my feet. He grinned, then reached for my hand and we walked back along the railway spur.

At supper time everyone had once again taken their meals into the lounge.

'Are you young people going to the dance?' Bill asked Phil. It sounded funny for an older brother to address his youngest sibling like that but then again, they were separated by sixteen years.

'Just try and stop us,' said Phil.

'Do you dance, Leanne?' Marge asked.

'Yes, I learned to jive in London but I gather that polkas are what's popular here.'

'Phil'll soon have you hopping around the dance floor,' Uncle Art assured me.

'I wish I had your confidence, Art.'

The conversation turned to what was happening the next morning with the pancake breakfast and church service.

After supper was finished Marge waved away my offer of help with dishes so that I could go and get ready. When Phil and I had talked about the dance prior to me coming to Canada, he'd indicated that people would be casually dressed. So instead of the short skirts that were popular at Ceroc, I wore my best pair of jeans and a pretty crossover black top, a faux jet necklace and earrings, and my hair long and fixed away from my face with sparkly black-velvet clips. I hoped Phil's advice was accurate.

The dance was held in a curling rink that doubled as a hall during the off-season. The building had a concrete floor which could be flooded during the winter to create the ice needed for curling. Around the sides of the room were trestle tables with benches either side where people could sit to rest from dancing or to visit. The room was fairly Spartan, other than balloons with tails of tinsel arranged at regular intervals around the walls.

No sooner had we entered the room full of people and chatter than a man's voice called out, 'Phil!'

'Hi Danny,' Phil replied, letting go of my hand to step forward and shake hands with the man. After a few initial comments, Phil turned and introduced me. He told me that he and Danny had gone to high school together.

While they caught up, I glanced around and found Phil had advised me well, most women were either in jeans and a top or a long casual dress. There was lots of laughter, and plenty of handshaking and hugs. Phil said goodbye to Danny and we went to take a seat. The band was setting up at the far end of the room and Phil recognised two of the musicians from school—Ronnie Anderson and Sandy Campbell. Wanting to visit with them, he looked for someone with whom I could talk. When he saw a woman he knew, he invited her over and after making us acquainted, he left to go and visit with them.

'How'd you come to meet Phil?' the woman asked.

I understood her curiosity as intercontinental relationships often came about through intriguing circumstances, ours being no exception. Having explained briefly I saw a chance to ask an important question. 'So, tell me about Phil—you've known him a lot longer than me!' I smiled, and then added cheekily, 'Are there any skeletons in his cupboard?' hoping it came across as an off-the-cuff question.

The woman laughed out loud. 'Phil? Not a chance, he's as honest as the day is long. What you see is what you get. You're a lucky woman.'

I felt guilty for probing but the woman's assessment of Phil was extremely reassuring. It was what my gut had told me but I was still learning to hear and trust what it was saying. Having ignored it with Karl, I was having to attune myself again.

Phil arrived back as the band started to play a country song.

'We can two-step to this,' he said and so we excused ourselves from Phil's friend and stepped onto the dance floor, joining many other couples who were already circulating around the room. Phil took my right hand in his left and held it about shoulder height. He placed his right hand on my waist as I laid my left hand on his shoulder. I felt a little nervous, not wanting to appear as the novice I was.

'Now what?' I asked.

'I'll talk you through the steps. Follow my lead. It goes "slow, slow, quick, quick." Here we go.' He applied pressure with his hands so that I moved backwards and matched his two quick steps and two slow ones with my own. We did this a few times, Phil turning me so that we could make a circuit of the room along with the other dancing pairs. 'You're doing fine,' he said.

Phil's praise was my undoing. Without him dictating the steps, I did a slow step instead of a fast one. His knee knocked into mine and we stopped abruptly. 'Sorry, can you count me in again?' I asked, frustrated with myself.

'Sure. Slow, slow, quick, quick, slow, slow . . .'

We continued on.

I loved dancing and it was heavenly to be held in Phil's arms but the two-step required intense concentration. With it being the easier of the two dance styles, it confirmed my hunch that polka would be out of my league.

Phil was patient and I started to get the rhythm of it after a couple of dances, although I was reliant on him initially reciting the steps. When he suggested taking a break, I was relieved. I longed for the freedom and fluidity of Ceroc where I never knew what step was to come next and I felt the exhilaration of being spun by my partner. To Ceroc well was to experience a physical joy I'd never known existed. I longed for him to see me Ceroc and understand why I took so much pleasure in it.

As Phil came back with drinks for us both, the band started up a fast-paced oompah-style number which I guessed was a polka. Phil placed his drink on the table and then excused himself to find a partner. Watching him, it was clear he was a skilled dancer with masterful footwork. After several dances with different partners he spent the rest of the evening two-stepping with me. As the routine became more familiar I enjoyed it more but the best part of the evening was a slow dance at the end when we held each other closely. Shutting my eyes, I inhaled the aromatic notes of Phil's Wild Country aftershave mingling with my perfume. I loved the strength and warmth of Phil's hands; it was a dance I wanted to last all evening.

'Pass the maple syrup, please,' asked Marge. It was Sunday's pancake breakfast and all Phil's family sat at the same trestle tables at which Phil and I had been seated last night.

'The pancakes aren't as good as yours,' Bill commented.

'Figuring I didn't have to cook them,' Marge said, 'I'm not complaining.'

The family chuckled and continued eating, in between sipping coffee from their Styrofoam cups. Everyone except me who was waiting for my hot water to cool. The kitchen had offered me tea but it was Orange Pekoe. I was on my own beverage-wise.

In some ways I also felt alone in Phil's family. They were courteous and kind but what I found puzzling and disappointing was their apparent lack of interest in me for they asked almost no questions. It was something I was noticing in Phil also.

I realised for the first time what skilled conversationalists my parents were and how outward-looking their social interaction was. Whenever we had visitors come to our home, mum and dad asked perceptive questions to draw them out. I had learnt and practiced those skills but it saddened me how infrequently others engaged me with similar questions. It seemed many people would prefer to talk about themselves and learn nothing at all about others. With this issue being a sensitive one for me, I was going to have to address it with Phil.

After the church service, Phil and I stayed on with his family to visit with neighbours and old friends. I'd had my fill of trying to stay focused on conversations that held little interest or relevance to me, but it felt rude to zone out and daydream. I made myself concentrate but I couldn't prevent yawning.

'Up late dancing?' Bill asked in his typically low-key but joking manner. It *had* been a late night but it had more to do with Phil and me talking and cuddling in the truck afterwards than the dancing.

As I sought for a suitable answer Aunty Betty came to my rescue. 'Oh, Bill, stop teasing the young folk.'

'Well,' Marge said, draining her coffee cup, 'lunch isn't going to make itself.'

'Haven't you got that figured out yet after all these years?' Bill said.

Getting up from the tables, and taking our dishes to the kitchen, we bid acquaintances farewell, walked to our vehicles and drove back to the farm.

Later that afternoon Phil and I went back to Amaranth for some live music. We said goodbye to his mum, brother, sister, uncle and aunties who would be returning home before we got back. Would I ever see them again?

On a grassy area a marquee had been erected on a flat-bed trailer and musicians had been setting up the sound system and instruments on the makeshift stage. Phil pointed out the two guitarists, Vince Anderson and his cousin, Gordon. I'd met Vince and his wife, Stacey, that morning as Vince had taken the church service. Evidently they'd been sweethearts since high school days. Vince had been a close friend of Phil's all through his school years starting from Grade 1 to high school, and they'd hunted and played sport together.

The band soon launched into their first set. We settled in to listen, sitting on the folding chairs Phil had borrowed from Bill and Marge. There were a few blues numbers which was a genre I enjoyed but the majority were country. The last 24 hours had illustrated two differences between Phil and me, those of dance and music styles. We had some cross-over areas as Phil had led me in some jive moves last night and we both liked Van Morrison, but they weren't large areas of overlap. Did it matter? And if so, how much?

'Are you bored?' Phil said, putting his hand on my arm.

I'd been trying to keep my dislike of country music muted, it seemed I hadn't been successful. How could I possibly explain my feelings about music he enjoyed without being disrespect-ful? It would have to be discussed but now was not the time.

'It's not my favourite,' I admitted, 'but my foot's tapping and that's good.' I had an idea. 'Can I make some recordings of music I like and send them to you?' Maybe Phil simply hadn't had much exposure to other genres.

'Sure, I'll try anything once.'

I squeezed his hand. 'Thanks.'

'Looks like they're taking a short break so I'm just going over to have a short visit. You okay?'

'Absolutely. Go for it.'

Glancing at Phil a few minutes later, he waved me over.

'Vince said that there's a jam session at his and Stacy's tonight. Do you want to go?' Phil asked.

'Yeah, that sounds good.' It would be great chance to get to know more people who were important to Phil.

After supper Phil drove us to Vince and Stacey's property. They ushered us into an outbuilding which was set up for playing music. I could see Phil taking close interest in the guitars which reminded me that I'd seen lots of musical equipment in Phil's basement. The men laughed and joked around as they tuned up. Vince and Gordon played initially, while Phil and I took a seat with Stacey.

After a few songs, Vince offered to give his electric guitar to Phil who readily accepted. He sat on a folding chair and settled into a comfortable position with the guitar. Phil was given his choice of song and as he began the band joined in. Phil's low-pitched voice resonated around the room.

Later he was offered Gordon's guitar and this time he stood up to play and sing. I retrieved my camera and took a couple of shots to add to the memories that would have to sustain me when back in London.

An hour or so later, it was getting late and people were starting to yawn.

Vince placed his guitar on a stand then went over to Phil. 'Well, brother,' he said, giving Phil a hug, 'we probably won't see you for a year or two so take care of yourself.'

'We look forward to seeing what develops between you two,' Stacey said.

'Plenty of photos, that's for sure,' Phil joked.

I winced inwardly. Was that all he thought was going to come from our trip?

On the way home I asked Phil to pull over so we could talk. Once parked we both undid our seat belts to make it easier to turn and face one another.

'What's on your mind, Leanne?' Phil asked. The cab was only faintly lit by moonlight and I heard rather than saw the smile in his voice. How I appreciated his willingness to talk.

God, please help me with this conversation. 'It's about when Stacey wondered what might develop between us and you turned it into a joke. It was clever, I admit, but it made me feel insecure. Is that all this trip has been about, just photos to look at? I'll go back to London and you to Jasper and we'll just have some photos to look at fondly in the years to come?'

'No, no, I was just joking.'

'Well, it made me feel unimportant. Like our relationship was unimportant. What are we doing, Phil?'

Phil looked bewildered. 'What do you mean?'

'What are we going to do after this holiday? What's our future?' I knew I was pressing hard but our time together was drawing to a close and I needed an answer. Were we thinking the same things? What did it mean that Phil had said, 'I love you?' I knew what I'd meant but what had he?

I wrapped my arms around my chest and gave a shiver. It was a little cool. Phil reached over behind the seat and drew out an old blue fleece of his.

'Here, put that on,' he said.

'Thanks.'

I pulled it on, zipped it up and waited. There was silence for a few minutes. Was Phil not going to say anything?

'I guess I need to answer,' said Phil finally, 'but I'm not sure what you want me to say.'

'If you only said what you thought I wanted,' I said impatiently, 'I might like it initially but it's hardly a good foundation to lay. I need to know what *you* think.'

'Yes, you're right,' Phil conceded. 'The thing is, I can't make any commitment to you until I'm divorced.' He reached across and took my hand. 'I want a future with you, Leanne, but I need time to sort out this mess.'

'What's taking so long? I thought things would be almost sorted by now.'

Phil groaned and rubbed his face with his free hand. 'There are registered retirement savings plans and superannuation funds to divide—it's not easy.'

'Oh.' Our fairytale balloon had popped and lay in tatters around us. 'Maybe it's just as well we continue to live a continent apart while we wait for your divorce to go through.'

Phil admitted that I had a point.

'However, I refuse to accept that God didn't bring us together. There are so many pieces to the puzzle of me coming to Jasper, let alone to Sheila's and then her introduction of us. It could have broken down at so many points. God's in it and we just have to give Him time to work it out.'

'I can do that, I'm a patient man.'

I cried on hearing that. 'I'm *not* patient. This is going to be very hard.'

Phil moved over on the seat, wrapped me in his arms and held me while I wept. 'I'm so sorry, Leanne,' he whispered.

Whether or not it was due to the stress of the legal proceedings facing Phil, he woke up on Monday morning feeling rotten. At breakfast, he didn't want to eat much.

'My throat's too sore,' he explained. 'It feels raw.'

'With you needing to get Leanne back for her flight on Thursday, Phillip, you'd better go see a doctor,' said Marge.

'But I'm not registered in Manitoba.'

'There's an A&E at Sainte Rose du Lac. They'll see you.'

After Phil forced down some food, we got ready and drove the long 80 km. At reception, Phil explained why he was there and after a short wait was called in to see a doctor. Phil invited me to accompany him. The doctor was female, in her 30's and attractive, and adopted a slightly flirty manner with Phil which did not endear her to me.

'Too much holiday fun,' she joked after Phil had briefly sketched out what had led up to his illness. 'Okay, let's take a look at your throat.'

After an examination she removed the tongue depressor, turned off the small flashlight and sat back. 'It looks like strep throat. I'll prescribe some antibiotics. Rest up, use a salt-water gargle and ensure you complete the course of antibiotics even if your symptoms resolve. Your romantic inclinations will need to take to take a back seat for the time being.'

She barely acknowledged me. I could feel myself bristling and was very glad to leave her office. Phil paid at reception and asked directions to a local pharmacy. Paying for his medication, we drove back to the farm in time for lunch. Mid-afternoon Phil went for a rest. Bill went outside to do some chores and Marge and I stayed chatting in the lounge. After a while we got up and I helped Marge prepare supper.

'You'd better go and wake up sleeping beauty,' Marge said as suppertime drew near.

'Yes,' I agreed, 'although I don't think I'll do so with a kiss.'

Marge laughed. 'No, best to avoid catching his strep throat.'

In the evening we watched some game shows on television, then Phil and I bid Marge and Bill goodnight and had an early night. I welcomed some time on my own in order to think. Already feeling insecure over our future, I'd been threatened by the banter that had taken place between Phil and the doctor. The encounter had stirred up feelings of jealousy and fear of me being seen wanting, with the possible result of me being passed over for someone else. I felt anxious and unsettled.

God had healed me from the pain of Karl's betrayal but I realised now that it had been from the position of a single woman. As a woman who was now dating I had to deal with another level of those feelings.

The next day was our last at the farm and continued warm and sunny. How I would miss this when back in dull-skied London. But the real sun in my days, despite our current difficulties, had been Phil—his presence, his smile, his companionship and laughter, his interest and listening, his kisses and physical closeness. How would I cope without him? When would we see each other again?

The day passed uneventfully as Phil was needing to rest. We had a walk in the morning before the temperatures climbed, and he had another nap in the afternoon.

At supper that evening, I thanked Bill and Marge for their hospitality.

'You're welcome,' beamed Marge, 'come again.'

'Thank you.' I wished it was that easy. The lengthy two-day drive back to Edmonton, the 12-13 hour flight to the UK, and then the additional travel by train and Tube from Gatwick to Kilburn was an expensive, lengthy and tiring undertaking. Bill and Marge had never left Canada and even Phil hadn't travelled further than the States, so none of them understood what such a journey involved. Still, I knew that Marge had not meant to dismiss that but to let me know they'd enjoy seeing me again.

'So, when will you all catch up next?' I asked, painfully aware I wouldn't be there.

'Come back for Thanksgiving, Phillip,' Marge said, 'and join with us for a fall supper.'

'Your pumpkin and Saskatoon pies would make the trip worthwhile.'

'Saskatoon?' I queried. 'What's that, other than the city?'

'You don't know?' Bill queried. 'They're berries.'

'No, I've never heard of them before. What're they like?'

'Small and delicious,' Phil said.

'Well, that really tells me a lot,' I laughed. 'That would probably describe any berry in existence.'

'When you come again,' Marge promised, 'I'll make you a Saskatoon pie and you can find out.'

Chapter Fourteen

Early the next morning our luggage was packed away in the box on the deck of Phil's truck, and he and I stood there with Bill and Marge. Marge looked a little sad; I could tell she had a soft spot for her husband's youngest sibling.

'Drive safely, Phillip,' she said as she hugged him.

She turned to me. 'You've got a good man there,' she said quietly as she hugged me. 'Take good care of him.'

'I will.'

Bill wasn't particularly demonstrative but I couldn't resist giving him a quick hug. I loved his dry sense of humour and his teasing manner, it made me feel noticed and liked.

Phil and I climbed into the cab of the truck, then Phil wound down the window for our last goodbyes.

'See you in the funnies,' called Bill as we drove off.

Phil turned left onto the shingle road and gave a short toot on the horn. I wiped away a tear. They were good, kind, straight-forward people and it had been heartwarming to be included in their family weekend.

'What did Bill mean, 'see you in the funnies?'' I asked as we turned onto Highway 50 and began the long journey to Edmonton.

'It's hard to explain but it refers to the funny pages in a newspaper. It means someone likes your company in the same way you enjoy the funny pages.'

'Okay ... interesting.'

We lapsed into silence after that. Phil still wasn't feeling one hundred percent and we were very aware that we had less than forty-eight hours together. It was time for some hard thinking.

We stopped at Yorkton for lunch. Phil took me to a restaurant that served Ukrainian dumplings called pierogis. He recommended ones stuffed full of potatoes and onions and served with cheese sauce, bacon and sour cream. To someone with Irish heritage who loved potatoes, I didn't need persuading.

'Mmm,' I said, as I bit into my first mouthful, 'delicious!'

'Best eaten on a cold winter's day but good any time.'

'What other Ukrainian dishes do you enjoy?'

'Borscht.'

'Which is ...?' I asked, spearing another pierogi with my fork and swirling it around my plate to coat it liberally with sour cream.

'Soup made from beetroot. Delicious.'

'I like cold pickled beetroot but hot in a soup?' I pursed my lips. 'Hmm, I'm not sure.'

'Don't knock it until you try it,' Phil said, pausing to take a sip of his drink.

'Okay, fair enough. But how do you know so much about Ukrainian food?'

'Easy!' Phil smiled. 'Lots of my friends were Ukrainian. I lived in Dauphin which had a Ukrainian festival every year, and we went to fall suppers which had lots of Ukrainian food.'

'How could you not?' I said, selecting another pierogi. 'Man, one could put on a lot of weight eating these.'

'Worth every pound!'

Leaving Yorkton we travelled on Highway 16. It was a couple of hours after lunch. With the landscapes on either side of the highway never seeming to change it felt like you were not making any progress; part of me longed for it to alter but it would only do so when we approached another city which would mark the door slowly closing on our remaining time together.

'I'm bagged,' Phil said. 'At the next truck stop I'm going to buy some sunflower seeds.'

After paying for a top-up of gas, Phil came back with a large bag of sunflowers seeds. I'd not seen them packaged before as snacks and was intrigued, even more so when I saw they were unshelled.

'How are you going to eat them like that?' I asked. 'Do you want me to shell them for you?'

'No thanks. I simply crack open the sunflowers with my teeth and then spit out the shells. Watch!' Taking a mouthful, his cheeks bulged and his jaws moved back and forth. I heard a few cracks—presumably the sunflower seeds and not Phil's teeth—then he grabbed the empty plastic cup he'd got at the gas station and periodically spat the shells into it, somehow keeping the seeds in his mouth.

'Wow, that's rather fancy mouth-work,' I said.

'Impressive, eh?' Phil grinned, chewing on the de-shelled seeds.

In Saskatoon that evening Phil wanted to celebrate our final meal in one of the city's most popular restaurants. He chose the memorable Saskatoon Station Place, built to resemble a train station with two old-fashioned dining cars.

Once seated, I unfolded my napkin and placed it over my lap, then opened up the menu. I skimmed over the choices. 'It's a little pricey,' I said.

'It's my shout so order what you want.'

'Thank you!'

After perusing the menu Phil chose steak and I a chicken dish.

Phil took a sip of his wine. 'What did you think of my family?' he asked.

'I liked them. They were easy to get along with. Marge is very kind and I thought Bill was a honey.' I fiddled with my cutlery, wondering how to phrase what I had to say next which wasn't as positive. 'I felt hurt though that they hardly asked me anything. I left with them knowing almost nothing about me.'

'That's just my family, Leanne. Don't take it personally. Did you hear them ask much about me?'

I gazed across the restaurant and considered. 'No ... no, I didn't,' I said, looking back at Phil. 'That's really sad.'

Phil chose not to comment. 'They like you though.'

It felt good hearing that but I wondered if Phil was just guessing in order to make me feel better. I asked him why he thought that.

'Because of the way they accepted you and carried on as normal with you there. They weren't putting on any airs or graces.'

I laughed at that. 'Yes, it felt really natural.'

Our meals were brought over, Phil's steak sizzling on its hot plate.

As we ate, an idea occurred to me. 'Phil, I said, cutting into my chicken breast, 'I'm planning on going home this Christmas. Would you like to join me? Then you can meet *my* family.'

Phil finished his mouthful of steak. 'That could work. I'm not busy during winter.' He smiled. 'I'd sure look forward to seeing you again so soon.'

My face lit up. 'That would be wonderful.'

We spent the rest of the meal discussing the dates and what Phil should expect from a Kiwi Christmas.

Back at the hotel it was our last chance to talk at length face-to-face. Our conversation grew more serious, from holiday fun to our future together.

'I'm just starting off in the backcountry,' Phil explained. 'It's been my dream since first becoming a warden. I love you, Leanne, but I don't want to give up this adventure to go live in London.'

I'd learnt that Phil didn't sugar-coat his thoughts and never less so than then. Tears threatened and I blinked several times to keep them at bay.

'I'm sorry,' Phil added. 'I don't mean to hurt you.'

'Thank you,' I acknowledged. 'I can understand you not wanting to give up the back country. The way you wrote about being in the upper Blue Creek Valley and especially Topaz, showed me how enamoured you are of it ... and of the lifestyle.'

'It's not a job I can take a break from and then step back into. The positions are sought after. I might not ever get another chance.'

I conceded that. As a teacher, especially one in London, I could get a position fairly easily but I could understand the backcountry warden positions were coveted and scarce. While in the excitement and fervour of new love it would be easy to submerge or minimize our needs and desires. But as a mature adult Phil recognised that naively promising to give up everything for the other wouldn't make for long term happiness. Part of me wanted Phil to make a passionate declaration in which he surrendered his dream to be with me but that wasn't realistic. He needed a vocation he enjoyed and the chance to fully live the dream with which he'd been presented. If I pressured him, he might be persuaded to give it up but he'd only come to resent me for it.

That led to another but equally difficult topic—children.

'I've already got a son,' Phil said. 'When I was younger I

wanted more children, in fact I'd have loved a cute little girl or two, but not now, I'm too old. I don't want to be a father to teenagers in my—' he paused a second to calculate, 'late 60s/early 70s.' He sighed and ran a hand through his hair. 'Sorry. I'm sounding selfish.'

I inhaled slowly and took time to consider what he'd said and how I felt about it.

'Part of me doesn't mind,' I began, 'as I've never desperately wanted children. I love teaching them and being with my nieces and nephew but I've never craved my own. However, I'm realistic enough to know that when we're married I might change my mind.'

Phil shifted his position on the couch to fully face me. 'I shouldn't be asking this of you, Leanne. Do you want to find someone younger who would like a family?'

At that I burst into tears. 'What?' I sobbed, 'you'd let me go just like that?'

'No!' Phil protested. 'I love you, Leanne, I don't want to let you go but I don't want to deny you children either.' He gestured towards me. 'Come over here.'

I slid along the couch and into Phil's arms where I continued crying until my tears were exhausted. Relinquishing the opportunity to have children was a huge concession for a woman but then again here was a man who loved me for who I was. In stark contrast to Karl, he accepted my sensitivity and didn't despise my emotions and tears. I'd never met a man like Phil. It was with a profound sense of finality I decided that I'd rather have Phil and no children than to lose him.

The next morning we loaded our gear into the truck for the fourth time. It had taken on the beginnings of a habit that was familiar and comfortable but it paled in comparison with the delightful routine of being with Phil from dawn to dusk. The thought that this was now our last day together flooded me with sadness. I had a choice—I could keep the feelings to myself or share them with Phil while I still had the chance to shelter in his arms.

'Phil,' I said as he held open the passenger door for me, 'I can't bear to think that this time tomorrow we'll be apart.' Tears had formed as I said this and they now slid down my cheeks. Phil opened his arms to me.

'I know,' he said, as he held me tight. 'Can't we just drive straight through Edmonton and keep going until we get back to Jasper?'

I choked out a laugh. 'I wish.'

Our route to Edmonton kept us on Highway 16. The scenes were much the same as our journey eastward and the land advanced flat and uninterrupted to the horizon, contributing to the feeling of desolation, as the trip I'd longed for was all but finished.

Phil chose Lloydminster in which to have lunch. I wanted every single thing we said to one another to have meaning and significance so I could treasure it afterwards. Unaware at the time that one of my love languages was words, I was unable to articulate this longing in a meaningful way.

What I *was* able to acknowledge was my desire for Phil to ask me about what my life in London entailed until we met again at Christmas. I now had a sound comprehension of his world, surely he'd want to know about mine?

'So you're heading back into Blue Creek next week?' I said.

'Yep, gearing up tomorrow and then heading out Saturday. I'm going to be busy.'

'Have you made out your shopping list?'

'I just use a standard one—it's plain cowboy cooking out there.'

'As long as you don't forget your veggies,' I teased, waving my fork at him with the floret of broccoli I'd just speared.

'You can't take out that stuff, it gets squashed too easily. You need compact vegetables like carrots or cabbage.'

I didn't say any more after that, giving Phil time to reciprocate. We ate in silence for some time.

'If you want a cup of tea and something sweet, Muffy, then you'd better do so quickly. We don't want to be late for your plane.' Phil had given me the nickname because of my predilection for ordering muffins with my tea. Other than a creepy boss who called me "Tiger" in my 20s because of a stripy skirt I wore, no-one had ever given me a nickname before. It felt good to be given a term of endearment.

'Yes, good thinking,' I said and eased out of my seat.

When I came back I was again quiet but still Phil didn't ask me a single question. Finally I couldn't stand it any longer. 'Phil,' I said, a little sharply.

'Sounds like I'm in trouble,' he grinned.

'Oh boy, you're too cute for your own good. But, yes, you *are* in trouble!' I said. 'I feel hurt that you haven't asked me anything about what I'm going back to, how I'm going to spend my summer, what work I've got lined up for the first term ... '

Phil didn't seem to gauge the importance of this. 'But if you want to tell me, you will,' he said with simple logic.

I sighed. 'I want to be asked! If I spout off about myself, how do I know you're interested? You might just be listening out of politeness. But if you ask me, then I *know* that you want to know. It's so much more rewarding to share when I know you have a genuine interest.'

'Well, I'll try but asking won't come naturally,' Phil said.

'Hmm' I said, my lips compressed. 'I understand that now, having met your family. But it would mean so much to me if you could.'

'It's not easy changing at my age but for you I'll try.'

I couldn't ask for more than that. But it now seemed I had two sets of pupils—my children at school and Phil.

When he began asking questions, I realised I'd not given much thought to the remainder of my holidays. My entire focus had been on my time with Phil. Now I couldn't avoid the fact the rest of my summer was going to be long and lonely. In my experience, women were usually able to project themselves into a future situation and fairly accurately predict their feelings. Men, I'd found, often couldn't. I was convinced that Phil would miss me as much as I'd miss him but he didn't seem able to imagine it in any detail. That hurt, for it meant I wouldn't hear his longing from his own lips but would have to wait until we were an ocean apart.

Phil pulled into a long-stay parking space at Edmonton airport. With a slam of the truck door, he shouldered my backpack then took my hand with his free one.

'Goodbye, truck,' I said, trying to keep things light.

'It's a constant reminder of you, my LPX.' Phil squeezed my hand.

Tears formed and I swallowed hard as we walked towards International Departures.

'You can't imagine how I'm going to miss your big strong hand holding mine,' I said.

'My big mitts?' laughed Phil.

'Please don't joke, I need your tenderness right now.'

Phil squeezed my hand again. 'Sorry, Muffy. I'll miss you more than I can say. Miss teasing you, miss your beautiful face.' My heart absorbed his words like water to a wilting flower.

Glass doors opened in front of us. We stepped through and I scanned the counters for KLM Airlines.

'There it is,' I said.

We walked over then Phil motioned he was going to stand back while I queued.

'No,' I pleaded. 'Please stay with me. I can't bear to be parted any sooner than necessary.'

Phil looked uncertain. 'They'll think I'm a passenger.'

'Let them!'

Phil acquiesced and stood close to me, his arm around my shoulders. We shuffled forward until we neared the counter when he slipped under the barrier and moved away.

Once I'd checked in my baggage and received my boarding pass, I stepped away from the counter and looked for Phil. There he was—lean and muscled with brown arms and legs, his tanned face with its broad smile that warmed me to my very core. The knowledge that in thirty minutes or so I would no longer see him caused a physical ache and I gulped down more tears.

Near Phil was an empty row of seating and we sat down. Each seat was separated by an arm rest; we were already being parted by degrees. We had half an hour before I had to go through the security checkpoint but it was hard making conversation. Anything other than our imminent parting seemed trivial and yet we couldn't keep talking about it or I'd break down. We compromised by reminiscing about our two weeks together.

The unavoidable time arrived and we stood up.

'Thank you for everything. It was wonderful … I love you, Phil.'

He gathered me in his arms. '*You* were wonderful,' he said, speaking quietly into my hair. 'I love you too, Leanne.'

Phil walked with me to the doors that led to the security checkpoint. I was working hard to swallow my tears. 'I'm not saying goodbye,' I choked out. 'Hasta luego, Phil.'

With a last lingering kiss, I joined the queue of passengers, had my passport and boarding pass scrutinized, and then walked through the doors. I turned to catch one last glimpse of him. Through my tears I could just make him out, his hand raised. I waved back then forced myself to turn and walk away, out of his line of sight and out of his presence.

Only God knew for how long.

Chapter Fifteen

I threaded my way through the pedestrians on Kilburn High Road, city noises in my ear: the squeal of a bus's brakes as it pulled over at a stop, the honk of an irate courier driver, good-natured shouts in an Irish brogue outside a pub. Approaching Safeway supermarket, I sidestepped a woman in a hijab pulling a striped shopping cart, walked through the open doors and began my weekly shopping.

It was jarring to be back in London. It was both the culture shock of exchanging mountain and prairies for a metropolis and also the shock of being without Phil. With me arriving back on 4 August, there were four months of separation before Christmas and they stretched ahead interminably, as unrelenting as the 7,000 km that divided us. But we'd forged something very real and precious and as Phil identified and valued the qualities of my character, God's love for me became real in a way and to a degree it had never done before.

For the first time I comprehended this was how God felt about me, although admittedly on a much greater scale.

As I walked back to my flat from the supermarket I thought of my conversation with Alison over the weekend. Before I left for Canada, she'd invited me to go and stay with her and Peter when I got back. It had been hectic—arriving on Friday morning then doing a quick wash of my clothes in order to pack again and head to Paddington for the 9 pm train.

I'd been excited to share my holiday with her and we sat up late talking. With her usual directness, motivated I knew by love and concern, she questioned my acceptance of Phil not wanting to give up his new backcountry position or have children. She wondered whether he would do the same for me. What did it say about him and our relationship if I was the only one making sacrifices?

Aware of how little scrutiny I'd given my relationship with Karl, I made myself seriously consider Alison's concerns. After we'd said goodnight, I wrote to Phil. As I began, I was struck with the irony of possibly going to live in Canada as it was the one country I'd vowed never to visit. Immediately the word 'vow' prompted recall of the one I'd made after Karl left—that I would live anywhere for the right man. God had taken my vow seriously after all! I had to laugh at the country He'd chosen. Whoever thought God didn't have a sense of humour?

This revelation cemented my belief God had brought Phil and me together. In Karl I'd chosen a man based on his looks—overlooking major flaws in his character and in the way he treated me. Only after I'd been won over by how courteous, kind, accepting and fun Phil was, did I come to find him physically attractive. I felt a strong sense of peace that this time I'd fallen in love with the man himself, with what was enduring and real.

Our pairing might seem unlikely but it also felt well-founded and solid.

I would still tell Phil of the concerns Alison had raised as our relationship needed to be strong enough to tackle thorny issues. Ultimately, however, I felt that what I would gain in Phil more than made up for my sacrifices. Regarding children, it was hard to think of it as a significant loss when it had only ever been a nice idea in the distant future and never a desire of mine. And as for leaving London, I would always treasure it—that amazing city had been a place of wonder, opportunity, fun and friendship—but what I'd longed for most was the intimate companionship in marriage with a man I respected and trusted.

In the only full day Phil had in Jasper before heading out to Blue Creek, he'd worked with urgency on the process of renewing his passport and booking flights. His travel agent secured not only the same flight I had booked from Los Angeles to Auckland, but adjoining seats. I was thrilled.

More importantly, Phil called his wife's lawyer to expedite his separation agreement. She informed him that his wife had a new lawyer from whom he would be hearing. I didn't think too much of that at the time, simply taking comfort from the speed at which he acted. I naively hoped that the matter would be completed by December so we could make a trip to New Zealand with Phil a single man in law as well as in practice. After all, he'd been separated from his wife longer than the necessary two years. I tried not to dwell on the frustrating fact that if he'd been proactive earlier on, the process could now be well underway.

His wife had made it clear from the beginning that there wasn't an atom of hope for reconciliation and their marriage was dead. It was only Phil's legal status that kept us from being able to progress our relationship.

With Phil now into his routine of being in the back country for two-week patrols and unavailable during that time, the remaining four weeks of summer holidays loomed long and lonely. They'd been bearable for the short time Phil was in Jasper and in daily contact with me but now they stretched out as endlessly as a prairie highway. For the rest of the summer and autumn it became hard not to wish away fortnights of my life each time Phil was away. I had to learn to live one day at a time because looking out across the sea of distance and time between us was simply too daunting.

We communicated by all means possible including phone calls, emails and letters. Many of Phil's missives were penned during his back country shifts—by lantern light in the evenings as he sat at the kitchen table and often written on paper bags. He was enchanted by the scenery in the Upper Blue Creek valley and became quite lyrical at times. I wrote almost every day, not only was writing a pleasure but it brought Phil close, as if he was in the room and I was talking to him. I took to spraying my perfume on my correspondence, and Phil did the same with his cologne. Closing my eyes and inhaling his scent, I could almost imagine him with me.

Romantic cards were another currency by which we maintained and strengthened our bond. Phil slipped in brightly coloured embellishments like musical notes, love hearts and little bears. I loved how they cascaded out of his correspondence when I opened them.

Along with the letters and cards we sent little parcels of chocolates and candies, bookmarks and small gifts. We also included newspaper and magazine clippings showing places we'd been, places we wanted to go to and even catalogue pages showing furniture, interior design, fabric and upholstery we favoured.

When I wasn't communicating in some form with Phil over the remainder of August, it helped to be busy with part-time work, volunteering and friends. On Sunday mornings I tutored three Muslim children who were a delight.

Grandma's had an outing every holiday for children who didn't have a regular volunteer and so I'd chaperone a child or siblings to and from their homes.

Friends-wise I was busy too. One of the girls who used to live in the flat had moved out into a bedsit nearby so I visited her. A current flatmate had a birthday party to which I was invited, and Jayesh asked me over for a meal to quiz me about Phil. I also met up with Gwen, as well as a Kiwi woman I'd gotten to know.

But although I kept myself occupied, thoughts of Phil were like a compass needle which, although it might swing to and fro, always came back to point north.

On Thursday night, 17 August, my phone rang late at night. Phil was the only one who rang at such times but we'd spoken on the phone last night so it wouldn't be him so soon, would it?

I picked up the receiver. 'Hello?'

'Leanne, it's me.' Phil's voice sounded strained.

'Phil! What's wrong?'

My concern broke his composure and I heard him sob.

'It's my sister, Vivian. She's been killed.'

'What?' I was incredulous. Only a few weeks before we'd been talking and sharing meals together at Bill and Marge's. Tears sprang to my eyes. 'Oh Phil, I'm so sorry. What happened?'

His voice choking up, Phil told me she'd been crossing a crowded street in Winnipeg when she had been hit and killed by a passing truck. It was unthinkable. How could a loved one die while simply out shopping?

'That's just awful,' I said, wiping away tears. 'I'm *so very* sorry.' My words seemed meagre but I was not going to offer platitudes. I'd enough thrust on me when Karl left to know how repugnant they were. Instead I trusted that my tone of voice, imbued with all the love and comfort I possessed, would touch Phil's heart.

'I wish you were here,' Phil said. 'I need a hug.'

I cried again at that. 'I wish I was too. I so want to hold you, and comfort you. Oh Phil, I'm so sorry. That's just devastating.'

We talked for a little longer but Phil had to go and make arrangements to take time off work in order to drive all the way back alone across the prairies to Manitoba for Vivian's funeral. Now I understood the great distance involved, my heart hurt even more for Phil as I contemplated the long hours he'd spend alone with nothing to fill them but grief.

Placing down the receiver and cutting off our connection was excruciating. From being "together" with Phil, in an instant we were severed again, half the globe separating us. Never had I felt so distant or so helpless to provide succour to someone I loved.

I lay awake in bed for a long time, wiping away tears as I dwelt on Phil's and his family's grief. This unwanted reminder that life was fragile made me long for Phil and me to begin our own life, and I cried for us too.

It was September.

For the first time ever I welcomed the close of the summer holidays because it meant that Phil and I were another month closer to being re-united in New Zealand at Christmas. I was working a full week, continuing with my special educational needs work at my Lambeth school Monday to Wednesday, and beginning my new Thursday and Friday job at St Agnes. The latter was small with friendly staff and well-disciplined children and I enjoyed teaching there.

Early in September Phil had a friend visit him. The man's reaction to learning about our relationship caused Phil great disquiet and he rang me to voice his own concerns. I was upset and torn for I acknowledged our situation wasn't ideal in that Phil was still married but I thought Phil's friend wasn't taking two important things into consideration. Firstly, we were now apart and waiting for Phil's divorce. Secondly, the way we came together was undeniably God inspired. Had only one step not occurred, the entire process would have broken down.

Over the phone I enumerated them to Phil: one, me putting a profile online; two, Richard responding; three, Hannah challenging me to give him a chance; four, Richard inviting me to Canada; five, me taking up his invitation; six, me buying non-refundable flights; seven, the school's educational psychologist encouraging me to use the tickets but go on to Jasper; eight, my dentist's receptionist telling me to do the same thing; nine, Christy's friend also encouraging me to go which finally decided me; ten, booking a B&B at Sheila and Joe's; eleven, Sheila setting up the blind date; and twelve, Phil actually agreeing to do so, as evidently he'd needed some persuasion!

No one could convince me that God had not orchestrated our meeting. We just needed to negotiate our relationship with wisdom and purity until Phil's divorce was secured.

By the end of our conversation, although it was hard for Phil to disagree with a close Christian friend on such a matter, he appeared to come to the same conclusion. The soul searching had been gut wrenching but the upside was that we began asking and answering tough questions in our correspondence—what did we have in common, what did we need and want from a spouse, how did a couple make a strong marriage, and weaknesses and areas in which we needed support. We also detailed what we valued in one another and our mutual affirmation was a boon that filled both our hearts.

For my part it was as if I was a flower garden and Phil was my gardener, pulling out weeds of worry, watering me with loving words, nurturing me with kindness and patience, and placing me in the sun of his sense of humour and laughter.

But about five weeks later Phil made a shock decision. His friend's concerns had been like a seed that I thought was dead but had taken root and had been growing unseen in Phil's private mulling. He rang to say that he was still terribly conflicted and had cancelled his flights to New Zealand. The legal proceedings were progressing so slowly that he didn't anticipate them being finalised by Christmas and couldn't in good conscience meet me in that state.

I was greatly upset but yet I didn't want Phil to act against his conscience. The fact he was resolved to do what he felt God was telling him, despite the pain to us both, reassured me that Phil was putting God first in our relationship; this was something I wanted.

But while I had a reluctant peace about Phil's decision, I wondered where it would lead. Would we not meet up for months or years if the divorce dragged on? I felt that his marriage was dead and just needed legal burying but was I wrong in thinking that? I needed to get someone else's opinion and my Christian counsellor in Auckland seemed an obvious choice. I respected his wisdom and deep relationship with God, and trusted that he would offer godly insight and practical advice. And so I asked Phil to email him.

My counsellor responded promptly to Phil. As he'd done with me, he asked Phil lots of great questions—about his relationship with God and his estranged wife, wanting to know what he'd learnt and what he'd do differently if he married me. Regarding our relationship, he didn't want to speak for God or tell us what to do. However, we were both encouraged by his acknowledgement that Phil's marriage was dead except for the paperwork.

His personal opinion was that we could meet while this process was being dealt with, providing we keep ourselves from acting married before we were, which was our desire also.

As a result, Phil emailed that he would fly to London in February which would give him extra time in which to finalise the divorce. It was the best Christmas present he could have given me. Our two weeks together had sustained me for months but, like fading perfume, its potency was diminishing.

Our peace wasn't to last long, however. A few days later another friend of Phil's called into Jasper to see him. Afterwards he sent Phil an email saying that he thought we shouldn't be conducting even a long-distance relationship until Phil was divorced. Once more this sent Phil into a tailspin.

This second blow was extremely tough. I was frustrated and angry with Phil's friends. Who among them had felt the pain and devastation of being deserted by their spouse? Which one of them had suffered having the fulfillment of their social, emotional, physical and sexual needs suddenly ripped from them? Who had endured years of the resulting loneliness and longing to have this restored? Who had invested in hours of counselling when it felt like all you were doing was paying someone to witness you weeping?

And it wasn't even as if we were seeing each other, we were an ocean apart! They seemed incapable of empathising, choosing instead to stick to the letter of the law. It seemed no coincidence that those who had never suffered great loss in their life were often the ones to make the harshest rules for others.

In the midst of the angst they stirred up, I kept coming back to the fact God had gone to considerable lengths to organise me being introduced to Phil. It reminded me of the way God brought Ruth to Boaz. Admittedly, our situation wasn't ideal but God had seen fit to bring together two lonely people who loved Him and longed to be remarried. And in acknowledgement of the inherent difficulty, he'd arranged that we'd spend the majority of our time apart until Phil's divorce was settled.

The desire to achieve this galvanised Phil to action. In view of the fact his wife remained adamant their marriage was irrevocably over, she needed to work with Phil to make it a legal reality. To my relief, Phil delayed a backcountry trip to meet with his lawyer and thrash out a way forward.

Chapter Sixteen

The year was coming to an end. My two schools had granted me a fortnight off in addition to the Christmas holidays and I flew to New Zealand on 7 December for a month.

I stayed with my parents and over Christmas we were going to be joined by my siblings. With each one of them married or with a partner, I worried I'd be very conscious of Phil's absence. But despite being in Canada, he soon made his presence felt.

A day or two after I'd arrived at my parents', Mum called out to me from the kitchen that there was a courier van approaching. My parents lived in the country and deliveries were rare. I presumed it must be a parcel for my dad who ran a herd of red deer in the eight hectares behind their house.

Mum dried her hands and went through the door into the entranceway. A moment later she came back.

'Leanne,' she exclaimed, holding a beautiful bouquet, 'you've got flowers!'

Phil! I leapt up from the couch where I'd been flipping through a magazine and joined mum who was beaming. She was a sensitive woman of strong faith with the kindest heart of anyone I knew. When Karl left me, I'm sure she'd felt my pain as if it were her own. She was absolutely thrilled that God had led to me a Christian man who clearly adored me and she was as excited as me about the delivery.

'He's not sparing any expense, is he?' she said with approval, handing me the bouquet.

'No,' I smiled, taking them from her and lifting them to my face to inhale their perfume. 'Oh, they're lovely.' Phil had asked for mum and dad's address but I'd thought that was to send me letters which I'd already begun receiving. I'd not expected flowers—I felt as sunny inside as one of the scented yellow blooms.

Mum and dad were naturally curious about Phil and I needed no persuasion to talk about him. Speculation abounded as to our future but I couldn't think much further than Phil securing his divorce. I was relieved to learn that considering the circumstances my parents didn't object to our relationship, with the unspoken proviso we abstained until marriage.

My four weeks went by quickly. I took many photos to show Phil when we next met. Asking to have photographs taken of myself was a new phenomenon. Previously I'd hidden from the camera; I'd felt very un-photogenic because I wore glasses and one of my top front teeth stuck out. Now, after wearing a dental plate for over a year, my tooth was in alignment. And I'd gotten contact lenses in August after I'd arrived back from Canada. But the most significant reason for my newfound confidence was that Phil found me beautiful.

My goodbye to mum and dad at the airport was tough, for my parents had been sweet and their support greatly appreciated. It was reassuring to count on their prayers that the divorce proceedings would be accelerated.

2001

Chapter Seventeen

Returning from holiday is always unsettling, especially so when farewelling summer and re-entering winter. London was dark and dismal, and my bedroom was pokey compared to the one at my parents'. However, I started school right away and had little time in which to ruminate.

Dominating my mind and producing anxiety, stress, and even a slight element of fear was a three-day visit by Ofsted to my Lambeth school in the first week of term. Most teachers dreaded these appraisals. Their professional standing, which impacted on the collective standing of their school, was determined on the "strength" of one or two observations. And from what I'd been told, the Ofsted inspectors offered little collegiality and empathy for the myriad of pressures and demands on a classroom teacher.

Because I was not teaching a classroom of students, there were far fewer variables to go badly. On the other hand the scrutiny would be more intense with there being only three or four students, the inspector and myself.

Luckily, my review proved to be less stringent than I'd feared. The inspector was easy to talk with and I didn't feel as if I was being grilled. In our initial meeting he asked me about how the special education needs programme ran. For my first inspection, he came in while I was teaching and stayed for a long one and a quarter hours. Afterwards he said he was very happy with what I was doing. He said I had a good rapport with the children and that the lesson was well-paced, keeping the children interested and involved which I was extremely pleased about. The second and final time he sat in on my lesson for half an hour while he checked my paperwork. He seemed satisfied, simply giving me some helpful pointers.

On the last day of the visit, the teachers were asked to wait at school until 6 pm by which time the Ofsted inspectors would have given their assessment of the school to the senior management team, and would then convey it to the remaining staff. Rather than wait in the staff room with my colleagues I used the opportunity to email Phil. I wrote about how fed up I was with working ten-to-eleven hour days.

My stomach rumbled and I looked at my watch. Five forty-five. I brought the email to a close having asked Phil to call that night, and walked downstairs to the staffroom where food had been provided for us by the school board. Speculation was rife as to what decision had been made. Would we keep our "good" status or slip back to "requires improvement?" Was it conceivable that with our new head teacher we would achieve an "outstanding?"

I hoped no single teacher was targeted for censure as I'd heard happened occasionally—how sickening it would be to feel you were the one bad apple, spoiling it for the entire school.

'Well,' Phil enquired, later that night on the phone, 'what was the verdict?'

I shifted on my bed to get more comfortable. It was late as usual given the time difference. After the intense three days I was exhausted and longing for sleep but my desire to talk with him was greater still.

'Good,' I said, then realised Phil might think I was just using the word generically. 'I mean that's the actual grade! We didn't go up a level to "outstanding" but neither did we drop a level. So everyone is relieved. And there was no negative comment about any particular teacher so no-one felt picked on.'

'That must be a huge relief.'

'It is! Some went to the pub to celebrate but I just wanted to come home. I'm knackered.'

Phil laughed. 'I still think that expression sounds rude! I'm not surprised you're exhausted though. We won't talk long.'

It was Friday night at the flat and I was in the kitchen eating tea.

'Mmm, lamb again,' said Dee as she came in to get a drink. I'd been surprised to find that lots of English people couldn't stand the smell of lamb but Dee was an exception.

Lu Ping, another of my flatmates, was in the kitchen preparing her own evening meal. 'It smell better Monday when Leanne has chicken korma,' she said, then changed the subject. 'What you do at weekend?'

'Just taking it quietly,' I said. 'You know, it's funny. Glenn is actually getting *into* dancing while I'm now going out less and less.'

'We'd noticed,' Dee said. 'While you were away we were discussing your decline as a party animal.'

I laughed out loud, almost choking on my food.

'Can you deny it?' she asked, taking a sip of her drink. 'There was almost a different man every week.'

I snorted.

'Well, every month maybe,' Dee admitted with a grin, 'but there were lots.'

'Just practicing my dating skills so I was ready for Phil,' I said with studied nonchalance, amusing Dee and Lu Ping.

They were right though. My yearning for male company had been the driver for me to make the effort to go to Ceroc after long days at work. But with Phil in my life that motivation was gone.

In late January my emails to Phil were dominated by the staffing situation at my Lambeth school. Three weeks into the new school term, teachers were already calling in sick. Admittedly it was winter when sickness always lurked but it seemed too soon after our Christmas break. I'd been there for four years and it was still not an easy place in which to work although behavioural issues were off-set by a robust schoolwide plan. The real issue in my mind, in addition to the unrealistic and crippling amount of paperwork expected by the Department for Education, was residual stress from the Ofsted visit.

For a week and a half I was used as a supply teacher as there was a serious shortage in London. My frustration turned to anger as the head teacher moved me from class to class and even sought and received permission from the St Agnes head teacher for me to work those two days at Lambeth.

Up until the Wednesday of the second week I hadn't managed to speak to Phil as I'd been too exhausted to stay up that late. So I was thrilled when he had kindly offered to come home and phone me during his lunch time.

'Hello?' I answered when my phone rang at 7 pm.

'Hello, my flower.' There it was, the deep, smooth timbre of Phil's voice.

'Oh, Phil, it's *so* good to finally talk to you.'

'And you, Leanne. What's happening?'

'I told the head teacher that I was very unhappy being taken away from my special needs work and he's worked extra hard to get a supply teacher. So now I can get back to doing my job.'

'Good, it's about time! They need to value what you do.'

'Thanks, Phil. I love it that you're on my side.'

'Always.'

I talked some more then asked him about his day.

'Boring. Desk work. Although I managed to get out of the office to patrol the Highway 93/93A loop to Athabasca Falls and back.'

I sighed. 'We live in such different worlds. Talking about that, what's happening with you coming to London?' I was desperate to have him visit but phrased it casually as I didn't want to put undue pressure on him. We'd realized that the one week I had off during half term in February wouldn't be sufficient time. If we could just hold out until April then it would give us two weeks together.

'I *need* to see you Leanne, so I'll have to make that happen. Give me a couple of days.'

'I'm just longing to have a date set that I can look forward to. Don't take advantage of what I'm going to say Phil,' I said with a forced laugh, 'but I almost don't care when it is, I just need a date that I can count down to. A concrete date though—not one you could change like at Christmas.'

'Yes, that was hard for you. For me too.'

'Yes, I know and I'm not trying to make you feel bad, I just don't think I can do that again.' My emotions welled up and a sob escaped.

'I miss you too, Leanne.' Phil spoke slowly to emphasise what he was saying, empathy evident in his voice. 'It's been far too long part. I *am* going to make it work for April.'

Sweet relief coursed through me although I knew I wouldn't be fully at ease until I beheld him walking towards me through the arrival gates at Gatwick Airport.

'How's Phil's divorce going?' Alison asked me.

I'd gone to stay with her for the first weekend in February. It was Saturday morning and we'd finished breakfast and were sitting in the lounge. Peter was working. Ordinarily, the sun would be streaming through her south-facing window but today rain dripped desultorily down the pane, reflecting both the depressing nature and sluggish progress of the divorce.

'It's not.' I gave a big sigh. 'Both Phil's and his wife's lawyers are moving slowly, and just when there's been some advance, then his wife seems to stall.'

Alison folded her legs underneath her on her chair. 'Life's so unfair sometimes.'

I agreed with her, knowing she was probably thinking also of the breakup of her first marriage.

We talked more about the situation but were unable to find any solution. Even if I badgered Phil, it would only stress him out and make us both unhappy. However, I really valued the chance to have a moan to Alison, knowing she was totally supportive. She had shown a healthy scepticism initially but only because she cared so much. And it hadn't hurt for me to be challenged—if our relationship couldn't withstand scrutiny then it was a feeble one.

Phil made good on his promise to sort out his trip to London and his flight was arriving mid-morning on Saturday, 7 April. I'd made the tentative suggestion that he stay on for an extra week. Phil could sightsee during the day while I was teaching and we'd have the late afternoons and evenings together. It was strangely reminiscent of my rejected offer to do the same for Richard in Vancouver. I was thrilled when Phil agreed. The only thing spoiling my joy was the fearful thought niggling at the back of my mind that he might cancel at the last minute.

I worked hard at giving that fear to God because dwelling on it destroyed my peace.

The winter months of February and March went by as slowly as the dripping of a melting icicle. I struggled against the dreariness induced by the dismal weather and the ubiquitous grey of tarmac, pavements, buildings, and sky. It wasn't until March that daffodils pushed their way determinedly through the soil and offered their brave yellow smiles to a cold world.

Work continued to be exhausting but through it all Phil nurtured me. If we'd phoned and he'd found me upset or down, he would head back out in the cold to his office after his supper to send me an extra email to encourage me the next morning. That he could support me so ably despite our physical distance was very precious and it comforted me while making me long even more for us to be together.

The only thing he couldn't do was accelerate his divorce proceedings but yet he seemed at peace with that. One of the things that had attracted me to Phil was his patience and it occurred to me that sometimes a trait that we admire, when taken to its extreme, can also be the very one that irritates us.

Frustration and powerlessness had a deleterious impact on my digestion and I began experiencing stomach pains.

As much as I knew I shouldn't worry, I found it so difficult to trust God in the situation. I was fearful something would happen and Phil would put off his trip again. Waiting was a task I struggled with. How to wait well is surely a hard-earned skill and one requiring a strong belief in God's goodness—something I was still developing.

Chapter Eighteen

It was finally 7 April.

The countdown had gradually reduced from months to weeks to days and now it was minutes. Phil's plane arrived in quarter of an hour. I stepped into a cubicle in the women's toilets at Gatwick Airport, lowered the toilet lid and placed my backpack on top. From it I removed high-heeled black suede boots, slipped off my flat shoes and pulled on the boots. I'd planned my outfit for weeks, a pretty black top and jacket with a short red skirt paired with these boots—sexy but sophisticated.

The concourse hummed with people. I threaded my way through them, and found a seat near Phil's arrival gate.

International airports were polarising places where sadness and imminent loss vied with anticipation and excitement. This time, for Phil and me, it was the latter. Waiting had been excruciating but the absolute certainty of Phil's arrival lent this final few minutes of waiting an exquisite pleasure. I don't think I'd ever waited so long for anything so significant before and I fizzed with joy like shaken champagne.

I glanced away from the doors for a moment and when I looked back, passengers were beginning to walk through them. I scanned the figures intently and suddenly I saw a black Western hat. My heart gave a jolt—it could only be Phil!

I stood up, threw my rucksack over one shoulder and moved into Phil's line of sight, waving frantically. Seeing me, he broke into that huge, boyish grin that lit up his face so handsomely. Swiftly covering the distance between us, he dropped his luggage and swept me up in his arms.

'Oh Phil, I can hardly believe you're here,' I said as we clung to one another.

We finally pulled apart to gaze at each other, reacquainting ourselves with the others' beloved features. I studied the full length of him. He wore blue jeans and cowboy boots and over his shirt he wore a sand-coloured duster. He looked so different than any man I'd ever wanted to date but he looked so good.

'I can, Leanne, it was a long journey! But I'm here now,' he said, and finally kissed me. When it ended we hugged again and

Phil whispered into my hair how sexy I looked. Mission accomplished, I thought, even if my feet paid the price on the way back.

On the train I snuggled as close as I could to Phil. We held hands—I'd forgotten how comforting it felt to have my small, often cold hand in his large, warm, slightly calloused one. After being physically apart for so long even such a small amount of touch felt sublime. I longed for the ultimate skin on skin of sexual intercourse but we were reserving that pleasure for marriage—whenever that would be. I desperately wanted to know a time frame.

Phil interrupted my thoughts. 'So this is jolly old England,' he said, as he looked past me through the window. Green fields and meadows flicked past, then a blur of blue as a train on the other set of tracks headed for the airport.

'Anywhere would be jolly if you're with me,' I smiled, leaning my head on his shoulder and squeezing his hand. 'It'll be a culture shock for you though.'

'Yes, what'll they make of this cowboy?' Phil chuckled.

'Pretty much anything goes in London,' I replied. 'I like being anonymous although occasionally people's tendency to retreat into themselves leaves you feeling alone.' I told Phil the story of being bullied by high school girls on a train and how the adults nearby had ignored my plight. 'I felt very vulnerable.'

'You would,' agreed Phil. 'Cowards.'

'The passengers?'

'Both—the passengers *and* the girls.' He leaned over to kiss me. 'You're safe with me, Leanne,' he said. And I truly did feel safe, emotionally and physically. It was something I'd longed for all my life without realising it. Now God had given me the desire of my heart—I would wait for this man as long as it took.

The girls at my flat knew Phil was coming to London and staying at Gwen's. Neither Phil nor I could have afforded to pay his accommodation so we were extremely grateful.

The first engagement in our busy three weeks together was a wedding that afternoon of a young couple from church. To save time Phil and I went straight to my flat. He wanted a shower after his flight and I desperately needed to get out of my boots.

I sat in the kitchen waiting for Phil to shower and change. When I saw him enter I was dismayed. Gone was the Western attire which, although new to me, I now realised suited Phil so well. Instead, he wore dress trousers and penny loafers with a cream-coloured sports coat. He looked pedestrian and ordinary; gone was his individuality and vitality.

'I feel like a new man,' Phil said, squeezing onto a cane couch beside me.

I wanted to say I preferred the old one but now was not the time for a discussion about couture.

Phil took my hand and looked around him at the kitchen. Through a newcomer's eyes it looked shabby and cramped. And now very noisy as both the Metropolitan and Jubilee line trains rattled past behind us.

'I need to get you out of this place,' he said.

'I know, I can't wait! But God *has* blessed me with this flat. It has everything I need plus it's safe and cheap—'

I broke off as I heard footsteps ascending the stairs. 'That's probably Dee. She said she'd be back about now. I'm so grateful for her too. She's been such a good friend— empathetic and a good listener, she remembers virtually every-thing I tell her.'

A moment later we heard the door to the flat open and Dee came into the kitchen. Phil and I stood up and I introduced him.

'Howdy Dee,' Phil said, 'I'm pleased to meet the first of Leanne's friends.'

'Hello, Phil.' Dee gave a cheeky smile. 'So you're real, not just a mystery man who sends Leanne mail and phones her late at night.'

We laughed at that and chatted for a short time then Phil and I left for the wedding.

The two weeks of my holidays fled as fast as only euphoric times can. Looking back on everything we crammed in, it must have been tiring for Phil who lived a much less busy life. I booked a large table at a cheap and cheerful restaurant in Kilburn and invited friends to come have a meal and meet Phil. One weekend, my cousin, Malcolm, picked up Glenn, Phil and I and drove us to Jill's home in Hertfordshire. Not only did Phil met her and her husband, Dan, and their two girls, but her mum, my aunty Raewyn, and her husband, David, who were visiting from New Zealand. Another weekend we took a train down to Kent to spend a day with Christy and Matt and their two girls. Back in London we had seats for a performance of Buddy Holly in Leicester Square, as well as a Van Morrison concert in the Royal Albert Hall. We also took a coach up to Nottingham where we stayed a few days with Ted, a distant family member of Phil's, and his wife Barb, who lived in Long Eaton.

It was while we were staying there that I received some sad news. Mum rang to tell me that her mum, who had been recovering from an operation for bowel cancer, had died. Always thoughtful and kind and mindful of others even in the face of her own pain, mum's parting words were that she was so glad Phil was with me to comfort me.

Phil and I excused ourselves and went for a walk. It was a dreary, overcast day with dampness in the air—very appropriate to mark the news of my Grandma's death and the knowledge I wouldn't be able to attend her funeral.

Narcissi and bluebells dotted the gardens we passed but their beauty was hard to appreciate.

'How are you feeling?' Phil asked.

'Thanks so much for asking.' I'd been coaching him for months to regularly ask that question. 'It's so hard to know where to start.' I paused, wiping away tears. 'Obviously I feel grief, not only at Grandma dying, but not being able to be there to say goodbye. You know from Vivian's funeral how good it is to be with family at such a time.'

'Yes,' Phil acknowledged, 'it was.'

'But the worst thing,' I continued, 'and I feel guilty about this because it sounds so selfish, is the reality that if I marry you, I'll never have a granddaughter to mourn me.' With that admission I wept.

We'd just reached a park so we stepped off the path and stood under a tree to gain a little privacy. Phil gathered me in his arms. I wanted him to say something to relieve the hurt but what was there to say? Having no children was not negotiable for him. But in accepting that, I was also accepting the now raw knowledge that I would never have a child to love and care for me when I was old, let alone grandchildren to mourn me.

'I'm sorry,' he said quietly, and I cried even more.

After a while the initial tide of grief ebbed away. As harsh and final as the realisation had been, I didn't want to reject the love Phil held for me to wait for a younger man who might want children, for he might never arrive. Nor could I imagine anyone else loving me as well as Phil did.

We resumed walking, discovering an empty playground where we fooled around like children on the swings and seesaw. It was a welcome tonic after the grief.

When Phil and I were back in London, we visited the vicar of St Gabriel's Anglican Church close by in Cricklewood.

I'd started attending there as it was a smaller church where I would be known and acknowledged, and I was delighted to have Gwen go with me. The vicar was a kind, approachable man who I respected. I'd asked whether he'd meet with Phil and me to help us lay a healthy foundation for our future. With two failed marriages between us we wanted to invest in our relationship and realised that creating a successful one needed intentionality and work. The vicar was pleased to help and gave me several pages of thought-provoking questions that I copied and sent to Phil.

The bus to Crickewood arrived and luckily we managed to find seats together. They weren't wide and I welcomed sitting close to Phil, our thighs pressed together. How I would miss this.

It reminded me of one of the questions. Why do you want to be married? Undoubtedly it was because of sexual desire—this need ran high for both of us, and our longing for the fulfilment of this was like a physical ache at times. But it was so much more than that. What I needed also was affirmation, encouragement, companionship and laughter. Phil provided all of these and I'd come to depend on them.

'How did you answer the question, why do you want to be married?' I asked Phil.

'So I don't need to keep saying goodbye to you!' he laughed.

I smiled but kept silent.

'But I can tell you want more. Let me think.'

A few minutes later we reached our stop.

Phil took my hand as we walked to the manse. 'Okay, to answer your question. Well, to make love to you obviously but it's much more than that,' he said. 'You have what I need, what I want—tenderness, compassion, understanding, a love for God ... intelligence, beauty ...'

While it was true Phil often needed encouragement and time to dig deep and say what was on his heart, if I gave him that space his words always touched me. 'Thank you,' I said quietly, 'that means so much.'

The meeting was beneficial and we were glad we'd made the effort. We left with some homework to do but also the assurance that what we were doing was creating a solid base for our marriage: being honest even when we felt vulnerable, talking issues through until resolution and without put-downs and going off on tangents, affirming one another, recognising and appreciating our differences, and viewing our strengths and weaknesses as complementary rather than cause for complaint.

Phil's trip to the UK wouldn't have been complete without a visit to see Alison. We took a National Express coach to Gloucester where Alison came to pick us up. As we stepped off and waited for our luggage to be unloaded, I heard Alison call out hello.

I turned and saw her approach in a short skirt and boots and her purple corduroy jacket; she always dressed so attractively. I gave her a big hug and then turned to introduce Phil.

She hugged him too. 'So, this is the cowboy you've been telling me about, Leanne.'

'Pleasure to meet you,' Phil said, tipping his hat.

Alison laughed. 'Let's head home. Peter's just catching up on some work.'

Our time together was short, only two days but it was so much fun. Alison and Peter loved Phil and we had interesting conversations and lots of laughter. Alison was once again a fabulous host and took us to fascinating places and pubs with great food.

When we came to say goodbye, Alison told Phil she'd had her doubts about him initially. 'But I can see you adore Leanne and so you have my blessing,' she said.

'Thank you, Alison,' Phil said, putting his hand on her arm. 'Leanne speaks highly of you so that means a lot.'

After farewell hugs, Phil loaded our luggage beneath the coach. Taking our seats we gave Alison and Peter a final wave through the window before they turned to go.

The highlight of Phil's visit was a long weekend in Paris during which we celebrated his birthday. We were easily the oldest couple on the coach tour and amused the rest by our obvious delight in each other.

Our tour company had pre-booked the first evening's meal in a chic little restaurant in Montmartre. During dinner a vendor selling long-stemmed red roses approached our table.

'This is for you, my Alberta rose,' he said as he paid for and handed me the bloom, making reference to the fact that the prickly rose was Alberta's provincial flower.

'Minus the thorns,' I smiled. 'Thank you, Phil.'

The weather though cool, was sunny, and enhanced our time. It was a memorable three days and delivered all the romance promised by Paris. We had our photo taken in front of the Eiffel Tower, Phil had a caricature of himself sketched by an artist outside Notre Dame, and we rode on a carousel complete with golden lights, prettily painted wooden animals and accordion music.

Early Sunday evening we were speeding our way from Dover to Victoria, London. We had sat in the back seats of the coach and with the dimmed internal lighting it made for a private and intimate setting.

'That was wonderful, Leanne, thank you,' Phil said. 'I even got to be on the ocean for my first time.'

'That's still hard for me to believe but then again, having travelled across Canada I realise the sea is a long way away.' I leaned my head on Phil's shoulder. 'Just like you're going to be in a week's time.'

Phil squeezed my hand. 'Yes.'

A few tears escaped and I brushed them away. 'When's this going to end?'

'The journey?'

'No!' I hissed quietly. 'Us being apart.'

'Sorry, I was still thinking about our wonderful weekend.'

'That's good but I want more than weekends.'

Phil turned his head and kissed me. 'I do too, Leanne. I'm sick of us being apart but I'm trying not to think about it.'

'I get that but I also want to be able to talk about it face-to-face when you're still here to comfort me.' I didn't want to push Phil but I couldn't let this opportunity pass. 'Can't you speed things up? Put pressure on your lawyer?'

Phil gave a big sigh. 'I'm trying but he thinks that putting pressure on my wife's lawyer might have the opposite effect. Also, every time I contact him it costs more money.'

My stomach churned. 'I'm so angry about it all.'

'I'm sorry,' was all Phil could say. He put his arm around my shoulders and pulled me close. It felt good and was comforting but I couldn't help longing for the ultimate comfort we could give one another. When would that time come?

Phil's final week was my first week back at school. I gave him my London A-Z book and left him a copy of the Tube map, as well as several suggestions of places to visit each day. The first day he visited the London War Museum which was on the south bank of the Thames and not too far from my Lambeth school. He arrived at school after the children left and I was able to introduce him to the staff.

'They seem to be a good bunch,' Phil said as we left shortly afterwards. I'd worked hard in the last couple of weeks before the holidays so that I was as up-to-date as possible with my work.

'They are,' I said, closing the school gate behind me and putting my hand in his outstretched one. 'I'm lucky to have found a school in which to put down roots. So, how was your day?'

'Good! The Imperial War Museum was worth a look. It was very informative and the WWI trench exhibit … you felt like you were actually there.'

On the following mornings Phil took walks in a park close to Gwen's and continued sightseeing in the afternoons, meeting me each day after school.

The week ended all too soon and with his early flight on Saturday in mind, I gained permission from the church for Phil to use the spare bedroom on the second storey on Friday night. We'd have more time together and be able to share breakfast.

Early on Saturday morning I put on my dressing gown and quietly let myself out of the flat. Downstairs, I tapped on Phil's door. I heard some movement and then the door opened.

'Good morning my darling,' I smiled, reaching out to ruffle his hair which was messy from sleep.

We hugged and then sat down on his bed.

'How did you sleep, Muffy?' Phil asked.

'Good thanks—when I finally got off to sleep, that is. I lay awake for ages thinking how much I'll miss you.'

'You too, eh?' Phil squeezed my hand. 'Having been to-gether makes our separation even worse. I need you with me.'

'I know but it's in your hands, Phil. I can't do anything.' I felt so utterly powerless and hated it.

'There's not much I can do either,' Phil said. 'I'm a patient man. I can wait her out.'

'It's all very fine for you,' I said sharply, 'but I've had enough of being patient!'

'Leanne—'

'No,' I interrupted, 'you have to do something! I can't stand this!' and started weeping.

Phil sighed, put his arm around me and gave me time to cry. As my tears ended he reminded me that August wasn't far away. During our time together we'd planned for me to visit him for the entire month.

'May, June, July… three months. I guess it's better than the eight months we endured last time.'

'Exactly. Hang in there, Leanne. With God's help we can do this,' Phil said and he kissed me tenderly.

As April turned to May, we were released from winter's bare-boned grip, and spring fully unveiled its buds and blossoms. Beauty was coming back in gardens, parks and flower baskets which helped raise my spirits.

My role at the Lambeth school expanded over the summer term with a host of new children with severe needs. However, my efforts to address them were being thwarted. The boy I'd been trying to get special funding for, was behaving so atrociously that he was in danger of being permanently excluded. That my work for him could all be for nothing was exasperating. A girl with severe hearing loss was being neglected by her mum who kept failing to present at appointments. And an anger management group I'd set up for two boys during the lunch-time was not taking place because they were only attending school part-time.

There were other frustrations as well and the stress was manifesting physically with me breaking out in cold sores, one particularly unsightly and painful.

I yearned for Phil; my longing relentless. It would abate when I was busy or corresponded or talked with him but afterwards it would surge back as strong as before. It was like trying to appease one's hunger with mere mouthfuls of food.

Chapter Nineteen

'Please put your tray table up,' instructed a stewardess, 'and ensure your seat is fully upright for our descent into Edmonton.'

I was almost there. Apparently the temperature was cool but Phil would keep me warm. Although it would be via fully-clothed hugs. Holding ourselves back from making love had been such a struggle in the few times we'd met. With us both having been married before, it was incredibly difficult to not resume this level of intimacy.

As we struggled to maintain this resolve, God helped us put even stricter limits on ourselves. With this came a greater peace and feeling of closeness to Him. Maintaining that peace became our guide. Meanwhile, after the absence of any touch at all, hugs, handholding and kisses would seem a feast to our senses.

This time Phil was driving to Edmonton to meet me at the airport. Not only would I not have to wrestle with my luggage, pay for taxis, stay at a B&B and then make my way to the Greyhound depot the next day for a long journey alone, I didn't have to wait an extra day to see Phil.

I retrieved my luggage and went through customs. Walking as fast as I could, I made for the exit, scanning the waiting area for a man wearing a cowboy hat—there he was! Almost running, I bee-lined for Phil whose wide grin matched mine. I dropped my luggage and nestled into his arms. Home at last!

We stayed at a hotel in Edmonton as it was too late to set out for Jasper. Seated at a table in the breakfast room the next morning, Phil was tucking into a cooked breakfast and I was enjoying some cereal and fruit.

A smile played on Phil's face as he looked at me.

'What's going through your mind?' I asked.

'That's for me to know and you to find out.'

'Ha, ha! However, I have asked so I'm waiting.' I drummed my fingers on the table for effect.

'Just thinking how great it is to have you for a whole month.'

'I know,' I said, reaching for his hand, 'it's amazing. And so is the fact you have all four weeks off.' He'd told me over the phone a few weeks back that, like me, he'd been suffering from stress—over the never-ending prolonging of his divorce and a couple of other personal concerns—and his doctor had prescribed a month of stress-leave.

I placed my empty bowl to one side and reached for a piece of toast. 'However, I can't help thinking that the situation must look a bit dodgy to your workmates.'

'I really don't give a rats,' Phil said, taking a sip of his coal-black coffee, 'but yes, there have been a few comments.'

'I love the fact you don't worry about what others think of you—I worry too much.'

'Sounds like a typical firstborn, setting super high standards for themselves and wanting to please people.'

I lifted up my hands in surrender. 'That's me.'

'Good thing is though,' Phil continued with a grin, 'firstborns are most compatible with the youngest in the family and that would be me.'

We paid for breakfast, finished our packing and took our luggage out to Phil's truck in the parking lot.

'This brings back good memories,' I said, handing my bag to Phil for him to pack into the box on the back of his truck.

He jumped down, drew me close and kissed me. 'Yes, doesn't it? Right, my Alberta rose,' he said, opening the passenger door for me. 'Let's blow this pop stand and head home.'

Oh, for that to be true in every sense, I thought, as I buckled up my seatbelt. For us to be married and this to be forever, with no need to part in four weeks' time. As the engine started up and it became too noisy to talk, I reflected on the many plans we'd drafted before making our final decision for me to move to Jasper once we were married.

After serious consideration of both New Zealand and the United Kingdom we realised that the wisest, most practical solution was to live in Jasper. Phil had a well-paid job that he loved, and a large and comfortable house for which he paid very reasonable rent. With me bringing virtually no savings to our marriage, the economic stability of this option made it by far the best.

With all our plans pivoting on the settlement of Phil's divorce, I was thrilled when he chose our wedding date—Saturday, 15 December. It gave us two weeks to organize the wedding after arriving in New Zealand in early December as well as time to honeymoon before returning to my family for Christmas. I had the blessed reassurance that we'd not enter another year apart. But most significantly, this commitment meant the purchase of airfares so Phil couldn't afford to be patient any longer, he had to make that date a reality.

As we turned off the highway into Jasper, Phil reminded me that a young man called Neil was boarding with him. He was a university student, many of who worked for Parks Canada in some capacity while spending their summer break in the mountains. But for now it was early afternoon and both Jason and Neil were at work. We'd have the house to ourselves.

Pulling back the screen door, Phil unlocked the back door and held it open for me. 'Welcome home, Muffy!' Phil said.

A feeling of contentment settled over me like a warm cloak. 'Thank you,' I answered and kissed him.

Stepping through the door I slipped off my shoes then ran up the stairs to the main level into the lounge. Everything looked much the same as I remembered—the slightly worn carpet, the ghastly pink curtain swag over the large south facing window, the outmoded blue-striped Chesterfield.

'It's looking a bit old-fashioned, isn't it?' Phil said, coming up behind me with our luggage.

'It needs a bit of a refresh but none of it really bothers me as long as we're together. Although,' I added with a laugh, 'after we're married I may well want to make some changes.'

'Fair enough.'

'Okay, I'm starving. Let's put away our luggage and groceries and have some afternoon tea.'

Jasper was hosting a folk festival in Centennial Park on Saturday and Phil had bought tickets. It wasn't my favourite musical genre but live music had an energy to it that made it appealing. Having arrived mid-morning, it was easy to claim a good spot in which to open out our folding chairs. The day was partly cloudy and cool and I was glad of the blanket Phil had packed.

Once settled, Phil saw someone he wanted to speak to. He checked if that was okay with me then threaded his way through the growing crowd. It was a pleasure to watch him, my handsome blonde-haired man attired in his jeans, duster coat, and cream shantung Panama cowboy hat. He moved easily with a confident, unhurried gait.

Phil was well liked and I received a warm welcome whenever we met an acquaintance of his. Unlike Karl, he didn't dominate social interactions and was happy for me to share the attention when we chatted with others, often prompting me to tell the story of how we met. He never seemed to tire of hearing me tell it, even though I'd fallen into the habit of using many of the same phrases each time.

We bought lunch from the food stalls while listening to a mixture of blues, folk and bluegrass. Most numbers got my upper body swaying and my fingers and feet tapping, I could never fathom how people could remain bodily unmoved by good music.

By late afternoon it had fully clouded over and there was a cool breeze. I gave a little shiver.

'Are you cold?' Phil asked.

'You know me well! Where are your gloves now?' I teased.

'I slipped up, didn't I?' Phil laughed. 'Shall we leave? I've heard enough.'

'Yes, please.'

'Let's go home for some hot chocolate. That'll warm you up.'

Walking from the garage to the back door we met Jason on the landing, putting on his shoes.

'Hi Jason,' I said. I didn't know how he felt about me but with me coming back a year later he must have figured my relationship with his dad was quite serious.

'What're you up to tonight, Jas?' Phil asked.

'Heading out to Chris's.'

Phil nodded.

'How was the festival?'

'For a small town effort it was quite good,' Phil answered, 'but I would have enjoyed it more if it hadn't been so cool.'

'I hope we don't get snow tonight.'

'What?' I gawped.

'Don't mind Jason, Leanne, he's joking.'

I laughed with relief as well as embarrassment that I'd been taken in. 'Have a good evening.'

'You, too,' Jason said, and walked down the path to the back gate.

In Phil's bedroom—which he'd kindly lent me once more while he slept in the spare bedroom opposite—I changed into warmer clothes. When I rejoined Phil in the kitchen where he was making our hot chocolate, I asked where Jason was working.

'The Sawridge.'

'Oh, yes, I think I know where you mean. What does he do there?'

'General housekeeping duties.'

'Okay. Not very stimulating for him, I imagine, but it's great he's got a job.'

'Yes,' said Phil, handing me my drink. 'Worst case scenario at least he'll know what he doesn't want to do.'

It was my third visit to Jasper but Phil hadn't exhausted new places in which to hike. He took me to Old Fort Point, a mammoth rock mass where we walked the loop around it under the shade of conifers and up onto the bare summit which gave panoramic views down the Athabasca Valley. Another day we followed a trail that began on the Bench and went up to Lake Hibernia. But of all the places we went to, Mount Edith Cavell was the highlight. Nothing else compared to its hanging glacier, glacial lake and alpine meadows strewn with wildflowers.

Not all of our time was spent alone. Sheila and Joe invited us to a picnic early one evening at Pyramid Lake. There were grassed areas edged with aspens on the south side of the lake and equipped with wooden tables and benches. Sheila was supplying cold meat and dessert and Phil and I were bringing salads.

When we arrived Joe and Sheila were already there. Joe was sitting at a table and Sheila was unpacking her food from a cooler.

'Hi Phil,' she called as he got out of the truck and came around to open my door.

'Welcome back to Jasper, Leanne,' she added as I climbed out. 'It seems we can't keep you away.'

'Hi Sheila, hi Joe,' I replied. 'Absolutely not! Phil's too good a drawcard.'

Joe returned our greetings as Phil carried over our own cooler and placed it on the table. He took out our salads and some drinks, then sat down beside Joe.

'You're not sitting next to Leanne?' Joe asked.

'I can see her better if I sit opposite her,' Phil said, winking at me.

I felt a little shy so quickly changed the topic. 'How's your B&B going? Have you organized anymore blind dates, Sheila?'

'They don't pay enough for that added service,' Joe joked.

'So,' Phil asked, 'how much did Leanne pay you, Sheila?'

She grinned. 'That's strictly confidential.'

Phil opened up the chips we'd brought and handed them around.

'Phil's told us about his trip to England,' Joe commented to me, putting down his can of Mike's Hard Lemonade. 'Sounds like a different pace of life. Jasper's not too boring in comparison?'

'That's what my London friends think. They don't realise I grew up in the country. I spent my childhood playing in the bush and riding ponies.'

'So you'll be going with Phil into the backcountry?' Sheila asked, taking a sip of her water.

'I would've liked to have accompanied him but he's not going out this month.'

Attention immediately turned to Phil. 'Dr Konkin's put me on four weeks stress leave,' he explained.

'Handy timing for you,' said Joe, with a glint of mischief in his eyes.

'You're not the first person to say that,' replied Phil, unperturbed. 'There's stuff going on at work, I'm concerned about Jason's future and the divorce is taking its time.'

'Well, it sounds like a month off with Leanne should be just what you need,' Sheila said.

'I hope so,' I smiled, reaching across the table top and placing my hand on Phil's. 'I want this man around for a long time.'

After some more conversation Sheila suggested we eat. The main meal was tasty but paled in comparison to Sheila's pièce de résistance which was something I'd never been served before—a fruit pizza. It was delicious—a perfect combination of pastry, cream cheese and summer fruit.

When the sun went down there was still plenty of light but the mosquitoes had started making their presence felt. Joe and Sheila were great company but it was time to leave.

Joe had asked if we were going to the Jasper Pro Rodeo as he would be attending. Phil had gotten tickets for us as soon as they were available, purchasing seats for the last night on Saturday as well as the dance afterwards. He appreciated the prowess of the cowboy athletes who took on the brute strength of the bulls and bucking horses, and the horsemanship of those who competed in riding events.

On the evening of the rodeo Phil drove down Pyramid Lake Road. It was lined with trucks but we managed to get a park not too far away. We joined the couples and small groups walking to the Activity Centre and made for the hockey arena. It was a multi-purpose space used for ice hockey in the winter, and now covered in dirt for the rodeo week. Phil guided me to our seats which he said were some of the best to be had—near the bucking chutes and close to where the action was.

'There's Bob Barker,' Phil said, once we'd sat down, directing my gaze to the whip-thin man with a full moustache, colourful cowboy shirt and big hat moving around the chutes. 'He's the chute boss, a bit of a legend around town. He was a backcountry park warden in the Brazeau. You'll meet him at the dance—he's always up dancing with as many pretty women as possible.'

The rodeo began with the playing of the national anthem, 'Oh Canada' and the cowboys' prayer; the audience stood for both. Settling back into our seats, the first event got underway. First was bareback bronc riding, followed by steer wrestling, team roping and calf roping. After intermission came the saddle bronc, the ladies' barrel racing and lastly the bull riding.

'Wow,' I said to Phil as the event concluded, 'that was impressive! In a different category to the rodeo dad took us to when I was a teenager.'

'Would you expect anything less?' he grinned.

We made our way through the departing crowd to another area in the Activity Centre which functioned as the curling rink in winter. A country band was tuning up as we found some seats to one side. While Phil went to get us a drink from the bar, I glanced around me. The men's attire was a given, jeans and western shirts with checks and piping, as was the women's, skirts or jeans with shirts. And almost everyone wore a cowboy hat and boots.

'Here's your lemon, lime and bitters,' Phil said, placing a tall glass with a straw on the table in front of me.

'Thanks. See many people you know?'

Phil chuckled. 'Most of them actually.'

As the band began playing, Phil jumped up and reached for my hand. 'Cadillac Ranch!'

I didn't know the song but it had a good beat. Getting to my feet, I asked Phil to count me in. It was almost a year since I'd last two-stepped and I didn't want to embarrass myself in front of Phil's friends and acquaintances.

He obliged, reciting, 'Slow, slow, quick, quick,' until I fell into the rhythm. There were three good songs in a row, then we took a break. As we sat down Bob Barker sauntered over.

'Phil,' he said while looking at me, 'are you going to introduce us?' Under thick eyebrows his dark eyes twinkled.

Phil did so and invited Bob to sit down.

'We've all heard about the New Zealand girl Phil's met,' Bob said. He had a low-pitched voice and spoke with a drawl. 'Are you living here now?'

'I wish!' I laughed. 'I'm here until the end of August and then I have to go back to London for the new school year.'

'Oh, you're a schoolteacher.'

'Yes,' I said, puzzled as to why Canadians used the phrase *school teacher* rather than simply *teacher*.

'How's Blue Creek?' Bob asked Phil.

'Having to do without me,' Phil said. 'I'm off on stress leave for the month.'

'You need to get your hairy arse back in the saddle and get out there where it's not stressful. What's stressful is being around town, especially those jokers in the office,' grinned Bob. He stood up. 'Well, excuse me but it's time for a dance. Nice to meet you, Leanne.' He tipped his hat to me and left.

'Time for us, too,' Phil said, and we moved back onto the dance floor.

Sometime later Joe came over to ask me to partner him for a dance—he was a good dancer and led strongly. The rest of the dances were Phil's and he threw in some Ceroc spins and turns. A few hours later when my feet became sore it was time to leave. The crowd had lessened but there were still lots of dancers two-stepping and people standing around visiting.

Walking back to the truck I glanced skyward. A myriad of stars issued cold white light. Even with my jacket on, I shivered. Phil put his arm around my shoulders to lend me his heat.

'It was a good evening,' he said quietly.

I leaned into him and laughed. 'Ever one for the understatement. It was wonderful!'

We didn't spend all our days away from the house. Like me, Phil valued time together at home—puttering as he called it. There were household chores, clothes to wash, shopping and gardening, as well as relaxing together. One afternoon while Phil weeded his vegetable garden in the backyard, I worked close by, creating a new flowerbed along the boundary fence between Phil's and his neighbour's section. It was too late to plant any flowers but I wanted the bed to be ready next spring when, God willing, Phil and I would be married and I'd be living here.

As I placed my foot on the spade to dig into the grass, I thought about how Phil had never actually proposed to me. We'd talked about wanting to be together for so long that it had almost negated the need for Phil to ask me.

Almost.

I leant my spade against the wooden fence and went over to the raspberry patch at one end of the garden. I picked a handful and walked over to Phil.

'Time for a raspberry break,' I said.

Phil anchored his hoe into the soil and stretched. 'My hands are dirty so you'll have to feed me.'

I placed a single raspberry into his mouth.

He swallowed it and then looked expectantly. 'Next!'

'Not until we discuss something.'

Looking at me sideways Phil smiled. 'Okay.'

'I'm not quite sure how to say this because I don't want to have to request it outright—that would take away from the romance of it.'

Phil looked confused.

'I'm going to hint instead. You know we plan to get married this December?'

'Yes ...'

'Well, there's a certain question you've never asked me. Can you please ask that question? But—' and I held my hand up so he didn't blurt it out now, 'not today, sometime when I'm not expecting it. It's really important to me.'

Understanding lit Phil's face. 'Yes, of course. I'd be honoured.'

'Thank you,' I said and kissed him. 'Now, here's the rest of the raspberries.'

One warm, sunny evening we went to an outdoor training centre called the Palisades, just north of Jasper, for a Parks Canada staff picnic. Many of the 120 strong contingent were there. Phil saw the back country crowd and we headed over to join them.

Phil's co-workers were aware of me being in Phil's life and I fielded a few questions, some about where I lived—there was a misconception it was New Zealand—but mostly I listened as wardens and their partners spoke of a life that was foreign to me. I felt like an outsider but my interest was piqued.

'So, Leanne,' said a warden as Phil and I made ready to leave. It was cooling down and the mosquitoes were coming out. 'When do you think you'll move to Jasper?'

It felt awkward to mention that Phil's divorce was still being finalised so I opted for a generality. 'I'm working on it,' I smiled. 'These flights are getting expensive.'

Those listening to our conversation laughed.

'You'll be welcome when you do,' another person said.

'Thank you!' I said, touched by their inclusion.

Phil had gathered up our plates and utensils into a rucksack then took my hand. 'Night, folks. Don't work too hard.'

Quick retorts and much laughter followed Phil's parting comment, as we turned to walk to his truck. I would never have had the nerve to be so cheeky, I would have been all apologies for not being at work. I loved the fact that Phil didn't get bogged down in guilt. It was definitely a lesson I could learn from him.

In one of our last afternoons Phil arranged with Jim Chesser, the barn boss at Jasper National Park, for Phil and me to ride two of the park's horses. They were kept at Maligne Range—a stretch of land that lay below a cliff face on the far side of the Athabasca and Maligne Rivers.

Jim had assigned us two sorrels. Not Phil's usual horses, they were almost as unfamiliar to him as they were to me.

Once mounted, we headed north. It was a warm summer afternoon and the sun's rays fell lazily through the trees. The timber was sparse and we were able to ride close together, soon reaching the tumbling waters of the Maligne River. Following alongside we came to where it united with the mighty Athabasca. There'd been some rain and the river sprawled from bank to bank.

Phil reined in. I gently pulled back on my own reins and my horse stopped beside his.

'How are you feeling?' he asked.

'A bit tender. I think I'll be walking funny tomorrow. Feels good though—psychologically, I mean. I'm not a sadist.'

Phil laughed. 'Heather mentioned going for a canoe ride on the Athabasca.' Heather was one of the ministering angels he'd referred to last year. 'Are you interested?'

'It's flowing rather fast at the moment,' I said, batting away a fly. 'Would it be dangerous?'

'No, we'll be fine.'

'Okay then, go ahead and organise it.'

Phil lifted his reins and drew them to one side to turn the gelding around.

'Let's get you back to the barn before you get too sore. You look quite at home in the saddle, by the way.'

'Thank you!'

I'd meant what I said to Phil—after years of riding as a kid, I felt comfortable being astride a horse again. There was a barely perceptible sense of danger that was exciting, but the attraction was more to do with determining the nature of your horse and engaging with their quirks to form a working bond. Not something you could accomplish in an afternoon but the ride brought back that memory. Horses were also beautiful and a pleasure to behold; I thought back to that telling game in an Oak Hall coach about favourite animals and smiled. If only they could see me now!

'See you at the Moberly buildings,' Phil called out to Heather. It was the following afternoon and she and a work friend with his dog were already on the water in her canoe.

'Race you there!' challenged Heather.

Adjusting our lifejackets, Phil and I clambered into his canoe and eased out into the Athabasca River, he in the back and me in front of him. It was partly cloudy and mild, although there was a breeze over the expanse of the river and I was glad of my jacket. The water was swift but calm with a slight turbidity, not the jewel colour it was when clear.

We didn't talk much, just enjoyed letting the current take us downstream, paddling occasionally while we gazed about us. I watched out for animals, studied the jagged outlines of the mountains that cut into the sky, and enjoyed the ever-changing cloud formations.

'Leanne?'

'Hmm?' I said, a little slumberous in the sun with the mesmerising slip of water against the side of the canoe.

'I love you, will you marry me?'

Oh, Phil! I thought. It was that precious question I'd so longed to hear but I hadn't gotten to see him say it—I didn't know whether to laugh or cry.

But I did know my answer.

'Yes, Phil,' I said, turning around in order to see his face. 'I'd love to marry you!'

'I'm sorry I don't have a ring but I wanted you to choose one you liked. Let's leave early for Edmonton so you can choose one at the mall.'

'Great idea! Oh, I can't wait! It would've been lovely if you'd had a ring but you're right—I really would like the opportunity to choose. And besides,' I laughed, 'imagine if it had fallen into the water!'

'That would *not* have been funny,' Phil said. 'Okay, Heather will be wondering what's keeping us. We'd better hurry up.'

As we paddled, I considered my engagement ring seriously for the first time. It would have to be simple as I didn't like large, gaudy jewellery, and I'd need to bear in mind that I would soon have an outdoors life and anything bulky might catch on clothing or gloves. The ring needed to be simple but elegant; it was going to be fun to choose.

Phil released my left hand as we stepped into Prestige Jewellery in West Edmonton Mall. 'You'll need it free to try on the rings,' he grinned.

It was a bittersweet occasion; choosing an engagement ring should have been the happiest of times but in only a few hours I would fly out and leave Phil behind. Excitement and sadness had vied with each other all day.

We approached the sales counter and a friendly sales assistant with the name tag, Alice, asked how she could help us.

'I've come to buy Leanne an engagement ring,' Phil answered.

Alice clapped her hands in pleasure. 'Oh, that's wonderful.' She turned to me. 'What kind of ring are you looking for?'

'Well,' I said, always keen to tell even a part of our story, 'I'm going to be moving to Canada, to Jasper actually, and I'm going to be spending time outdoors. So I'm thinking that I don't want a ring with a stone that's too high.'

'That makes sense,' Alice agreed. 'You don't want it catching on things.'

'Exactly.'

'Especially reins,' Phil added.

Alice looked baffled.

'Phil is a park warden,' I said. 'During the summer he rides into the back country on horseback. I'm hoping to join him.'

'Oh,' Alice said, 'how exciting.'

'Yes!'

'Well, in that case have you considered a low-profile ring?'

It was my turn to look perplexed.

'Come over to this display cabinet and I'll show you.'

Alice pulled out a tray of rings. The diamonds were set much lower than those with a traditional prong setting.

I took my time examining each one. There was a plaited ring—it was unusual but I didn't like it; several had low-set rectangular stones but those didn't appeal; one ring had a low circular diamond but I didn't find it attractive either. I was beginning to wonder how many jewellers we'd need to shop at to find something suitable.

In the middle of the last row one finally caught my eye and I pointed to it. 'Can I try on this one please?'

It was a wide-band gold ring with bevelled edges and small diamonds set into a shallow central groove spanning half the circumference. I slipped it on and was captured by its unusual style and how the arc of diamonds glimmered as I turned my hand.

'This is it,' I said. 'I love it.' Then came an unpleasant thought and I turned to Phil with a grimace. 'Oh dear, I hope this isn't when we find out it's horribly expensive.'

'Alice?' Phil asked.

'Firstly, I think it's beautiful. And no, it's one of our medium-priced rings.' She named the price and I inhaled sharply.

'No, it's fine, Leanne,' Phil answered me. 'I was expecting a similar price. You're worth that.'

Alice beamed.

'Thank you!' I said. 'I think it's a little large though.'

Alice agreed. 'Yes, we'll need to resize it. It should only take a couple of days.'

My face fell. 'I'm flying back to London tonight,' I explained.

'Oh no!' she said, almost as disappointed as me; clearly it wasn't part of the fairy-tale ending she wanted for us.

'Don't worry,' Phil said. 'I'll post it to you.'

'Make sure you insure it for its full worth,' Alice said, looking concerned.

'Don't worry,' he said, 'I don't want to end up paying for two!'

We sat side by side in the international departure lounge. Phil held my ring-less hand.

'Are you feeling sad?' he asked.

'Yes. It's the first thing women say after you tell them you're engaged—"Show us your ring!"'

'Sorry, Muffy. I'll hopefully have it to you in a few weeks.'

I gave a tight smile. 'Thanks.'

Phil squeezed my hand. 'Only three months 'til I get to marry you. I can't wait.'

'Neither can I. I'm so fed up with waiting! I know I'll be busy working and winding up my life in London but three months is still plenty of time to miss you like crazy.'

I looked around and saw couple after couple travelling together. Two more solo flights then Phil and I would be able to do the same. I felt my heart fill with pleasure at the thought, then fear deflated it just as quickly.

'Do you really think your divorce will be done by then?'

'It should be.'

'Should? I want certainties, Phil, not 'shoulds'. We can't get married on a 'should. '' I gave a deep sigh. 'It has to be definite.'

'I know. Roger and I will do everything we can. Keep praying.'

'Oh, I will! Mum and dad are praying too.'

'We can't do more than that, Leanne.' Phil said, putting his arm around me.

'Can you please pray?' We had started every day with a time of Bible reading and prayer, and I would greatly miss it.

We put our heads together and closed our eyes. Phil asked for God to go before us and expedite the divorce, and to give us both peace and patience.

'Thanks so much,' I said, as he finished.

'You're welcome, Leanne,' Phil pulled me to my feet, enveloped me in his strong arms and kissed me. 'The next time I see you will be in Los Angeles and then we'll never be apart.'

Chapter Twenty

Back in London I was buzzing with excitement to share that Phil and I were engaged and I would be leaving. But I felt I had to contain it somewhat as I didn't want to hurt my friends. I was realistic enough to know I would miss them all—and many aspects of London life—but I'd waited a painfully long fifteen months to be with Phil and my remaining time in London could not rush by quickly enough.

There were only two things dampening my joy. The first was that I wasn't going to have the pleasure of wearing my ring in London, for when Phil had taken the resized ring to Canada Post, he discovered they didn't insure such items. I would have to wait until we met in Los Angeles. I felt so cheated.

The other was my dread of the divorce not going through in time.

We were so close to the fulfilment of our dream that it seemed to make the fear of it not happening even greater. I found myself on a merry-go-round of committing it to God, picking it up and worrying about it, then giving it back to God again. It was very stressful.

The new school year started almost immediately. With me working a shortened term I was concerned that I wouldn't get a two-day position to supplement my Lambeth school work. But the wonderful team at Teachers'R'Us managed to find me a job at Mayflower School in East London for which I was very grateful. It was a super school, small enough to be welcoming, with well-mannered Muslim children.

At my Lambeth school I was exceptionally busy. In addition to my usual duties, I needed to complete outstanding paperwork, make final assessments and cull files of anything outdated or extraneous. I'd given the position and the students my absolute best but I was relieved that the years of pressure were finally coming to an end.

Early in October Phil rang very late one mid-week night. I'd just gone to sleep and was very groggy as I said hello but became instantly alert as soon as Phil mentioned the name of his wife's lawyer. Evidently there was a further delay in the divorce settlement.

'Unbelievable!' I muttered. 'I want to say some very bad words.'

'That's understandable.'

'Just a second, I need to put on my dressing gown. The heat's gone off and I'm cold.'

'I'm back,' I told Phil a few seconds later.

'The heat will stay on all night at my—our—place,' Phil assured me.

'Oh, I can't wait,' I said. The idea of something so domestic was a tangible reminder of what we stood to lose. I wanted to both cry and scream but made myself refocus on what Phil had said. 'I can't bear to even say it but do you think this delay will mean we can't get married on the fifteen?'

'My lawyer assured me that it's not a big deal. He thinks it can be sorted quite quickly.'

I let out my breath audibly. 'Thank God.'

We didn't talk much longer as Phil was conscious I needed all my strength for teaching. I wanted to keep chatting because it felt like he was right beside me, but it touched my heart that his priority was my well-being.

Eager to make my move to Jasper a practical reality, within a week of being back, I had ordered some large boxes to be delivered by an international moving company. In them I started packing all the personal items I could manage without until February when they would be delivered to Edmonton. It was tricky as I used so many things on a regular basis, and I couldn't store away my summer clothing because I'd need it in New Zealand.

One weekend in October I packed a fridge magnet I'd kept displayed on the metal heater in my room. A little wooden box full of colourful vegetables, it had caught my eye in the souvenir store of the hotel in Narita, Japan at which I'd stayed overnight upon my initial flight from New Zealand to London.

The flight had been five and a half years ago and I'd been broken and lonely. God had steadily built up my confidence in His love and ability to look after me. Through Phil, who had named and valued my attributes like no-one else ever before, I could see who God had made me to be. At age thirty-nine, I was finally comfortable with and loved who I was.

But as contented as I might have been, God hadn't finished with me. Phil sent a card in which he quoted from an article about time management and learning to say no. It was an 'ouch' moment—my situation at my Lambeth school clearly spoke of the need for me to evaluate my workload in order to reduce my hours. Learning to say no was a telling struggle for me. Without counselling and practical advice on how to address my people-pleasing nature, I didn't make any head-way. But it was on Phil's radar and he was to pick up on it again.

That wasn't all Phil had been focusing on. He'd been thinking ahead to me applying for permanent residency once in Canada and he strongly suggested I should have my fingerprints taken for police clearance purposes. Fitting in the appointment around my long working hours was difficult but I managed to do so.

Infinitely more stressful was the discovery of a lump in my breast. When twelve years old I'd had a benign tumour removed from one of my breasts and I feared another one was growing. There was also the dreadful thought that this time it was cancer. I tried to suppress it but it was like trying to submerge an inflatable object, as soon as you pushed down one side, up popped the other.

A friend recommended a specialist and he saw me on an emergency basis. He was a kind and sensitive man and after examination gave me the hugely relieving news that he thought the lump was a fluid-filled cyst which he aspirated with a fine needle.

It was a great outcome but there remained one further issue, also a deeply personal one. Ever since Karl's desertion I had wondered about his sexual history and health and how it might have affected me. He had claimed not to have had a sexual relationship with Amanda but in light of his lies I was doubtful of that. And had he even started his second relationship *before* he left me?

The possibility that I could have contracted a sexual disease from Karl, hounded my thoughts, as it did Phil's.

'I hate to ask, Leanne,' he said one night on the phone, 'but it would be wise to get tested.'

With everything else going on, it suddenly seemed too much and I gave a sob.

'I'm so sorry, Muffy.'

The kindness in Phil's voice fully released my tears.

After a few moments I blew my nose and wiped my eyes.

'What happens if I test positive?' I asked. Then my mind went a step further to my work with Grandma's. 'What if I have AIDS?' I added, starting to cry again.

'We'll deal with that if it happens,' Phil said quietly, 'but you said you've had no symptoms. I'm sure you'll be okay.'

It was scant comfort.

I had the testing done at the Royal Free Hospital in Camden and in a few days that seemed more like months, the test results came back. They were negative. Relief was tangible, settling my stomach, and dropping my tensed shoulders. The only hurdle that remained was for Phil's divorce to go through in time for us to get married.

Late October, Dee and Gwen had told me the amazing news that they were planning a farewell party for me. They were calling it, 'Oh No, I'm Nearly 40!' as I would turn forty in February. They asked me for contact details for Phil, Glenn and my friends but kept all other information secret.

The big night was Saturday, 17 November and it was held in the church hall on the first storey of our building. Alison came to stay for the weekend and Christy and Matt drove up from Kent. Glenn and his fiancé, Melanie, were there as were many London friends and colleagues—Hannah from my Lambeth school, and her husband, Augustine from Ceroc, Steve, and friends from church.

Not content with a social evening with drinks and nibbles, Dee and Gwen had gone all out and planned for the occasion to include a meal with the main course being korma! After we ate there was an opportunity for people to share their favourite memories of time spent with me. It was uncomfortable being the centre of attention but I felt so loved hearing my friends speak. Their memories were captured forever as another of Dee and Gwen's great ideas had been for everyone to send a photo and message which they made into an album for me.

The evening culminated in the tables being cleared away so those who wanted to could dance. I had a last few Ceroc dances with Augustine and boogied the rest of the night away, pausing only to say goodbye to guests as they began leaving.

The farewell party, permeated by celebration rather than sadness, is indelibly etched in my memory as one of the most thoughtful and generous gestures with which I've ever been blessed. To know that Dee and Gwen devoted hours of time and energy to plan, prepare and host such a large event touched me profoundly. No-one else had ever done anything like it for me before.

It still makes me smile to think about it.

I had only two weeks left in London before I flew out from Heathrow on Sunday morning, 2 December for Los Angeles. There I'd meet Phil and we'd stay overnight before flying on to New Zealand. I had agreed to work up until the end of my last week, and there was still so much to do.

In spite of all the last-minute busyness, one thought overrode them all—when was Phil's divorce going to be granted? The fifteen of December was rapidly approaching and the pressure was intense. Would the date come and go? Would we be able to be married at all during the six weeks we'd be in New Zealand? What would happen then? Would I go to live in Canada but have to stay at Sheila's until the divorce came through? But if so, then my family wouldn't be present at our wedding!

My thoughts swung back and forth like a weather vane in a storm. I knew God was the master of last minute reprieves and rescues and yet doubts assailed my mind constantly. It was such a battle to keep giving my fears to God and trust Him in spite of how our circumstances looked.

The last day at my Lambeth school was Wednesday, 28

November. Saying goodbye to my students and colleagues was hard as it had been the backdrop to my five and a half years teaching career in London.

Friday was my final day at Mayfield School and the staff put on a farewell morning tea, generously gifting me an exquisitely embroidered cloth. They had no idea that the upcoming event they were celebrating was, at that moment, still a legal impossibility.

That evening I was in the flat making a final list of domestic chores to do, like washing my sheets which I wasn't taking with me. Dee was lending me a pair of hers for my last night in London.

My last night. Our wedding was due to take place in fifteen days but the divorce had still not been finalised. I should have been excited but joy seemed increasingly absurd.

Suddenly the phone rang. Who was it? Maybe Alison or Christy making one final phone call. I put my pen down and picked up the receiver.

'Hello?'

'I've got it!' It was Phil.

For a moment I was afraid to assume that I knew what he meant. 'Do you ... do you mean your divorce?'

'Yes, Leanne! I'm free!' Phil shouted—something he never did.

I burst into tears, probably not the reaction he was hoping for but the release of all that tension was profound. Then, like the sun coming out after rain, my own excitement burst through.

'Wahoo!' I yelled. 'Oh, sorry, Phil,' I added in a quieter voice, 'I've probably perforated your ear drums.'

'Close!' Phil said. 'Maybe don't do it again if you want me to be able to hear the minister read our wedding vows.'

I laughed at that like I hadn't laughed in a long time, giving full expression to my joy. The huge, seemingly insurmountable barrier to our union had been eliminated. Thank you, God! You're amazing!

The doorbell rang in the flat. Dee left my room, where she was helping me cram remaining items into my luggage, to answer the bell.

'Hello?'

'It's Gwen.'

Dee pressed the door release and returned to my room. We soon heard Gwen's footsteps climbing the stairs. In a minute she entered the hallway through the door Dee had left open for her.

'Are you ready?' Gwen asked, as she came to stand in the doorway to my room.

'Not yet,' I grimaced. 'I should have squeezed a few more things into my boxes.'

'Have they gone?' Gwen asked.

'Yes, they were collected yesterday.'

Dee zipped shut the last of my bags. 'There, I've squashed in those last few clothes.'

'Oh thank you!'

On my desk, now strangely empty of my teaching materials and other personal items, was my map of the United Kingdom. I reached over and picked it up. 'Do either of you want this?'

'I will, thanks,' Gwen said.

I passed it to her and then looked around the room. The shelves above my bed held only my washed and folded single bed sheets.

'I'll leave the girls in the flat to fight over those,' I said and Dee and Gwen grinned.

Finally, I checked the wardrobe to ensure I hadn't left anything but it was bare and awaiting the belongings of the room's next occupant.

Dee and Gwen sensed I needed a moment alone so they each reached for a bag.

'Feyzo's parked just a few spaces up the street,' Gwen said. 'We'll take the bags down and see you in a moment.'

I thanked them and sat down on the bed, the room now as empty as I'd found it when I first moved in five and a half years ago. Looking back, I recognized the courage it had taken to move halfway around the world while I was still grieving. God had been so faithful in providing me with this haven, income on which to live and surplus to use for travel, sterling friends, and—incredibly—a godly man to cherish me. When many of my girlfriends were still single, I felt extraordinarily blessed to be given a second chance at marriage.

Thank you, God! Bless the next woman who lives here.

I picked up my handbag and coat, and closed the door to the room in which I'd dreamed, despaired, cried, longed and loved long distance.

For the final time I descended the three flights of stairs. I let myself out of the building and walked down the street to join Gwen and Dee. As I climbed into the back seat of Feyzo's car, he turned to me with a smile. He was an Albanian man with an invalid sister and Gwen had taken them both under her wing.

'Thank you so much, Feyzo,' I said. 'This is so kind of you.'

'No problem,' he said in his increasingly fluent English.

Dee got in beside me, we closed the doors and Feyzo started the car, eased out of the park and made for Cricklewood Broadway. My anticipation and excitement were suddenly supplanted by the reality that my time with these two dear friends was about to close, as surely as the door to my bedroom, the flat and the building had clicked shut behind me. With my emotions mounting it was hard to focus on making conversation but I asked about their plans for Christmas and the coming year. For their part they made me laugh by joking about me being a lady of leisure until I was granted a Canadian work permit.

'Well,' I said, looking at the departure board, 'it's getting pretty close to boarding time, so I should go through the security gates.' I was conscious that my voice was suddenly shaky.

I stood up and turned to Gwen. 'Thanks for everything—all the movies and concerts, having me stay at Christmas and especially for having Phil stay at Easter.' My voice broke at this and I choked out, 'I'll always be grateful.'

We hugged and I saw tears glistening in Gwen's eyes as she released me.

'Dee,' I said, hugging her next. 'How can I say thanks for your friendship over the years?'

'Thanks for yours,' Dee said. 'How will I manage without you? You've been the social glue of the flat.'

At her compliment and the enormity of leaving, tears began to flow.

'Don't miss your flight,' Gwen said, ever practical.

'No,' Dee said, 'Phil would never forgive us.'

I managed a weak laugh, which gave me the strength to hug them both once more and say goodbye but as I turned away I began crying in earnest. With tears streaming down my face and my throat working, I couldn't speak as I approached the customs officer and handed him my passport and boarding pass. He took a cursory look at my documents, nodded, and then waved me through.

Before I did so I turned to catch one last glimpse of Gwen and Dee. With tears blurring my vision I wasn't able to see the expressions on their faces, they were simply two outlines to whom I waved. I hoped my tears spoke of my love for them.

Greeting Phil in Los Angeles held the same intensity of feeling as in Heathrow but this time it was joy instead of sadness.

'I can't believe it,' I said as Phil and I clung to each other. 'It's finally happening.'

'They can't stop us now,' he laughed, kissing me tenderly, then with increasing passion.

'Whoa, cowboy,' I laughed as we drew apart, 'there's still twelve days to go.'

'Point made.' Phil reached for my hand. 'Let's go and get your bags.'

Once in the hotel room Phil zipped open one of his bags.

'Look away for a moment, please,' he asked.

I moved to stand by the window and looked out over the darkening Los Angeles nightscape, hearing Phil rifle through his belongings.

'Muffy,' he said, and I turned around.

He bent down on one knee before me. In his hand was my ring displayed in a black velvet box. 'I love you, Leanne. Will you marry me?'

I didn't know whether to cry or smile. In the end I did both while saying an emphatic yes.

He stood up and placed the box on a table. Lifting out the ring, he took my left hand in his and slipped the ring on my finger. Engaged to Phil since August, I finally had the visual proof—the gold-encased, eleven diamond evidence of our promise to marry. Sparkles of light glinted from the cut faces of the stones.

'Thank you,' I whispered, 'it's beautiful.'

'Just like you,' Phil said, and kissed me.

Chapter Twenty-One

One further airport encounter remained.

I don't know who was happier when I walked hand in hand with Phil through the arrival gates at Christchurch International Airport—mum or me. Her smile was as wide as I'd ever seen it. Having felt my pain over the years I was alone, I was thrilled she was now experiencing my joy as well.

'We meet at last,' dad said, shaking hands with Phil while I hugged mum.

Phil turned from dad to mum. 'Pleased to meet you, Lesley,' Phil said, 'I can see where your daughter gets her good looks from.' Mum blushed but I could tell she was pleased at the compliment.

'Your cowboy's got a golden tongue, I see,' said dad as he gave me a hug.

'That reminds me,' I said excitedly, holding out my hand. 'Look at my ring!'

'Oh Leanne, it's lovely,' Mum said. 'It looks expensive.'

Phil put his arm around me. 'Only the best for my bride-to-be.'

Now it was my turn to be embarrassed.

'If the compliments are over,' dad joked, 'let's get your bags and head home. Your mum has lots to show you.'

Mum was a born organiser and had taken much pleasure in making all the arrangements for our wedding—the guests, venue, catering, flowers, as well as working with dad to transform the attic over their double garage into a bridal suite for Phil and me. She and dad motioned for us to climb the stairs that wrapped around the far right-hand corner of the garage. We ascended the stairs and crossed a small landing to walk through the open doorway into the attic room.

Lengths of carpet and rugs covered the wooden floor. A queen size mattress had been placed in its centre and was covered in new linen and duvet. Furnishing the sides of the room under the eaves was a chest of drawers and a bookcase on which mum had placed a vase of cut flowers.

'Oh, mum and dad, you've done wonders! This is lovely.'

'It's nothing flash,' Mum protested but I could see she was pleased with my reaction. 'Phil, this will be your room before the wedding.'

Phil turned to mum. 'Thanks for all your hard work, Lesley.'

'And Brian!' Mum said, but dad protested it was mainly the results of her efforts.

'Phil,' dad said, 'why don't you move your luggage up here while we show Leanne to her room. Then let's have a cup of tea and some of Lesley's baking.'

Phil's transition into my family was seamless; he and dad had a lot in common and dad was fascinated by Phil's career with Parks Canada. Mum immediately seemed to have a soft spot for Phil and he was very gracious towards her which touched my heart as well as hers.

The first family to meet Phil other than mum and dad was my brother Dale, his wife, Michelle, and their two children, four-year-old Jamie and one-year-old Matthew, as they lived nearby. Phil didn't meet Wendy and her two girls, four-year-old Brittany and one-year-old Maya, and my sister, Carmen, until they arrived one or two days before the wedding. Glenn and Melanie of course were in the United Kingdom.

Our twelve days rushed by. Phil and I went to Christchurch to obtain a marriage license and to meet our marriage celebrant, Rev. Blair Robertson. Mum and I double-checked the finger food and wedding cake she had chosen—she had excellent taste and I had no changes to make. I made a visit to mum's hairdresser to discuss how I wanted my hair.

Phil and I also went to Dale and Michelle's where we typed then printed our wedding service sheets onto pretty marbled paper. Phil created stencils to represent our respective countries which he imprinted onto the upper corners of the sheets—the pohutakawa flower for me and the maple leaf for Phil. And just before the big day I accompanied Michelle to a friend's house to pick red roses whose plucked petals Brittany and Jamie would have in their wicker baskets to scatter onto the aisle of the church.

The day before the wedding my long-time friend, Linda, came out to my parents' place to paint my finger- and toe-nails. She was the wonderful sort of friend you might not see or even hear from in years and yet when you next met it was like you'd been together only the day before.

Saturday, 15 December dawned fine with an expected high of 25° C, perfect for the dress I'd chosen. A traditional white wedding dress had seemed inappropriate so I'd scoured London's shops for something special, finding a sheath dress with shoestring straps that skimmed flatteringly over my body. It fell to my ankles in an abstract pattern of black and grey, brightened with red roses. With the dress had come a small scarf. Not intending to wear it, I'd sent it to Phil so he could choose a scarf of the same red hue. I'd also bought some strappy black summer shoes with low heels.

'Your aunty's getting married to Phil today,' Wendy said to Brittany at the breakfast table, as she buttered her toast for her.

'Will I wear my dress?' Brittany asked, putting down her glass of milk.

'Yes, Bee. You finally get to wear it.'

I smiled at Brittany. 'You and Jamie are going to look so pretty. Thanks for being our flower girl.'

'Your rose petal girl,' Carmen quipped and we laughed.

'Mum,' I said, 'won't you come and have breakfast with us?' She was close by in the kitchen.

'No, thanks. I had something earlier,' Mum answered, opening the oven and placing in a quiche she'd made for us to have as an early lunch before the wedding at 2:30 pm. 'There's too much to do to sit down.'

I felt bad but mum was hard to budge from her kitchen. She liked to do things in her own way and time.

'Where's Grandad?' queried Brittany.

'He's busy getting things ready for the wedding,' Mum said in a tone that indicated she wasn't going to elaborate.

I shot a look at Wendy and Carmen but they just shrugged their shoulders. Clearly they had no more idea what dad was up to than me.

Having finished my cereal I took the empty bowl to the kitchen. I rinsed it, placed it in the dishwasher then put my arm around mum's shoulder and gave her a soft kiss on the cheek. 'Thank you for *all* you are doing to make this a wonderful day.'

'It's my pleasure,' she smiled.

Mid-morning Mum and I had our hair appointments in town. The finished look wasn't nearly as casual as I'd intended—instead of my hair flowing in long sexy waves, it was styled in tight ringlets that were very old fashioned. They made me look like a saloon girl at which I gave a reluctant laugh—at least I'd be a match for Phil in his Western wear.

After lunch Mum had invited me to dress in her and dad's bedroom. Warm sunlight poured through their large, north facing window.

'I'm delighted for you, Leanne,' mum said, as I slipped on my dress. 'When you left for London I was so worried about you. I clung onto the verse in Psalms about the Lord watching over your going out and your coming in, and He was faithful.'

'Thank you.'

'I prayed you'd rebuild your life after Karl but I didn't have much faith that you'd meet someone special.' She stopped and gave me with a look of apology. 'I'm so sorry.'

'That's fine, mum,' I said, reaching out to give her a hug. 'I didn't either in the end. There were so many guys I liked and so many knockbacks. I started to think it would never happen.' I sat down on the bed and motioned for mum to sit beside me.

'After Karl left the second time I still longed to be married again—but to a godly man who would cherish me. I vowed to God I'd go anywhere in the world if He found that man. I never thought He'd take me seriously.'

Mum reached over to take my hand. 'Well, He definitely did. Phil's such a wonderful man and it's clear he thinks you're very precious—as you are. I couldn't be happier for you.'

'Thank you,' I said, squeezing mum's hand. 'God sure kept his side of the bargain and in a few weeks' time I'll have to keep mine! I've come to love Jasper and the Rockies but I do fear the cold.'

'Phil will keep you warm,' Mum said with a rare cheeky twinkle in her eye. 'Talking about Phil, don't let's make him wait. Let's see how the garter fits.'

On the newly-mown lawn of a country church, an assortment of cars were parked in two rows. Mum and I drove onto its grounds and she parked alongside the last vehicle. Dad had come earlier in order to greet people with Phil. He and I had wanted a small intimate gathering so we'd only invited—in addition to immediate family—aunties and uncles, my Nana, Linda and her partner, Ed.

The Anglican church was a small, gable-roofed building clad with white-painted weatherboard. Earlier in the week Phil and I had been delighted to discover that while the exterior may have been plain, the interior was charming. It glowed golden with native rimu timber that lined the walls and ceiling. On either side of the church were two decorative mullioned windows, while three exquisite stained-glass windows were set in the recessed chancel at the front of the building, as well as the back wall of the entrance.

Dad met us, saying that all our guests had arrived and were seated. As he and Mum went inside I talked with Wendy and Michelle who were waiting for me with Brittany and Jamie.

'Leanne, you look lovely,' said Michelle.

'Thank you!' I smiled, then crouched down in front of the girls, each clutching a single red rose to complement my bouquet of a dozen.

'You girls look *so* cute.' Their sleeveless dresses were white net with satin bows at their waists. Over these each girl wore a white velvet jacket with a feathery collar that fastened at the neck. On their feet they wore little white sandals.

'Do you remember what to do?' Wendy asked them. 'Walk down the aisle in front of Aunty Leanne.'

'Yes,' the girls answered.

'Good, just don't walk too fast, you don't want Aunty Leanne to have to run to keep up with you!'

The girls looked at each other and giggled.

Judging that enough time had lapsed, we entered the church. Michelle took her seat next to Dale in the front row, Wendy staying behind with her camera to photograph the girls. She signalled to Dale that we were ready and he started our first song which was Van Morrison's, "Moondance." As it began, Wendy whispered to the girls they should begin walking down the aisle.

As they did so I stood looking at Phil standing at the front of the church, barely noticing the large red Christmas bows fastened to wooden pews, the floral arrangements with red wattle, the array of guests, or even the jaunty beat of "Moondance" that always had my foot tapping when it was played at Ceroc. Instead, like a magnet to steel, my eyes locked onto Phil's.

There was my very own cowboy in black dress jeans, white shirt and black frock coat with a red scarf at his neck. Black lace-up ropers and a black Stetson completed his outfit. Under the wide brim of his hat, Phil smiled broadly, laughter lines bracketing his mouth and his blue eyes shining. How could I ever have thought he looked ordinary? This man was not only rugged and mature but he was handsome.

The girls had reached the front, Jamie going to sit with her Mum and Dad, and Brittany beside Wendy who had slipped down the aisle behind them. This was my cue and I walked to join Phil, only a few metres and a short ceremony away from being his wife.

As I approached Phil his hand reached for mine. It was warm and his grasp firm.

Once Reverend Robertson welcomed everyone, Phil picked up one of the two guitars resting against the wall. He sang, "Look at Us" by Vince Gill, having altered a few words to acknowledge it was God who had brought us together. As the song progressed, the weight of longing and pain of separation fell away like unfastened shackles. All the obstacles we'd encountered had been overcome, all the battles won. The words from Psalms came to mind, "weeping may endure for a night but joy comes in the morning."

After Phil came to stand by me, the minister spoke.

'Phil and Leanne have asked that I share two verses which are special to them.' He opened his Bible. 'The first is from Jeremiah 29. "For I know the plans I have for you," declares the LORD, "plans to prosper you and not to harm you, plans to give you hope and a future." The second from Ruth is very appropriate for

Leanne,' he said, smiling at me. '"Where you go I will go, and where you stay I will stay. Your people will be my people."'

Dad then took up his guitar to accompany Carmen as she sang Fleetwood Mac's exquisite, "Songbird." There was such beauty in my sister singing that our union was appointed and there would be no more crying.

Afterward came the making of our vows and exchanging rings, ending with Reverend Robertson pronouncing us husband and wife. 'The groom may kiss the bride.'

Even as I thrilled to Phil's kiss, it paled in comparison to what awaited us this evening when there would no longer be any boundaries. All my longings for Phil while alone in London would be fulfilled. That God had delighted to plan these pleasures for us caused me to blink back tears.

As we signed the register I'd asked for that special song by Steve Apirana to be played. The faint hope that "Something Beautiful" had instilled all those years ago had indeed blossomed into a miracle. God was so good.

Finally, after a closing prayer and benediction, Phil and I left the church to, "Have I Told You Lately?" by Van Morrison. In front of us were Brittany and Jamie, reaching into their wicker baskets and scattering rose petals on the carpet.

'They'd normally get into trouble for doing that,' whispered Phil into my ear, making me laugh with sheer joy.

Outside, family and friends congratulated us before our wedding photographer got us all together for a group photo-graph. The church was in the background—to its right a stately oak tree spread its branches and to the left stood a conifer, adding a welcome Canadian touch. As warm sun filtered down through the leaves and needles, I felt God smiling at us.

Mum and Dad had worked incredibly hard to prepare their lovely home and garden for our wedding reception. After the photos had been taken, the finger food was served, followed with a large carrot cake smothered in coconut icing served with tea and coffee.

After the reception Dad gave a speech. Being an ex-principal he was a skilled public speaker and his humour won much laughter. When he finished, Phil stood up, inviting me to come and stand with him.

He thanked all those who had contributed to our wedding, then turned to my Dad's mum. 'Thank you, Nana, for your life and influence on Leanne.'

I was thrilled that at 93 she was still alive to witness the results of her prayers that I know she prayed daily for me and all her grandchildren. She'd been a wonderful grandmother and I was touched that Phil should honour her in this way.

He concluded by saying, 'This is the day I married my friend, the one I laugh with, the one I live for, the one I dream with, the one I love. Thank you for coming to share these moments, this special day, with us and for witnessing our vows to each other.'

'Here, here,' Dad said, raising his glass.

My heart was full and I turned to Phil and kissed him. 'Thank you my darling,' I said quietly. 'That was beautiful.'

'Hold on! You're only allowed the one kiss today and you've already had that,' Dale called out, causing laughter to erupt.

With the speeches over, our extended family began to depart, with many hugs and kisses and good wishes for our new life in Canada. Some gave us monetary gifts which was very much appreciated. After they left we finally got to discover what Dad had gotten up to that morning.

'Leanne,' directed Dad, 'could you go and sit in the plaid recliner.'

'Sure,' I said, shooting a questioning look at Phil.

Dad went up the stairs and came back down with a large wrapped box. He placed it in front of me to open.

I ripped off the paper and lifted up the flaps. Inside the box was what appeared to be footwear. Lifting out one of two identical items, I saw it was a red gumboot fastened to a tennis racket.

'What on earth?'

'It's a snowshoe,' Dad explained. 'For getting around Jasper.'

We all laughed, including Phil. 'She won't get far in those,' he said, 'but full marks for creativity.'

Dad's "gift" prompted my recall of the massive cardboard poster above the sign to the turn-off from the main road to the church. I knew from the handwriting and artwork it was his handiwork. He'd drawn wedding bells and a love heart, as well as a graduate cap for me and a guitar for Phil with the phrase, 'Jasper—or bust!'

'Dad, we loved the sign you made. I guess that's one of the things you were doing this morning that Mum kept so quiet about.'

'Yes,' she smiled, 'I was sworn to secrecy.'

'Great sign, Brian,' Phil said, 'except the guitar was missing a few strings!'

'What about the possum?' Carmen asked. 'Jamie and Bee, did you see the possum Grandad hid behind the plants in the church?'

'No!' they chorused.

Dad darted away again and came back with his right hand behind his back. Brittany and Jamie looked on with anticipation. Dad brought his hand forward, on it was a possum puppet that he made talk in a gravelly voice. The girls squealed in delight.

Suddenly I had the urge to yawn.

I tried desperately to quash it because I didn't want anyone to notice and tease me. Our wedding day had been as wonderful as I'd wished but it was tiring being the centre of attention and I now longed to be alone with Phil. From exchanging surreptitious glances with him I could tell he was thinking the same thing.

'Well, I said, 'I think it's time for us to be going. We've got a meal waiting for us.' Mum and Dad had generously gifted us the wedding present of a night's accommodation in a nearby stately home. It came complete with an evening meal and breakfast the next morning.

'Yes,' Dad said, 'you'll need to keep up your strength.'

'Brian!' Mum whispered.

'Right, everyone,' Wendy directed, 'let's let Leanne and Phil get away without any more ribald comments. We've got children here.' She stood up and began collecting up the box and torn wrapping paper.

Phil took our honeymoon luggage and stored it in the Toyota Corolla parked on the gravel driveway. With Dale so knowledgeable about cars, we'd asked if he'd purchase a bargain vehicle for us with money we'd sent him. He'd done a great job.

All the family stood at the front doorstep waiting to say goodbye.

Carmen stepped up. 'I won't be here when you get back,' she said, 'but I'll see you when you get up to Auckland.' She gave me a big hug. 'I'm so glad for you, sweetie. Phil's a lovely man and it's wonderful to see you happy.'

'Thanks, Carmen. Thank you for coming down and thanks again for your beautiful song.'

'You can't beat Fleetwood Mac.'

I hugged Wendy, Brittany and Maya who were staying on at Mum and Dad's and who we'd see when we got back on Christmas Eve. Dale and Michelle came up next, Dale holding his one-year-old son, Matthew, and Michelle with Jamie. We said goodbye to them, and then turned to Mum and Dad.

'What can I say?' I said, 'None of this would have happened without you. Thank you seems insufficient.'

'Leanne's right,' Phil said, 'you've both been amazing, you especially, Lesley.' I loved the way Phil singled Mum out for the praise she deserved.

We all hugged, and then Phil and I walked to the car where he opened the passenger's door for me.

'She's got you well trained!' joked Dale.

Phil laughed. He got into the driver's seat and shut the door. As he started up the engine, I turned to wave at my family. Each one was precious and I felt so loved and honoured as they had all given of their time, talents, and energy to make our wedding day so special. Thank you, God!

The tyres crunched on the gravel as we drove down the drive and turned right onto the road. Alone at last! I put my hand on Phil's knee and he covered it with his own.

'It's just you and me now, husband,' I said. 'It only took a year and a half.'

'Mrs Minton, you were worth waiting for,' Phil said, raising my hand to his mouth to kiss.

Acknowledgements

Top billing belongs to God for without Him I wouldn't have such an amazing story to tell, one that took me from great loss to great adventure. He is the original and best storyteller.

The second thank you goes to my late beloved mum who suggested I try online dating which became the first step in the journey to meet Phil. The honour of the introduction to him of course goes to Sheila Couture to whom I'll always be grateful!

My dad, an author himself, has shown continued interest in my writing and I'm so grateful for that and his encouragement over the years.

Karen Gardyne and Christine Nikoloff are two close friends of long-standing who have been very supportive, encouraging me and maintaining interest in a project which has taken years, and who read and commented on early drafts. Thank you.

Thanks to Verna McFelin and Carol Brokenshire who also read early parts of my manuscript and made comments and corrections.

Shelley Pegman has come into my life more recently. She very generously gave of her time to read my original, lengthier manuscript and as a writer herself made exceptionally illuminating and helpful suggestions for which I'm very grateful. I'm also extremely appreciative of the copy editing she did for me. Thank you, Shelley! I'm thankful too for your talented husband, Chris Pegman, who gifted me his time and expertise to take my author photograph.

Another author, Chris Tracy, provided encouraging feedback.

I've been very appreciative of my sister, Carmen's interest in and enthusiasm for my book. You kept me going at the end when it got really tough!

My niece, Maya, and MacKenzie Frew provided early drafts of a cover for me. I didn't end up choosing either of their beautiful drawings but I thank them for partnering with me on my journey.

Thank you too to Lynne Frew who invested the time and energy to read the entire completed manuscript and give me valuable feedback. Her comments on the book cover I was considering at the time were perceptive and led me to search for something quite different and more fitting.

I'd like to acknowledge Jo and Tara from PrintABook who kindly answered my many emails about formatting and gave me much assistance. You're amazing!

I'm very grateful for Rebecca Rhodes' passion for my book and for the beautiful cover she created. Thank you so much, Bex.

A huge thank you to Rosetta Allan, my developmental editor extraordinaire who provided helpful professional reading material and excellent recommendations, the implementation of which have significantly improved my memoir.

Lastly I want to thank my darling husband, Phil, for without you my longings in London would never have been fulfilled. Thank you for recognising, valuing and loving who God made me to be. I am so grateful for the time you took to painstakingly read my manuscript and provide corrections, and for believing in me and this project. I love you!

Afterword

My writing journey began as a child when an entry of mine was accepted by the children's section of the New Zealand Woman's Weekly. The publishing of this snapshot of my rural life birthed the desire to write a book.

During my teenage years I wrote both prose and poetry but they were neglected once I finished high school and moved into the world of work and marriage. Nor did I return to my writing while living in London.

After marrying Phil and moving to Canada, I travelled with him on horseback into his district of Blue Creek and kept detailed diaries. On my return I wrote lengthy emails to friends and family about my experiences. Several women encouraged me to turn my accounts into a travelogue, and Blue Creek Bride was the result. But, despite the book's title, I largely skipped over the amazing God-incidences that lead me to Canada and Phil.

Years later God gently but insistently suggested I write a prequel to Blue Creek Bride and focus on our romance. Like most women I enjoy the romantic aspect of books so why was I reluctant to detail my own? God had gifted Phil and me with an incredible story and He challenged me to write about it and use it to bring Him glory, as well as encouragement to hurting women.

With some trepidation I embarked on the project. Phil and I had kept all our emails and letters which enabled me to re-experience this difficult but remarkable time in our lives. They were an invaluable resource in the writing of my memoir.

It wasn't easy recalling the eighteen months of longing to be with Phil. But even more painful was reconstructing the tale of my first marriage—revisiting the confusion and pain, and grieving for the naïve and weak young woman I was then who submitted herself to ten years of emotional and verbal torment.

It's my fervent hope that if you are a woman in a similar position of abuse and desertion you will discover you are not alone in your emotional prison and that God wants to set you free. My story is an example of how He can restore you and give you a hope and a future. He is the God of second chances.

Lastly, for those who are wondering whether I have an encyclopaedic memory for conversations—no, I don't, although I do have clear recall of the gist of many significant ones. In resorting to my imagination for the rest, I strove to create verbal exchanges with as much fidelity as possible to the situation, the people involved and their character. I sent excerpts to many friends and family for them to approve the words I placed in their mouths. If, however, after reading the book, anyone feels misrepresented I sincerely apologise for I endeavoured to accurately present each friend, family member or acquaintance.

Thank you to each of you for being part of my story.

About the Author

Leanne resides in New Zealand with her husband, Phil, and is passionate about her work with children with special needs. Fascinated by history, she loved living in the UK with its proximity to ancient sites, medieval castles and gorgeous manor houses. She also enjoyed the opportunity to travel to Europe and North Africa. In addition, Leanne likes reading, gardening, going to the movies, spending time in nature, taking photographs, listening to music and dancing when she can.

Reach out to me at:
bluecreekbride@gmail.com

www.ingramcontent.com/pod-product-compliance
Lightning Source LLC
LaVergne TN
LVHW052018080426
835513LV00018B/2077
* 9 7 8 0 4 7 3 7 4 6 0 9 4 *